Confessions of a Good Christian Girl

Confessions of a Good Christian Girl

Tammy Maltby
with Anne Christian Buchanan

Published *by*
Thomas Nelson™
Since 1798

www.thomasnelson.com

CONFESSIONS OF A GOOD CHRISTIAN GIRL

Copyright © 2007 by Tammy Maltby

Published in Nashville, Tennessee, by Thomas Nelson, Inc.

Thomas Nelson, Inc. titles may be purchased in bulk for educational, business, fundraising, or sales promotional use. For information, please e-mail SpecialMarkets@ ThomasNelson.com.

All Scripture quotations, unless otherwise indicated, are taken from The Holy Bible, New International Version. Copyright © 1973, 1978, 1984, International Bible Society. Used by permission of Zondervan Publishing House. The "NIV" and "New International Version" trademarks are registered in the United States Patent and Trademark Office by International Bible Society. Use of either trademark requires the permission of International Bible Society.

Scripture quotations noted NLT are taken from The Holy Bible, New Living Translation®. Copyright © 1996. Used by permission of Tyndale House Publishers, Inc., Wheaton, Illinois 60189. All rights reserved.

Scripture quotations noted MSG are taken from The Message by Eugene H. Peterson. Copyright © 1993, 1994, 1995, 1996, 2000, 2001, 2002. Used by permission of NavPress Publishing Group. All rights reserved.

Scripture quotations noted NKJV are taken from The New King James Version® Copyright © 1982 by Thomas Nelson, Inc. Used by permission. All rights reserved.

Library of Congress Cataloging-in-Publication Data

Maltby, Tammy.
    Confessions of a good Christian girl / Tammy Maltby ; with Anne Christian Buchanan.
        p. cm.
    Summary: "Dealing with the secret pain in the lives of Christian women"—provided by publisher.
    Includes bibliographical references.
    ISBN 13: 978-1-59145-531-8 (hardcover)
    ISBN 10: 1-59145-531-6 (hardcover)
    1. Christian women—Religious life. 2. Maltby, Tammy. I. Buchanan, Anne Christian. II. Title.
    BV4527.M237   2007
    248.8'43—dc22   2006102337

Printed in the United States of America
07 08 09 10 11 QW 1 2 3 4 5

Thank You, my faithful Father, for saving me—
then rescuing me over and over again.
Oh, my heart longs to see You face to face,
to run into Your strong embrace
and forever experience Your awesome, tender ways.
Until then, my King, use the fragments of this broken child
to reflect Your healing love . . . Your abiding peace.
For I am banking my whole life on the amazing reality
that with You all things are new.

Contents

Writing a book like this was an amazing journey. It would have been impossible without the help, love, and support of so many.

I would like to thank first and foremost the courageous women who lived these stories of personal pain and dared tell them to me. The depth of respect I have for you is overwhelming, and your God so big. May you find purpose in your pain as other women find hope and healing in your transparency.

Anne Christian Buchanan, my dear cocreator of *Confessions.* You are a profoundly talented woman and writer. Thank you so much for capturing my heart and vision for this message. For listening to me for hours—hey, I was sick of listening to myself; I can't imagine how you did it!—and giving your time, energy, and passion to seeing women set free. You are a dream God just dropped into my life!

To the excellent people at *Integrity Publishers,* especially Joey Paul, for catching the vision for this message and giving me a tender, encouraging heart when I needed it.

To *Bill Jensen,* my agent and friend, for telling me all along that I needed to write this story.

Acknowledgments

To *Karla Ver Meer*, who was incredibly helpful to me in setting up interviews with a variety of good Christian girls and whose own incredible story of turning pain and shame and failure into something wonderful for the Lord inspired me deeply. (Karla, you're not in this book by name, but your spirit shines through it.)

And to my dearest friends . . .

Maryjo Valder: Thirty-four years of friendship and growing strong. You are not only the most beautiful woman I have ever known on the outside, but your beauty is unparalleled on the inside. I am deeply proud of the woman you have become.

Joyce Anne Dickinson: You little chef, you! Thank you for traveling around the country with me, for the tender ways you listen, for easy tears and outrageous laughter. Girl, I am just crazy about you!

Erin O'Keefe: You are such a strong fortress of a woman. Thank you for giving me perspective when I had lost it, for calling me to hope when I couldn't embrace it, and for telling me the truth about myself and my God.

Lisa Black: Girl, you are just the craziest fun around. I love your heart . . . your passion . . . the way you totally get what is real in life. Thank you for being there for me and my children. I'm awed by what you are and what I know you will become.

Leanna Tuff: You have taught me more about God's wild grace than anyone. To know what you have lived through . . . and yet to see how centered and amazing you are is clearly a testament to what He can do. You, my deck, and a fur coat . . . I will never forget!

Lynn Brown: You little cheerleader, you! I love you and Steve so much. Thank you for being there when I was at my worst and loving me anyway.

My sisters, *Twyla Beyers, Terri Johnson, and Trudy Delich*: For reading my endless e-mails when my world was crashing in . . . for helping me to see God's miraculous grace for the day . . . for reminding me of what truth looks like. When I was overwhelmed with fear, you brought me the gift of life. I love you all dearly.

Ken and Ramona Hanson: I love you, Mom and Dad. Having praying parents is a gift unlike any. Thank you for modeling godly lives for me and your grandchildren.

Tom and Emily Davis: I know for certain you are the most faithful, loving, honest, genuine, and authentic friends I have ever had. I'm amazed that people as young as you can "get it" so deeply. Thank you, thank you! God kissed my heart when He brought me you, and I know your devotion is one reason I'm still here.

Finally, to my precious children, whom I love more than life. *Mackenzie, Tatiana, Sam,* and *Mikia*, you will feel the impact of this book more than any. You have seen the reality of this very broken mother, a mother who often failed at loving you as she so longed to. Forgive me for those times. Thank you for bringing gentle graces to me, forgiving me, and releasing me to share my story . . . which in many ways is your story too. You are the greatest and most amazing gift your father has ever given me. I stand humbled to be called your mama.

1

"Daddy, Are You There?"

*I pray that Christ will be more and more at home
in your hearts as you trust in him. . . .
And may you have the power to understand,
as all God's people should,
how wide, how long, how high, and how deep
his love really is.*
—Ephesians 3:17–18 NLT

A story is told of a carefree young girl who lived at the edge of a forest, where she loved to play and explore and take long, adventurous journeys. But one day she journeyed too deep into the forest and got lost. Evening approached, and as the shadows lengthened, the girl grew worried. She tried one path after another, but none looked familiar. And none led her home.

Deeper and deeper into the forest the frightened girl ran. Her skin was scratched from limbs whipping her as she pushed her way through the overgrowth. Her knees were scraped from tripping in the dark. Her face was streaked from her tears. She called for her parents, but the forest seemed to swallow her words.

After hours of trying to find her way home, the exhausted child came to a clearing in the forest, where she curled up on a big rock and fell asleep.

Meanwhile, the girl's parents were frantic with worry. They searched the forest for her, cupping their hands and calling her name. But there was no answer. As night fell, the parents' search grew more intense. They enlisted the help of friends and neighbors. They even asked strangers from town to help them search for their lost little girl.

Over the course of the night, many of the searchers went home. But not the girl's father. He kept on combing the woods, even when his wife left to tend their other children. He searched all night and on into the next morning. Finally, at the first light of dawn, he spotted his daughter asleep on the rock in the middle of the clearing. He ran as fast as his legs would take him, calling her name.

The noise startled the girl awake. She rubbed her eyes. Then, reaching out to him, she caught his embrace.

"Daddy!" she exclaimed. "I found you!"[1]

It's a beautiful story. A familiar story. And if you've been a Christian for any time at all, you probably guessed the punch line.

Yes, I'm that lost little girl.

The thought of it still produces an ache in my heart.

I bear the scars of many wayward travels, painful journeys through grasping briars and dark forests. Places where I came to believe no one could really rescue me—or no one would want to. For, oh my goodness, if people really knew who I was, what I was like! If people could see my great lack, hear my silly mumblings—this broken girl huddled in a pile, bruised and broken. Was I even worth rescuing?

My Father thought so. He never gave up on me.

And when I finally stopped running, He was right there, ready to wrap His loving arms around me and carry me back home where I belong.

Just as you thought—a lost girl found.

But there's a twist to this particular story.

You see, it's not about an unbeliever who finds Jesus after years of wandering and is saved. Because when this story happened, I already knew Jesus. I was already saved. In fact, I was the quintessential good Christian girl.

And I still needed rescuing.

I still sinned, was sinned against, made mistakes, got confused, and strayed from the path—more than once. I desperately needed my Father's gracious, tenacious love to go after me and bring me back to Him.

> *To be alive is to be broken.*
> *And to be broken*
> *is to stand*
> *in need of grace.*
>
> —BRENNAN MANNING[2]

And then I needed more.

I needed healing for my wounds.

I needed forgiveness—oh how I needed forgiveness!

I needed guidance and strength.

And grace. I needed loads and loads of loving grace.

Even though I knew my Savior, I kept coming to points in my life when I needed more of Him than I ever thought possible.

And I'm not the only one. In fact, most churches I know are packed with terrified, wandering little girls.

These are good Christian girls who look at their lives and see little but disappointment, rejection, shame, and brokenness. Women who struggle in secret with painful experiences like abuse, addiction, and mental illness. Women who have affairs or seek divorces or suffer in silence in a loveless marriage. Women who live with the constant, desperate sense that no matter how hard they try, they just don't measure up.

These women long for lives that are rich and free and victorious. But most are just hanging on, trying desperately to get by. They're wondering how they got so far off course—and whether the One who saved their souls can do anything with the mess they've made of their lives.

These are not nominal Christians I'm talking about, but evangelical, Bible-believing, born-again women. They have a usual place to sit on Sunday mornings . . . and often Sunday evenings and Wednesdays too. They host Bible studies and attend women's retreats. They make casseroles for potlucks and serve in soup kitchens. Many know Scripture backward and forward— they can recite all the right answers to life's questions. But still they're broken . . . hurting . . . desperately in need of help and healing.

I understand how these women feel, because I've been where they are. In some ways, I'm still there.

And yes, I'm a good Christian girl too. I grew up in the church and learned Scripture along with my ABCs. I accepted Christ at a young age and attended a Christian college, even took my fair share of theology courses. Though I've occasionally strayed from the church and its teachings, I've always come back. I have been involved in ministry for most of my adult life. I am raising four teenagers in a Christian home.

But my life, too, has been full of pain and sin and shame and brokenness. I've been divorced. I've experienced abuse and known the terrible relational fallout that can stem from abuse in a loved one's life. I've had sex when I wasn't married. My life has been touched— not gently!—with the reality of addiction and mental illness in my family and massive disappointment in my own life. I have known hopelessness so oppressive I could barely breathe. There was a time when I took steps to end my own life.

Not a very Christian way to live?

That's exactly my point!

I was a Christian during all my lost times. At times I've been not only a good Christian girl, but a prominent one. A speaker. A media personality. The wife of a man who knew just about everybody in the evangelical world. We entertained Christian celebrities in our home. We worshipped and broke bread with evangelists and talk-show hosts. And still I was lost and stumbling, struggling with the secret sins and pain in my very visible life. And as much as I tried—God knows I tried—I couldn't find a way out to the other side.

To the place I had heard of called forgiveness and redemption.

A place warmed by the presence of a Father who saw me, knew me, loved me.

A safe place where I could run into my Daddy's strong and tender arms and say, "Daddy, I found You!"

And where He would whisper with a loving embrace, "Oh my baby . . . I've been searching for you all along."

And that, too, is the point of this book.

Because I did find my Father—or

Jesus wants you to know that when you are broken, shivering, alone, or afraid, with nothing left and nowhere to go, then you can turn in His direction and lay yourself at the foot of His love. . . . God wants you to know that when everything else is gone, that makes more room for Him, and every time there is more room for Him, you are blessed.

—Angela Thomas[3]

rather, He found me. And He found me right in the middle of my pain. In the moments of my despair, I heard the gentle whispers of a gracious God who seeks the lost, a God who lives to forgive, to restore, to heal, and to give hope. I learned firsthand that good Christian girls need the grace of Jesus just as much as unbelievers do—and that grace is abundantly available to anyone who is willing to be honest about her pain and cry out for help.

But honesty can be a problem, especially for us good Christian girls, because we are so used to thinking of our lives as before-and-after stories.

When I was growing up in a conservative Baptist church, I loved to hear the testimonies of those whose lives were broken and painful before they came to the Lord. As an adult in women's ministries and as a Christian talk-show host, I loved them even more—those heart-touching tales from those who were lost and then found, those whose lives were changed by an encounter with the ever-gracious Savior. They're wonderful, juicy true-makeover stories with irresistible happy endings.

The trouble is, the "before" in those stories is almost always "before I knew Christ." And the implication is that once a person accepts the Lord, she stops sinning and lays all her brokenness outside the door.

The implication is that churches are populated by those who are joyfully and triumphantly healed.

And that's just not true—or it's just a fraction of the reality most good Christian girls I know experience.

Most Christians know that. We'll admit it if we're pressed. We'll even make a point of telling people that "we're all sinners." Yet we're pretty quick to cover up our deeper failings. There are things we'll confess and others we don't dare mention to anyone—even, sometimes, to ourselves.

Why the cover-up? We tell ourselves we must "keep a good witness"—you know, keep God looking good. More often, I think, we do it to keep ourselves comfortable. To help us feel safe. Because we don't know how to handle pain or because, deep down, we're not sure if God can really handle who we really are and what we've really done.

We cover up the ugly stuff to protect ourselves.

But when we do, we send the message to those who are hurting, who are broken, who are truly weary and heavy laden, that they are not welcome in our churches and our lives. Especially if those hurting, broken people are already Christians! Especially if they're honest and admit they're losing the battle and don't know where to turn.

And when we send that message—even to ourselves—I believe we're actually working against God. Because broken, hurting, and honest people are exactly who God wants in His churches. Those are the people He wants on His side, because they're the ones He can really do something with.

You see, God can work miracles with pain. He can make short work of sin and guilt. It's pride and dishonesty and self-deception that slow down His rescue efforts. And as often as we good Christian girls have heard that, we sometimes have trouble remembering it applies to us.

I've certainly had a hard time remembering it!

Looking back, I can see that part of God's purpose in my own pain was bringing me to a place of complete brokenness and dependence on Him. The gospel I once believed—that the Christian life was a simple before-and-after tale and that believing in Jesus would automatically give me a victorious life—was a false one, and God was obligated to set the record straight. Tenderly but relentlessly, one by one, He

7

pulled down my false idols and reminded me that victory over sin is a battle I will never win here on earth.

As long as I'm here, I'll have to live with the confusing reality Paul described in Romans 7: "For what I do is not the good I want to do; no, the evil I do not want to do—this I keep on doing. . . . For in my inner being I delight in God's law; but I see another law at work in the members of my body, waging war against the law of my mind and making me a prisoner of the law of sin at work within my members" (vv. 19, 22–23).

As long as I live, I'm going to sin. So will you. We'll all have to live with the consequences of our own failings and the fallout from the sins of others.

We can try to do better.

We can grow and improve.

But we'll always be in danger of straying from the path and losing our way. There's just no way around it.

But look at what Paul said next! Some days, this incredible message of grace has been all that keeps me going: "Therefore, there is now *no condemnation* for those who are in Christ Jesus, because through Christ Jesus the law of the Spirit of life set me free from the law of sin and death. For what the law was powerless to do in that it was weakened by the sinful nature, God did by sending his own Son in the likeness of sinful man to be a sin offering" (Rom. 8:1–3; emphasis added).

Do you hear that? The Lord has no condemnation for those of us who try to follow Christ and still find ourselves lost.

None.

He knows what we're like, what we're capable of, what we've actually done. And He can handle it. He's going to stay with us through it all—redeeming our mistakes, covering our sins, teaching us through our transgressions, and going after us time and again when we stray far from home. There's nothing we can throw at Him that He cannot handle and help us with—as long as we let Him.

All of which leaves me with two choices.

I can work hard on my "good Christian girl" image and keep my brokenness hidden. For the sake of my "witness," I can pretend to be found when I'm really lost and wandering.

Or I can choose to open up my life and depend absolutely on the love and forgiveness of the One who has found me again and again . . . who loves me so much that He gave up His own life so I could live free of condemnation . . . who wants me to trust Him with my sin and brokenness so He can teach me what it really means to be a whole, healthy, "found" human being.

Through my own lengthy process of learning what costly forgiveness is all about, even walking it through with others, and then ending the journey in my own backyard, I believe God has been showing me something of His heart. He's teaching me that honest pain can be healed, but secret, hidden pain cannot. And that when we truly take that truth to heart, we start living

> *My Lord is more ready to pardon than you to sin, more able to forgive than you to transgress. My master is more willing to supply your wants than you are to confess them. Never tolerate low thoughts of my Lord Jesus.*
>
> —CHARLES HADDON SPURGEON[4]

in a completely different way—a way that gives life to ourselves and those around us.

Psychologist Brent Curtis once said that we can never be healed emotionally or give life to others unless we look at our own sin and the other person's pain. Most of us tend to do just the opposite—we look at our pain and the other person's sin. But when we finally get honest with ourselves and others about just how lost we are, that's when we start to be found.

It begins with the most loving and difficult of all acts: forgiving ourselves, embracing our humanness, and believing that somehow God can turn our brokenness into beauty. It begins with understanding the reality that Christ died for sinners, which means all of us—good Christian girls as well as those who don't know Him at all. It begins when we open our eyes and our hearts in wonder to His grace.

Because, in the end, it's all about grace.

Loving, forgiving grace.

Passionate, overwhelming, truly amazing grace.

That grace is the reason I've written this book in the first place. Because, in so many ways, it's the story of my life—and I want to tell you why. So this book is my confession to you about times I've lost my way. And about the many times I have been sought out and rescued by a persistent, lovesick God.

I'll also introduce you to other real women who know what it's like to wander, women whose complicated lives defy the good-girl myths and yet bear vivid testimony to the power of transforming grace. Some are close, personal friends of mine. Others are women I've met in my work as a speaker and interviewer. (Their stories are true, although in some cases, at their request, I have disguised names and specific details.)[5] And still others are women I met in the pages of the Bible—women whose stories remind me that God has been in the business of rescuing lost little girls from the very beginning.

All these women have helped me understand the many painful and messy ways that good Christian girls can stray from the path . . . how, by grace, we can get found . . . and how we can reach out to one another in love and compassion and be agents of grace to one another. This book tells their story too.

But the real story at the heart of this book—the one that I hope shines through all my confessions—is not about good little girls at all. Not even about lost little girls.

Remember, the little girl in the woods thought she had found her father. But the father was really the one who found her. He was the hero of the story. And that's true for the good Christian girls in my book as well. Especially for me.

Because my true bottom-line confession is not that I've been lost, but that I keep being found.

Not that I strayed and messed up, but that I've been rescued and given another chance . . . and another . . . and another.

Not that I'm a good Christian girl, but that I serve a good God. And that I'm growing in His grace—with a lot of help—to be the woman He always wanted me to be.

And yes, some days it feels hopeless. Some days I just don't feel up to being good. But hopeless feelings don't change the reality of my hope.

So that's what this book is really about. It's the story of our persistent, lovesick Father who keeps on seeking us whenever we're lost, who loves us too deeply to let us stay there, and who longs to reach out and pull us back into His arms of grace, no matter how far we stray.

He loves you that way too. Can't you hear Him now, wherever you are?

Come home, sweet baby. The lights are on . . . soup's on the stove, warm bread in the oven. Just come home and let Me hold you, protect you, cleanse you from the world that ravages your very soul. I know you. I know what you have done and what has been done against you. I know how hard you have tried to be good and how defeated you feel. But you can rest now. My yoke is easy, and My burden is light.

You don't need to be a good Christian girl.

Just be who you are—My beloved child.

WORD OF GRACE TO ALL GOOD CHRISTIAN GIRLS

Come home to Christ. And He'll do all the rest.

2

"I Can't Take It Anymore"

The Desperate Pain of Suicide

Praise the LORD, O my soul;
all my inmost being, praise his holy name.
Praise the LORD, O my soul,
and forget not all his benefits—
who forgives all your sins
and heals all your diseases,
who redeems your life from the pit
and crowns you with love and compassion.
—Psalm 103:1–4

I was the last person anyone would ever expect to attempt suicide.

I was the very last person *I'd* ever expect.

I just wasn't the type.

I'd always been a happy, cheerful, sanguine girl. I'd grown into a tough, resilient woman who loved my family and loved the Lord. I had faced my share of loss and disappointment, and I'd handled them well. I was independent, self-assured, confident.

And yet there I was in my garage that bitter-cold January night, slouched in the driver's seat of my SUV with the motor running and praise music on the stereo.

Sobbing. Empty inside. Chilled to the point of numbness.

Just waiting for the fumes to do their work so I could wake up in heaven and leave my whole impossible life behind me.

How did someone like me end up in a place like that?

The same way anyone can—even the most cheerful, resilient good Christian girl. No one in this fallen world is immune from the kind of pain and stress that brought me to the end of my rope . . . to the point of despair . . . and yes, to the point of taking my own life.

Winter had descended on my soul. I couldn't stand the cold any longer. And that's where this story begins . . .

The Winter of the Soul

How does a woman enter the winter of her soul? And why? When? The early signs are hard to see. But one day you wake up and it's rattling your windows—pounding, howling—an icy wind that numbs you through and through.

Never mind that you didn't invite the bitter visit. Really, you prefer warm and sunny weather, sandy beaches, calm. You've worked very hard to keep your life in order. In control. You have worked hard at looking good, feeling good . . . even faking good.

Most of all, you want to be good. You desperately want everyone else to think so too. And then you reach the point where it's just not working.

I had worked hard to be beautiful, to do beautiful things, to be everything to everyone. And for many years, I had done so well. I'd spoken to thousands of women who really seemed to care what I had to say. I'd written words that people seemed to want to read. I'd mothered four kids, worked on a difficult marriage, kept an immaculate showplace of a home.

I was just so damned successful. And I use the word on purpose because damned was what I felt. Nothing on my outside matched the inside. The gap between the life I'd planned and the life I was experiencing widened into an icy chasm of disappointment.

Emotionally and relationally, my world was falling apart, and I was holding on for dear life to keep it from collapsing entirely and leaving me out in the cold. But nothing I tried seemed to work.

I dredged up endless Bible verses. They all sounded empty in my ears.

I prayed desperately for relief. It didn't come.

I read countless self-help books. Their pat answers and quick fixes just annoyed me.

I cried, fasted, begged God to rescue me. The chasm just widened, and the winter wind howled even louder.

Been there? Felt that? Is your soul even now aching from an icy winter reality?

I know.

Really, I know.

Stay with me here. Because my heart is to let you know that when I finally let go of my sunny, successful facade . . . when I finally dared to acknowledge the cold in my heart . . . when my false reality shattered and I finally reached the end of myself . . . God was there.

At the bottom of my personal pit—that's where I rediscovered His outlandish, outrageous, incredible grace.

A Winter's Tale

That particular January was a bitter one in our part of the country—with day after day of biting winds and temperatures in the teens or below. I was feeling pretty wintry inside as well—physically, emotionally, and spiritually. I had had my period for ten weeks straight. My iron levels were dangerously low, I was far too thin, and I dissolved into tears at the least provocation. I cried every day for hours.

> *We must learn to realize that the love of God seeks us in every situation, and seeks our good.*
>
> —THOMAS MERTON[1]

I know now that my hormones were completely out of whack, and I was suffering a deep depression. But I couldn't see it then. I just kept telling myself I needed to get a grip because I was driving everyone crazy.

I was driving myself crazy.

Maybe I *was* crazy.

But the problems weren't just with me—deep inside, I knew that. My husband and I had hit a crisis in our often challenging marriage, coming to terms with more than twenty years of life together that seemed to be anything but . . . together. On the surface we were a picture-perfect family—two successful careers in the Christian world, four teenagers, a showplace home, friends around the world. But we had spent far too many days and nights and weeks apart because of his career and mine. On top of that, my husband was dealing with some devastating issues from his childhood that had erupted into our life together—revelations that threatened to tear our lives apart.

I loved my husband, and I knew he loved me. I was desperate to keep our family intact. But I couldn't handle the loneliness, the shame, the sense of failure. I wasn't sure we would make it.

To make matters worse, word had gotten out about our problems, and everyone I knew seemed to have an opinion about what was going on. Some of our friends disappeared; they just couldn't deal with what I was going through. Some felt honor-bound to tell me where one or the other of us had gone wrong. Others just looked helpless . . . or looked away.

Have you experienced a time like that in your life? A time when the pain and shame of the past seem to meet up with the pain of the present and swirl together into a dark pit you just can't escape? Some days it's all you can do just to summon the energy to survive.

And sometimes, well . . . you can't.

It was a day like that for me—though it had been building for months. Week by week, as the stress in my life mounted, I had moved into a mind-set of escape. And I don't mean just drinking a bit too much . . . or buying a few too many pairs of shoes . . . or eating too much ice cream. No, I craved real release. The ultimate escape. The final freedom.

I'd reached the point where all I could think about was heaven.

I was obsessed with going there, living there, being there. I read everything I could about God's promises of life after death. I loved the thought of heaven—music, beauty, intimacy with Jesus, singing, laughing, joy, peace. Yes, peace—that's what really drew me. The sense of complete release. The promise of freedom from all the pain I was feeling.

And of course I wasn't thinking straight. Emotionally, I was a wreck. Physically, I was depleted. And something had obviously gone spiritually haywire, because I had begun to believe the lies that the enemy was whispering in my heart. That my family would be better off without me. That life would not be worth living if anyone knew the truth about my marriage. That I was a complete and utter failure.

No wonder I wanted out of my life. I wanted out as soon as possible.

Looking back now, I can't say I actually wanted to die. (I've learned that many suicides are ambivalent like that.) But I didn't want to live anymore. Not the way I was living. Not with this hurt and emptiness that I couldn't seem to fix.

And so on a bitter January night when my husband was away on business and all four teenagers were out of the house, I decided it was time. I went into my kitchen, I walked over to my purse, and I thought, *I'm ready.*

I took the keys from my purse, telling myself I would take a drive. I walked through the mudroom into the big, half-empty garage and got in my car.

Turned the key in the ignition.

Rolled down the windows.

Pushed the CD into the player.

Then leaned back in the seat and waited for the fumes to do their work.

I honestly don't know how long I sat there. I do remember a sense of looking at myself from the outside, knowing that killing myself wasn't the answer but still yearning to be free from the pain and the shame and the devastating sense of failure.

That's when I heard the Voice.

Now, I've never been a Christian who regularly hears God speaking. I mean, the Lord often communicates to me through Scripture and through silent "nudges" and impressions, but until that moment I had never had a clear sense of the Holy Spirit speaking literal words to me. And to this day I honestly don't know whether I heard it audibly or in my spirit, but the words were unmistakable—and a bit confusing.

What God said to me was, *Go get a drink of water.*

Water? Really?

Looking back, I'm both touched and amused that my first direct word of wisdom from on high was about getting hydrated. But that's what I heard. God said to me, *If you get a drink you will feel better. You need to drink water.*

Well, I'm a water drinker, so my first thought was that I probably had a bottle of water in the car. I fumbled around for a minute, checked under the seats—no water. So I left my car running—fully intending to come back and finish what I had started—and walked back into the house to get a glass of water.

As I walked through the mudroom into the kitchen, I heard my cell phone ring. I felt compelled to pick it up—and heard the alarmed voice of a friend.

"Where are you?" he asked.

"I'm here at home," I answered.

My friend persisted. "What are you doing right now?"

I hesitated. "Uh, nothing really. Getting ready to go out . . ."

"Well, don't go," he said urgently. "Listen, the Holy Spirit has just said to me that you are in grave danger right now at this very moment. You need to—"

That's when I started to sob. And I do mean sob. Uncontrollable pain and shame began to pour out of my very being.

"Tammy," my friend asked, "what is happening?"

"Oh," I managed through my tears, "I'm just having a hard night." Even at this point, I was reluctant to admit what was really going on—though by now it was obvious something was really wrong.

"Stay on the phone," my friend urged. "I'm going to call someone to go over to your house right now."

"No, no, no, no," I wailed unconvincingly. "Everything's fine. I'll be fine." But I stayed on the phone with him while he called a close friend of mine on his cell. I was still clutching the receiver and weeping when Emily rang my doorbell, but by that time the immediate crisis was over. Something had switched in my spirit. The pain and fear and shame and stress were still there. But the hopelessness, the longing for death, the lie that ending my life was the only way out of my problems—all those were gone.

Emily stayed with me for several hours that night, comforting me and confronting me. She was just the right person—this vibrant young friend whose own mother had committed suicide many years before. She said, "Tammy, I think you have many things colliding in your life at once. We need to pray, but I also think you need to see a doctor."

She was right, of course. I can't believe it hadn't occurred to me before. I'm a fairly intelligent woman. But after ten weeks of hot flashes and bleeding and crying every day, it still hadn't crossed my mind that something might be physically wrong. I took Emily's advice and visited my doctor, who diagnosed depression and a hormonal imbalance related to perimenopause. After eight weeks of treatment with hormones and an antidepressant—plus lots and lots of prayers—I began to feel a lot stronger.

No, my problems didn't go away. If anything, they would grow more difficult in the days to come. But now I had the physical and emotional ability to deal with them in a stabilized state. Even more important, something had changed in me spiritually—something that made all the difference.

I had learned some things deep in my soul that I only dimly comprehended before, including a few I was just too stubborn—or maybe too cheerful and strong and resilient—to understand. Some things about my own limitations and the power of God's limitless love . . . the depths of the Father's mercy and how hard it is to move beyond it. For even in the dead of winter, at the end of my rope, in the chasm of my despair and disappointment . . . He was there for me. He truly had redeemed me from the pit and crowned me with compassion.

And knowing that forever changed the way I looked at life, death . . . and even winter.

DESPERATE MEASURES

So what does all this say about suicide?

In a sense, not much—especially since my suicide attempt did not succeed.

In fact, if you were expecting an essay about the issue of suicide, this chapter might be a disappointment to you. I have no intention of sorting out all the pros and the cons or passing final word on the legal and ethical or even theological implications.

I simply want to make the point that good Christian girls do attempt to kill themselves from time to time. And some succeed. Ask any preacher who has had to conduct a funeral service for a member of the youth group . . . or a despondent young mother . . . or an eighty-year-old woman with inoperable cancer.

For one reason or another, Christians do get desperate enough to take their own lives. And that's a reality we don't usually like to face. Suicide makes us uncomfortable. It frightens and unsettles us. It makes us quick to turn away or to pass judgment. And it brings up a lot of questions.

For instance: Are Christians who kill themselves really Christians? Can someone who really knows the Lord ever take so drastic a step? Can someone who takes her own life get into heaven?

Well, I'm no theologian, but I know that I am a Christian. A broken one, yes. A fallen one, certainly. A sinner, absolutely. But my salvation was taken care of years ago when I said yes to Jesus. My sins were forgiven once and for all. I have been saved once, and I have also been rescued again and again by a loving Lord who knows I am "prone to wander."[2] I really have been a good Christian girl in many ways. Wanting to serve God with all my heart. Living sacrificially for others. Delighting in His law. My desperate attempt to end my pain through suicide didn't change any of that.

And yes, God did pull me back from the brink through an amazing, miraculous intervention. But what if I had heard God's voice and then spent a little too much time in the car looking for a water bottle? What if my friend had been a little less sensitive to the Holy Spirit's prompting—or if I had chosen not to answer my cell phone? What if my friend Emily hadn't been available to come over and talk to me?

Would a God who loved me enough to intervene at my point of deepest need have let such minor circumstances keep me away from Him?

In my heart, I just don't believe it.

But please understand—I'm not saying suicide isn't a sin. I absolutely believe it is.

For one thing, suicide is a form of murder, a sin specifically forbidden by the sixth commandment. Suicide, like the despair that drives it, surely reflects an alienation from God, an acceptance of the deceiver's lies. And that's sin. It's a failure of faith, a presumption that God can't handle our pain. Sin again. It's a waste, a tragedy, a permanent solution to a temporary problem—all the clichés apply. And it deeply wounds the people who are left behind—yet another indication of sin.

I think of people like my dear friend Emily, who helped me when I was so low—she was just twelve years old when she found her mother's body. And then there's Kathi Curtis, whose CEO husband stabbed himself to death in a motel near their home. Both Emily's mom and

Kathi's husband were devoted Christians, and their families, friends, and colleagues suffered deeply as a result of their suicides. To cause such pain to others is surely a sin.

But is suicide the unforgivable sin? Some Christians hold that the very act of taking one's own life guarantees eternal separation from God. And that I just can't accept.

I believe God knows our hearts. He knows our sins, our weaknesses, our unspoken cries. And He loves us so deeply and passionately that He was willing to live on earth as a human being and even to die for us. His gift of salvation includes forgiveness of sins both past and present.

Would such a God let a person's eternal destiny hinge on a single decision made on a day—even a moment—when she's stretched beyond her limits to cope? While I cannot claim to know everything about what God would do, my personal conviction is that He wouldn't.

At any rate, we cannot know what goes on in another person's heart and mind in the final seconds before a death by suicide. So any speculation as to whether a particular person was really a Christian or is in heaven or hell is purely that—speculation.

Another Desperate Story

The Bible, interestingly enough, is relatively quiet on the subject of suicide. Although it contains a few accounts of people who killed themselves and a few passages that could be—and have been—interpreted as applying to the subject, we have no explicit pronouncements about how God views suicide. We do have stories, however, of how God encounters good Christian boys and girls who are literally at the end of themselves physically, emotionally, and spiritually. And I think these stories tell us a lot about what God can do with desperate people and even suicidal ones.

One of these is the prophet Elijah, who fled from the wicked Queen Jezebel after a dramatic confrontation with her henchman, kept running until he collapsed under a broom tree, and basically begged God, "Kill me now" (see 1 Kings 19:4). I find it very interesting—and very touching—that God's response to Elijah's melodramatic but heartfelt plea was similar to the one He gave to me in my pain. It was a tender parent's response: "You're totally worn out. You need to eat and drink." Only after the prophet was past the crisis of suicide did God get on to the task at hand, which was teaching Elijah more about how God speaks (in a still, small voice) and handing him the next divine appointment.

That was the way God treated me, too, when I was at the end of my rope—with a tender reminder of my physical needs. He reminded me that I was thirsty, hinting that what I needed most was to address my physical issues. And He used the wise advice of my friend Emily to direct me toward an earthly physician for my hormonal imbalance and depression. It's just like the psalm reminds us: "As a father has compassion on his children, so the LORD has compassion on those who fear him; for he knows how we are formed, he remembers that we are dust" (Ps. 103:13–14).

But the biblical story that really speaks to my heart in this regard is another person who came to the end of herself and reached out to Jesus. Her story is told in Matthew, Mark, and Luke. She's commonly referred to as "the woman with an issue of blood."

We have no way of knowing if this poor woman ever considered suicide, but I suspect she might have. She was certainly at the point of desperation when we meet her in the Gospels. She had suffered from a discharge of blood for twelve years.

Twelve years! I can hardly imagine. I was sick and depleted after only ten weeks—and I wasn't living in a culture that considers such a condition "unclean." In Jesus's day, even a normally menstruating woman was expected to isolate herself from normal society, and anyone who touched her had to carry out certain rituals to be "cleansed." As for a woman who continues to hemorrhage, Leviticus 15 specifies:

When a woman has a discharge of blood for many days at a time other than her monthly period or has a discharge that continues beyond her period, she will be unclean as long as she has the discharge, just as in the days of her period. Any bed she lies on while her discharge continues will be unclean, as is her bed during her monthly period, and anything she sits on will be unclean, as during her period. Whoever touches them will be unclean; he must wash his clothes and bathe with water, and he will be unclean till evening. When she is cleansed from her discharge, she must count off seven days, and after that she will be ceremonially clean. On the eighth day she must take two doves or two young pigeons and bring them to the priest at the entrance to the Tent of Meeting. The priest is to sacrifice one for a sin offering and the other for a burnt offering. In this way he will make atonement for her before the LORD for the uncleanness of her discharge. (vv. 25–30)

Now, can you imagine what that woman's life must have been like?

Chances are she had a husband and a family, since such bleeding problems most typically arrive in midlife. But for twelve years of her life, this woman had been practically an untouchable—cut off from her family, her friends, and normal society. She had to have been physically weak and depleted as well—twelve years of constant hemorrhage will do that to a person. And Luke tells us specifically that she was financially drained, having spent all she had on doctors who did her no good.

I imagine her living in a little hut a distance away from her home, subsisting on charity from her family and neighbors, spending what little energy she had on washing out her stained garments. Surely she had long ago given up on the idea of going out. What kind of life did she have?

Then she heard that Jesus was in the area and that He could heal people. And she made up her mind to try one more time.

After all her frustrated hopes, I wonder how that poor woman even summoned the energy to seek Him out. Surely He was her last hope—perhaps her final effort before attempting something more drastic. But she was willing to give it one more try. She gathered up her absorbent rags (no Kotex in those days) and somehow made her way to where she had heard Jesus was supposed to be. And she found Him in the midst of a great, surging crowd.

That presented a problem: how could she get to Jesus? She caught a glimpse of Him through the crowd—huddled with His disciples and a distraught man who was yelling something about his daughter. She tried to push her way past elbows and knees, praying not to be noticed, hoping no one would cry out about being touched by an unclean woman.

But she was unclean—and that was another problem. Leviticus made that abundantly clear. No one wanted to touch her or be around her. Surely this holy man would be repelled by the very sight of her.

The familiar despair threatened to engulf her once more, but she shook it off. This was her last chance. She couldn't miss it, no matter what.

Maybe . . .

A tiny hope glimmered in her heart, a minute glint of faith in her black despair.

Maybe He wouldn't have to see her. Maybe she could just work her way in close enough to touch the edge of His cloak.

Steeling herself, she pursed her pale lips and pushed forward through an opening in the crowd . . . reaching, reaching for just the edge of the Healer's garment.

And you know what happened next, don't you?

In the middle of all that shouting and shoving and pushing, Jesus said, "Who touched Me?"

I have always wondered why Jesus asked who had touched him when He surely knew . . . Why create tension and discomfort for the poor woman, who probably just wanted to be healed and go on her way? . . .

Jesus waited for the woman to acknowledge His question because He honestly desired to see her face, to acknowledge her pain, to heal her body and her soul, to encourage her spirit.

He allowed the discomfort because he loved her.

And because He had something even more lavish to do with her than ease her symptoms. He wanted to make her whole.

—SUSIE DAVIS[3]

The disciples laughed. "What do you mean, who touched You? Everybody's touching You." The worried-looking man at Jesus's side inhaled anxiously, clearly wanting Jesus's full attention.

But Jesus repeated, "Who touched Me? I felt the power go out from Me." He turned to look and the crowd fell away, revealing a thin, astonished-looking woman in bulky, stained garments.

"It's stopped," she said as her pale cheeks flushed. "I can feel it."

"What are you talking about?" someone blurted. "Hey, are you all right?" For the woman was trembling. She dropped to her knees before Jesus. And then in a quiet voice, with her eyes glued on her Healer, she began to tell her story. How she had been afflicted for twelve long years. How she had almost bled out of hope. But how merely touching Jesus's robes had healed her.

Her voice was weak at first. The crowd pressed forward to hear, then drew back as they realized she was still ceremonially unclean. If they touched her, they would have to go to all the trouble of washing and still wouldn't be clean until sunset. Better to stand back.

The woman looked around, and her heart sank. She had touched Jesus—just barely, but enough to render Him unclean as well. Would He shrink from her? Would He take the healing back?

But Jesus looked at this woman with loving eyes and called her a name she hadn't heard in years.

"Daughter," He said gently, "your faith has healed you. Go in peace."

Surely she held her head high as she walked away, reveling in the energy she had almost forgotten. She had things to do—clothes to wash, plans to make. She needed to talk to her husband, to her children. Tell her neighbors what had happened.

And then make arrangements to buy a couple of doves for the temple, so she could get on with her life . . .

What God Can Do

Isn't that a fabulous story? It's such a beautiful picture of Jesus's response to those of us who have come to the end of ourselves, reached the end of our rope, bled out our lives, and lost our way in the dead of winter. It's a word of comfort to those who are drowning in shame, a word of hope to those who can see no way out, a word of strength to us who have worn ourselves out trying to do it on our own, to heal ourselves, even to live for Him under our own power.

"Daughter," He says to desperate Christian girls, "just come to Me. Muster whatever last spark of faith you have and reach out, and I will be there for you. I can do so much with so little. I can save your life and send you on your way in peace."

And by the way, the word translated "peace" in the story of the woman with an issue of blood is a Greek version of the Hebrew word *shalom*, which carries many more shades of meaning than our English word *peace*. "Go in peace" doesn't just mean "don't have conflict." It means to be completely well, completely sane, completely whole, with nothing missing, nothing broken. That kind of peace is Jesus's gift to us in our despair, a healing word that changed my life that desperate winter day and has carried me so often in the difficult days that followed.

Our Lord knows our weaknesses. He knows our failings. He knows how hard we try and how hard it is sometimes to turn to Him. He knows our faith can grow dim and our hopes can sputter. But I'm convinced He can take whatever tiny bit of faith we can manage and then use it for our healing.

He heard Elijah's exhausted whining, provided sustenance, nursed him back to health, and then taught him how to really listen.

He responded to a desperate woman's feeble touch at the edge of His cloak and restored her to health.

He heard the halfhearted prayers of a woman in a garage who couldn't stand her life any longer and sent her the one message she could respond to in her weakened state.

So please hear what I'm saying: *He can do it!* Whatever your state of desperation, the One who loves you as a daughter can bring you peace. Even better, He can make you whole.

And yes, I know that not every suicide story ends like mine does. Not every suicide is averted, and even good Christian girls succumb to despair. Honestly, I don't know why. I can't know the state of another person's soul. But I do know my loving, infinitely gracious Lord, and I know that His power is greater than any of our despair.

Just the tiniest bit of faith can transform a desperate situation into an opportunity for God's outrageous grace.

That's what I found when I was literally at the end of my rope.

Treasures at the End of My Rope

The word *despair* literally means "without hope"—and that's dangerous. Despair can drive good Christian girls to the brink of suicide and beyond. It can also cause God's people to become angry and bitter or even to turn their backs on Him. I've known people like that, haven't you? People who have stopped the hemorrhage in their hearts by letting them grow hard.

Yes, despair is a dangerous thing.

But despair can also be a gift, as I learned in my brush with suicide. Desperation can be a motivator. It can slice through our pretenses, show us our lack, and make us willing to do whatever it takes to stop the pain.

If we let it, it can drive us into the arms of God.

That's what happened to me that cold, bleak winter season. I had to get really desperate before I was willing to give up my quest to be the best little Christian girl ever and let God remake me into the kind of daughter He wanted. I had to get to the end of my rope before I started to put my trust in God, where it belonged. I had to give up my hope in myself before I could accept the hope my Savior has to offer.

It took an icy, blustery winter to shatter my safe, false reality—but thank God it shattered. In many ways it was the end of what I knew as "me." But it was a new beginning of who I really am in Christ.

So I learned there is value in our desperation, hope in our hopelessness, if it drives us into the arms of Jesus. There are treasures to be found in the darkness, dangling at the end of our rope, if we can just manage to reach out from there to the only One who can bring us *shalom.*

I know that God used my own desperation to change me, to teach some heart-deep lessons that still echo every day of my life.

One of these is *trust.* For me, this is a no-brainer. How can I not trust a God who has treated me with such loving and personal attention? A God who took my shame-warped, hormone-riddled

---

It comes down to this: God's best is available only to those who sacrifice, or who are willing to sacrifice, the merely good. If we are satisfied with good health, responsible children, enjoyable marriages, close friendships, interesting jobs, and successful ministries, we will never hunger for God's best. We will never worship. I've come to believe that only broken people truly worship. Unbroken people—happy folks who enjoy their blessings more than the Blesser—say thanks to God the way a shopper thanks a clerk.

—LARRY CRABB[4]

faith and used it to rescue me? A God who provided me with loving, sensitive friends—just the friends I needed at just the right moment? (I really believe that timing is God's primary link to this dimension.)

These days I trust God more than ever because He proved so trustworthy in my time of greatest need.

You see, it's one thing to trust God in innocence, because nothing bad has ever happened to you. Or to trust God theoretically but still handle all the hard stuff yourself.

But when you've fallen into a chasm and have been lovingly and heroically rescued, you develop a different kind of trust—an absolute confidence in God's love and His ability to intervene in your life.

So *trust* is one gleaming treasure I found at the end of my rope.

Another is the gift of *compassion*. I've found that enduring winter in my own soul has made me far more loving and understanding of good Christian girls who are struggling with their lives and not making much headway.

I've never really thought of myself as judgmental. But looking back, I wince at how impatient I was with pain and difficulty—both others' and my own. I knew all the answers, and I was quick to spout them off.

Did someone I know have a weight problem? Obviously, she just needed to eat less and exercise more.

Was a friend depressed or anxious? She needed to "let go and let God."

Had someone sinned? She needed to confess the sin and ask forgiveness.

And again, those are all right answers. I offered them kindly and sincerely. I really wanted to help. But I now believe I was way too quick to give advice to people who were struggling. I had always been strong, able to handle anything life threw at me, but struggle and failure made me deeply uneasy. My quick answers were basically a way to make myself more comfortable.

I'm different now that I've lived through that awful winter of my soul. I choose to be more loving, more understanding of human failing—including my own. I'm more willing to suspend judgment, to acknowledge the limits of my own understanding, to give the benefit of a doubt. And I am far more eager to reach out and do what I can to help others who are suffering, because I know firsthand what that suffering feels like. That kind of compassion, I believe, is a gift found only in the darkness of despair.

Yet another treasure I discovered at the end of my rope is *honesty.* I've learned that what hinders God's work in our lives more than any other is our insistence that everything is "just fine." I've learned to be more honest about my shortcomings because, as Dr. Phil McGraw is fond of saying, you can't change what you don't acknowledge. And I learned to be more honest about my suffering because it's hard to heal when you won't even admit you're sick.

I've learned that God can do a lot with our honest pain but very little with our good Christian girl facades. And that's not because He lacks power, but because He chooses to let us choose. If we're determined to pretend everything is fine, He's going to let us keep on going our own way. And because we are fallen, sinful creatures, we're going to

> *Honesty keeps us in touch with our neediness and the truth that we are saved sinners. There is a beautiful transparency to honest disciples who never wear a false face and do not pretend to be anything but who they are.*
>
> —BRENNAN MANNING[5]

mess it up. Our motives will be mixed. Or we simply won't be strong enough to survive the inevitable disappointments of this life.

No, we might not reach the point of suicide. But we still might live futile, defeated lives. We still might be crippled with disappointment and bitterness. We might fall into blatant hypocrisy or lukewarm ineffectiveness. We might settle for what Henry David Thoreau described as "quiet desperation," doing our best but always knowing our best isn't going to measure up.

But we don't have to live that way. There really is an alternative.

It's trusting, compassionate honesty—which feels a lot like courage.

It's looking our disappointment right in the face and daring to let go of our compulsion to be good Christian girls.

It's admitting who we are so God can make us into something new and better.

It's admitting we're so desperate we're willing to do anything just to touch the edge of His garment.

A New Look at Winter

I've often said one of the most important changes we can have in life is a change of perspective. At this point of my life, I'm rediscovering how true this really is.

As I write this chapter, you see, it's January once again. The winds howl, the aspens shiver, the grass is brown and dry. All of creation seems to huddle in the cold, just as it did on that bleak January evening when I almost took my own life.

And I still have my struggles, of course. Who doesn't? Not everything that once drove me to desperation has been resolved.

But things are different now. *I'm* different. My perspective has changed. And because of that change, even winter looks different to me. I'm beginning to see that just as there is hope at the point of despair, even wintertime has its purposes.

In fact, wintertime is just as necessary to growth as spring and summer and fall. Seeds need quiet and cold to prepare for germination. Soil needs rest to support new growth. Trees and bushes need winter dormancy before they can be pruned and shaped.

And even a wintertime of the soul can be useful if it helps us see reality more clearly . . . and if it drives us into the warm arms of God.

I can't honestly say I'm *happy* for the problems and the despair that led me to attempt suicide. I would have preferred to learn the lessons of trust and compassion and honesty another way. And yet I'm glad for what grew in me that particular bleak winter. And I'm spectacularly grateful for the saving presence of God in the midst of my despair.

That's what I wish for you, my friend, in all the seasons of your life—winter included.

That you will have faith enough, when life makes you desperate, to believe you can still have life.

That you'll have hope enough, when times are dark, to reach toward the light.

That you'll open your heart to the love you need to carry you through your coldest winters.

And may you discover, as I did, the deepest truth of all—that no matter where you go, even into the pit, even to the end of your desperate rope, God will still be there.

If you give Him the slightest chance, He will rescue you from the pit.

Heal the hemorrhages of your heart.

Call you daughter.

Bring you peace.

And never leave you. Ever. No matter what the season.

WORD OF GRACE FOR DESPERATE CHRISTIAN GIRLS

The One who loves you as a daughter can bring you peace.

3

"I Just Want to Be Loved"

> *Jesus said . . . "I am the light of the world.*
> *If you follow me, you won't be stumbling through the darkness,*
> *because you will have the light that leads to life."*
> —John 8:12 NLT

It's fuel for the tabloids, fodder for the headlines.

Illicit acts exposed, secret shame revealed.

And it's happening, right now, in places you might never suspect. Even in the lives of good Christian girls.

Yes, I'm talking about sex. About the pain and brokenness that results when love goes wrong and God-given passion goes astray.

Make no mistake: I'm talking about myself here. Chances are, I'm talking about you too.

How would you feel if somebody turned a spotlight on your sexual history? What if everyone you met suddenly knew the details of what you had done and what had been done to you?

Scary thought, isn't it? It is for me. Because although I've known Jesus a long time and deeply desire to honor Him with my life, there are aspects of my sexual past and present I'm not proud of. I have my own particular form of sexual brokenness. And you, too, may struggle with a secret shame you would cringe to have someone else discover.

Someone like your boss. Or your Bible study leader. The children's pastor in your church. The Christian school principal. Your children's parents. The folks next door.

What if they could just look at you and know about that one-night stand you'd rather forget about? About the affair you ended years ago . . . or the one you're involved in right now? What if they knew you slept with your husband before you married him? That you've struggled with a same-sex attraction or dabbled in Internet porn or masturbated compulsively?

> *The world thinks intimacy occurs in the dark, but God says real intimacy occurs in the light! There is no intimacy without honesty.*
>
> —RICK WARREN[1]

What if everyone knew you'd been sexually molested as a child? Or raped as an adult? Or that you've never even had sex—and sometimes feel like a second-class citizen as a result? That your husband stopped being interested in you sexually years ago? That you've been rejected and cheated on? Or that you've used your sexuality to manipulate or even abuse others?

What if people knew that you think about sex all the time?

What if they knew you can't handle sexual intimacy at all?

Sexual brokenness has so many faces. And more often than we want to admit, it's the face of a good Christian girl. In fact, my years in women's ministries have convinced me that more of us are sexually wounded than anyone knows.

Anyone except God, of course.

Because no matter what we manage to keep covered up, God sees everything about us. Including our sexual acting out. Including our most intimate pain. The things we've done, and the things that have been done against us.

Think about that for a minute before we go on, because I'm not writing just to titillate. I'm not writing to expose "juicy" little secrets or glorify sin. But I do want to proclaim from the beginning a reality I've seen at work in the most painful circumstances.

Hear it now. The God who knows the secrets of your inmost heart also knows the sexual secrets that touch your places of tenderest pain. The God who knows you most intimately knows your most intimate wounding. And knowing all that, His response to you is profound. He grieves for your hurt. He loves you more deeply and passionately than any lover could. And He will shine His light on the path that leads you out of the trap of shame.

This is the God who longs to make you whole. Which means straightening out your crooked thinking and twisted desires and filling the empty places that leave you vulnerable to sexual sin. It means healing the sexual neediness . . . the one-night regrets . . . the porn movies . . . the lesbian attraction . . . the left-out feeling of being unpartnered in a hooked-up world.

Best of all, this is the God who can actually do what He promises.

He offers you grace and healing at the depths of your body and soul. Covering for your shame. Correction for your bent desires. Fulfillment for your yearning hunger. Healing for it all.

WHEN THE GIFT GETS BROKEN

Can you relate to what I'm saying?

In a way, for your sake, I hope you can't.

You see, I believe with all my heart that God's sexual best for us is purity if we're single and faithful, loving intimacy if we're married. I believe God created sex as an incredible gift, a source of joy instead of pain. And we were always meant to enjoy an intimate, shame-free relationship with our Creator. Good Christian girls were never meant to live in shame and brokenness because of sexual transgression.

But we do—far more often than many of us want to admit. The specific problems range from regrets over a long-ago past to full-blown sexual addiction—using sex compulsively to control others or mask pain. But no matter what the specific circumstance, the reality of brokenness is the same. The isolation. The fear. The overwhelming sense of being tainted or second class. The soul-deep questions about our ability to love and be loved. The terrible sense of loneliness and isolation in one of the most intimate areas of our lives.

That's the reality Claire lived with from the moment she became a Christian. The sexual compulsiveness that had plagued her for years didn't go away when she gave her life to Christ at a Young Life meeting. Instead, the habits that started early in childhood, when she was sexually molested, proved almost impossible to shake. Habits like compulsive masturbation. And Internet flirtations that inevitably turned into one-night stands. And periods of "sexual anorexia," in which she invested inordinate amounts of energy into not having sex. Her written memoir of those anguished times is so poignant:

> I knew I loved the thrill of sex. I also knew I hated the idea of sex with someone I knew, or I thought liked me. I would play the game, show some interest, conquer, and run . . . leaving some poor guy crying and my friends trying to gather some pieces of his heart to give back. I was blind and confused. I knew if I ever got married,

I was incapable of being faithful. . . . I knew my rebellious heart couldn't be trusted in a marriage covenant, and that qualified me for punishment.

I was a Christian now! Supposedly victorious. How could God ever forgive me? I was beating up my already bruised heart more with guilt and shame. Every night I lay down hating who I had become. Hating sex and loving it. Masturbating. Still trying to conquer all the lies that constantly remained a step ahead. Hurting. So much pain.

Finally I just opted to exist, giving up on my battle. I hardened my heart. I quit on the future. I lived for the moment, doing the best I could. I worshiped God, knowing I was defunct. Sex, masturbation, and God. Until one more moment of crisis fell upon me. I was diagnosed with the herpes simplex virus, a common STD with no cure. . . . While the consequence was difficult, it did not outweigh the jolt reminding me of my state of sin. I had a window . . . a moment. My heart was soft, vulnerable, and willing to exchange exposing my story for an opportunity to live.[2]

Even after her decision to seek help, Claire's full-blown sexual addiction required many months of counseling and years of learning a new way to relate to others. But those who know her rejoice at the beautiful, godly woman she has grown to be.

Cheryl Field, Claire's counselor, also knows the pain of sexual addiction firsthand. Before becoming a Christian, she was married three times—twice to men who were sex addicts themselves—aborted two babies, bore two sons by different fathers. She estimates she slept with nearly a hundred men during a nineteen-year period. And she continued to struggle with the implications of her brokenness long after she committed her life to the Lord, married a Christian man, and even began training as a therapist. But today she is a true minister of God's grace and healing to others—a Christian therapist specializing in sexual addictions.

Of course not all sexual brokenness takes such extreme form as Cheryl's and Claire's. Sexual brokenness has many faces among good Christian girls.

I think of a close friend of mine, a well-known Christian woman and a notable author, who discovered her husband had been involved in a long-term affair, probably seven or eight years. That marriage ended, but within a month my friend found herself deeply involved in an affair with another married man.

I think also of Jennifer, who wrote me to confess that though God healed her of a cocaine addiction and a promiscuous lifestyle, she continued to fight an ongoing battle with Internet porn. She told me it "gives me a stash of images that help me get where I want to get sexually."[4] Without an ongoing commitment to the Word and a steady program of renewing her mind, she knows she will give in again to the illicit temptations of cyberspace.

I think of a new friend who struggled with the fact that her husband never seemed to want her sexually . . . then learned he was spending thousands of dollars on call girls and escort services. He

> *The first step [to healing] is truly the hardest, but it is absolutely essential and critical—that you make yourself known. The greatest fear is being known. The hardest part of that is initially letting yourself be known, fighting through that shame.*
> *The truth will set you free—that truly is the bottom line.*
>
> —CHERYL FIELD[3]

kept saying, "It's not about you." He said he loved her and wanted to be married. And she even understood that was true in a way, but understanding didn't ease the pain.

And I think of myself as well. My struggles with this issue have been very real and my failures very damaging. I can't say I've ever struggled with a sexual addiction, but I've certainly used my sexuality to get love or to escape rejection and pain. And though it pains me to admit it, not all the sex I've experienced has happened during marriage.

I especially remember the embarrassment and shame I felt when my teenage daughter asked me point-blank whether I was a virgin when I got married at twenty. I couldn't be honest and tell her yes. She asked about her dad and me . . . had we waited? Again I had to say no—a reality I regret for many reasons, including the difficulty of teaching a young woman to do as I say, not as I do.

Back then, the possibility that one day I would have children and would be accountable for my choices seemed light-years away. Now here I was, my own sexual brokenness exposed to a daughter I desperately wanted to protect.

WHY FALL?

How does a good Christian girl get herself in such a place? Each circumstance is different, of course. But when I look at the stories of sexually struggling women I know, it's easy to pick out common threads and familiar themes.

First, we want to be loved. Oh, that one is so basic. We want to feel special. We yearn to be desired. And women especially hunger for intimacy, for true closeness.

But our sexual neediness is often more complex than that. We may fall into sexual sin simply because we want to experience pleasure . . . or distract ourselves from pain. Some of us have bought the lies of a dominant culture that proclaims it's impossible to live a full life without sexual experience and that sex between consenting adults is no big deal. We may want to feel affirmed as women. We may fear missing out on fulfillment—and we've bought the lie that we can't be fulfilled if we're not fulfilled in a sexual way.

Some of us sin sexually because we're bored. Or craving the comfort of someone's arms. Or because we've become dependent on the physical release of sexual excitement. Or as a way of acting out our anger with others or rebellion toward God. Or for the ego boost of being desired and the sense of power that comes from sexually attracting others. (Women have known for centuries that sexuality is an effective tool for getting what we want.)

Like my author friend, we may want revenge for rejection or abandonment—to prove to those who mistreated us that we are indeed worthy, attractive, lovable.

Or we may want something more specific. A child, perhaps. Or some kind of material gift.

Sadly, some of us may have suffered sexual abuse and other forms of mistreatment—abuse that confused us and taught us lies and awakened a heightened sense of sexuality. Early experiences may have caused us to fear real intimacy and compulsively seek to control others with fake intimacy.

Under all these reasons, all these motivations, I believe, is that deep desire to be seen. Really seen. To be fully, intimately known . . . and loved for who we are.

Aren't you hungry for that, deep inside? I am, even when I'm most worried that someone will know about my sexual brokenness.

It's really a kind of paradox.

We live in terror that our dark secrets will be discovered, yet we crave the light.

And secretly we wonder if we'll ever emerge from the shadows of shame and darkness.

Not the Only Sin

Sexual sin, like most human sin, is a good thing perverted, led astray by human selfishness, human greed, human fallibility. And like all sin, apart from Christ's saving grace, its wages is death. The apostle Paul even says that sexual sin has a special seriousness and warns us, "Run away from sexual sin! No other sin so clearly affects the body as this one does. For sexual immorality is a sin against your own body" (1 Cor. 6:18 NLT). Sexual sin, in other words, messes us up in a deeper way than a lot of other sins because it affects some of the deepest aspects of our personhood.

> *[Our] hunger for intimacy with God is echoed in all our yearnings for relationship as well. Sometimes it leads us away from the Source and we look to others to fill that God-shaped place in our souls . . . But God, who uses everything, can use even illegitimate longings to draw us eventually toward more legitimate relationships.*
>
> —Michael Card[5]

Yet I've sometimes wondered how we've gotten to the place where the word *sin* automatically makes us think of *sex*. I believe it's dangerous to think that way. It's as if sexual sin is the only sin . . . or the only unforgivable one. So that when most people hear the word *morality*, they automatically think *sex*.

Jesus didn't think that way. Yes, He supported the Old Testament teachings about sex. He never condoned sexual immorality. Yet when you read the Gospels, you'll see that sexual issues just weren't a major priority for Jesus. He paid a lot more attention to sins of disbelief and disobedience, to injustice and mistreatment of the poor, to spiritual pride and arrogance, than He ever did to sexual behavior.

I think that's important to recognize when we look at issues of sexual brokenness. I'm not saying sexual sin is all right. But I do want to put it into perspective.

And here's something else that's interesting: of the episodes in Jesus's life where we see Him responding to sexual issues and sexual sin . . . most of them involve women.

Have you ever thought about that? The reality of that?

There's the "sinful woman" in Luke 7 who anointed Jesus's feet, for instance. Or the Samaritan woman at the well who had had five husbands and was living with a man she wasn't married to. Or Mary Magdalene, who according to tradition was a prostitute—though the Bible makes no such claim.

There are places in the Gospels where Jesus answers the (male) Pharisees' theological tricky questions about divorce or teaches about the inner reality of lust. But the Gospel passages showing real people with sexual problems are invariably about women.

Even more important, they're about wounded women who discovered grace and healing for their sexual wounds as they encountered the Light of the world.

Women like the woman whose title sums up her indictment. We know her as "the woman caught in the act of adultery."

Caught red-handed in her own brokenness . . . on a day that changed her life forever.

A CASE OF EXPOSURE

She knew it the minute they rushed in the room in the early morning. Knew it when her lover wouldn't meet her eyes. Knew it as they dragged her from the room, barely giving her time to throw on a robe, let alone sandals.

For some reason she'd been set up. Betrayed. Exposed. But why? What was going on?

She'd known all along that she could get caught. But her need was so great, the desire so strong, the risk had almost seemed worth it.

Now the very thing she feared had come to pass.

They dragged her from the house, her bare toes stubbing against the road. The stone-faced Pharisees refused even to look at her. They just hurried her on, tense hands gripping her forearms.

From the corner of her eye, she saw one stop to pick up a jagged rock from the side of the street.

The possibility chilled her. *Surely not . . .*

Her lover had sworn that the Scripture-prescribed penalty for adultery never happened these days. (Where is he anyway? Why haven't they accused him too?) The Romans claimed the sole right to capital punishment; they wouldn't let the Jews stone anyone. But watching the Pharisees' tight lips, their determined faces, those white knuckles clutching the stones . . . she had to wonder.

A part of her even wished it would happen. Maybe death would be easier. Better than living in shame and disgrace.

Disgrace . . . A fresh wave of fear washed over her. Her guilt was devastating, unmistakable. And about to be announced to the whole city. But why single her out? Why should they care so much about one woman's sin?

It wasn't until they reached the temple court that she began to see what was really happening. That it wasn't about her at all—although she would bear the consequences.

What these Pharisees really wanted was to trap the man named Jesus. She was just the object lesson, the visual aid. Their real target was the quiet man in the center of the hubbub. The man with the strange eyes that managed to look both fierce and gentle.

He watched in silence as the Pharisees dragged her across the courtyard and dropped her at His feet. She lay there crumpled, clutching at her gaping garment. Not daring to look up as the men spat out their challenge.

And then, for some reason, she had to look. As she met the man's gaze, she felt her spirit grow strangely calm as well. What was it about this man?

"This woman has been caught in the act of adultery," one of the Pharisees was saying. "Our laws say she should be stoned to death."

They're trying to get Him in trouble with the Romans, she realized. The Roman authorities forbade the Jews from following the letter of the Torah law and stoning adulterers to death. *Or catch Him dismissing our laws. He's being set up too.*

She wondered if this Jesus knew it. If His thoughts were racing as hers were.

If He would condemn her as everyone else did.

As everyone had a right to do.

But He didn't look worried. He wasn't even paying attention to the

Pharisees. Instead, He squatted down and began to write something in the dust.

She craned her neck, but she couldn't really see what He was writing. So she watched the faces of her accusers. Watched the emotions parade across—discomfort, guilt, disbelief, embarrassment. They blinked as if staring into a bright light. Then one by one, still blinking, heads hanging, they dropped their rocks and turned away.

The wrinkled, gray-haired ones were the first to leave—and they were the ones in charge of the show. Then the middle-aged men turned and left. The last one to leave was a dark-haired man not much older than her son.

She watched as one by one they slunk away, trying hard to hide the shame on their faces. But she saw it, because it was her shame too. Because no matter that she'd been set up, she was still guilty—and everyone knew it now. There was no going back. Soon, she knew, the loss would hit her. For now, she just watched with numb curiosity.

As the last of her accusers slunk from the temple, the man Jesus turned to her. And finally, for the first time, it really was about her.

Somehow, she found courage to meet His eyes. And in the face of the man who'd boldly faced down the Pharisees she saw nothing but . . . compassion.

And something else. Something different from the look of her lover. Something far removed from the Pharisees' crafty stares and the crowd's scorn and pity.

For once again she was exposed.

Once again all was revealed.

But this time, for the first time in many shame-filled years, the light was her friend. Though her life as she knew it was over, for the first time in many years she felt . . . safe.

He asked the obvious. "Does no one condemn you?"

She looked around the courtyard. Onlookers still gaped, but her accusers were all gone. She shook her head.

A little smile played around His lips, almost as if He were enjoying a private joke.

"Well, I don't condemn you either."

And the strange thing, when He said it, she knew it was true.

All was known. The truth was out there. And somehow, because of this amazing encounter, everything would be all right.

He really didn't have to speak the next words, but He did: "Go, and leave your life of sin."

She almost laughed. Where could she go . . . except to follow after this man who had transformed her world? Slowly she got to her feet, only dimly aware of her scraped knees, her stubbed toes, her disheveled hair and clothing. She kept her eyes on Him, wondering what He would do next.

What He did was preach a little sermon.

"I am the Light of the world," He told the remaining crowd.

She tilted her head at the words. A strange statement for an exceedingly strange morning.

And then, suddenly, it hit her.

Light.

That was what she had been missing all these many years.

Light that showed the truth, that illuminated who she really was.

The light she had feared for so long.

Now she stood in its full glare and found it wasn't fearful at all. It was warm. It was kind and loving. Because this man with the light in His eyes wasn't giving her orders. He wasn't accusing her. He had no hidden motives or desire to use her.

He was simply stating a fact: *Who I am changes everything.*

She believed it. She'd seen it.

As to what came next, who knew?

She just knew she'd be sticking close to the One who saw her sin exposed and loved her anyway.

The One who could show her how to live in light instead of darkness.

THREE TRUTHS

So what does this say to good Christian girls who have been broken by sexual sin? I see four crucial truths in the Lord's encounter with this woman.

First of all, *sin is sin.* Though Jesus doesn't overemphasize sexual sin, He never pretends it isn't serious. And don't be fooled—He'll find a way to shine the spotlight on the sexual sin in your life and its damaging consequences. A stray e-mail, an overheard conversation, a suspicious intuition, an awakening conscience—one way or another, in His own time, He'll reveal your brokenness.

But not to shame you. (Shame is never from Christ.)

Not to set you up.

No, the purpose of the light Jesus shines is to heal your heart.

Which brings us to the second truth, which is that *the truth really does set you free.* Jesus said that in John 8:32, and it's as true of our sexual secrets as it is of any other aspect of life. Though most of us hide—and hide from—our sexual brokenness, though we fear exposure more than anything, though we are used to fiercely protecting our intimate selves . . . the truth is that we only find freedom when we make the choice to stop hiding and to live in the light.

Cheryl Field, the former sex addict who now counsels sexually broken people, makes this point quite specifically: "The first step [in healing] is truly the hardest, but it is absolutely essential—that you fight through the shame and make yourself known. . . . The truth will set you free, that truly is the bottom line, and facing the truth is going to lead to a much greater life than that hidden shame, that hidden secret you have to work so hard to keep."[6]

And no, that doesn't mean you have to tell everyone everything you've ever done—or that you should. There is a place for privacy. There is a place to protect others. There is even a place to protect ourselves. Given the judgmental attitudes in many churches, I would certainly recommend caution about whom you trust with your intimate brokenness. Christ doesn't condemn you, but quite a few Christians might!

At the same time, when it comes to our sexual brokenness, we will never find healing until we learn to open up about the issues we usually relegate to darkness. At the very least, we need to be honest with ourselves and with God—to confess our brokenness specifically, repent of our sins, and ask for guidance and healing. In addition, we need at least one other carefully chosen person—a friend, relative, pastor, or counselor—to come completely clean with. Someone who will accept us despite our failings and yet call us to continue living in the light. I have found that when I get serious about opening up this way, the Holy Spirit is faithful to show me who the right person is.

Beyond that, within the limits of kindness, decency, and wisdom, there's a tangible benefit to living as openly and transparently as possible. The more we open up to others, even about our failings, the more we'll know the joy of living in the light.

I know this is true with me. Though I still struggle with issues of what to share and what to hide, when to talk openly and when to keep silent, I know that my healing works best when I adopt a general policy of transparency about my life and even about my mistakes. When I resist the urge to keep my struggles secret, I almost always find my honesty opens the way not only to healing but to ministry. When I come clean about my pain, I find I am sought out by others who are struggling with the same issues.

That was certainly true about the day my daughter asked me hard questions about my past sex life. Hard as it was, I chose to answer her truthfully. But after that, I was able to truthfully share my heart about the consequences of mistakes, the reality of forgiveness, and the importance of living in the light. While I lost the chance to set an example of purity, I believe I was able to set an example of integrity, to show that the truth really can set us free.

But why is that exactly? Why are truth and light so healing when it comes to sexual sin? I think it's because we can't hide our shame without hiding our hearts as well. And if we're hiding our hearts, we'll never really trust the love that's offered to us. We'll always be thinking, *If anyone really knew . . .*

But of course Someone does know. Jesus sees you, really sees you. Your pain. Your failings. Your deep longings and your most grievous sin. He knows what you have done, what has been done against you. And what the pain of brokenness has caused you to do—for those who have been sinned against almost always end up sinning themselves.

Jesus sees all this, and He still wants you . . . in the most loving, most intimate, most pure and wholesome way possible.

Do you hear that?

You might feel like damaged goods. You might squirm with embarrassment to realize the Lord of the universe knows your intimate secrets. You might be so used to hiding yourself that light feels downright painful.

But no matter what you've done, no matter what has been done to you, no matter how dirty or shameful or frustrated or confused you feel, you are beautiful to Him. You are desirable—so much so that He was willing to give His life for you. He never wants to see you hurt, because He loves you more than life itself . . . and He has better things in store for you than you could possibly imagine.

Which is the third message this story has to deliver. No matter how sordid or shameful or embarrassing your past may be, *your past is not your future.*

> *"Go! And sin no more."* . . . *is an empowering word. It encourages the sin-sick soul that we needn't remain stuck in our destructive sinful ways. In modern day speak Jesus might have said, "You go girlfriend! You can live a life free from sexual sin."*
>
> —MARIO BERGNER[7]

That's exactly what Jesus was saying when He told the woman caught in adultery to leave her life of sin. Some Scripture versions translate that as, "Go and sin no more." But surely Jesus didn't think she could walk away and never commit another sin!

No, what Jesus was telling the woman, and what He tells us, too, is that we can change directions. We can move away from the patterns of pain and abuse and selfishness and twisted desires that keep us away from the true intimacy we long for. Though we may feel trapped and hopeless, helpless in the face of our fears and our desires, terrified of letting ourselves be known, He can show us how to move beyond this brokenness into a new kind of life.

It's really possible. We can do it. Jesus said so.

54

And that's the real kicker—just as it was for the woman caught in the act of adultery.

It's not just about facing our destructive behavior, though that's crucial.

It's not just about God's forgiveness, though that's real.

It's really about "What happens now?" About how we can move beyond our sexual brokenness and experience wholeness on a daily basis. How we can leave our shameful secrets behind and learn to live in the light of His love.

Not that it's easy. As so many of us good Christian girls have discovered, issues of sexual brokenness reach deep. Sinful habits can be hard to break, and the agonizing consequences of our brokenness may stick with us for a long time. The compulsion to hide our shame and control our pain may make healthy intimacy a struggle for years to come.

We may need counseling (and thank God for wise Christian counselors like Cheryl Field). We will definitely need support from friends, from family, from others who have walked the path we're trying to take. We will need time to heal, a healthy dose of forgiveness for ourselves and others.

Most of all, we'll need a daily walk with the only One with the right to condemn us . . . and who chooses to love us instead.

Which brings us to the final message of this remarkable story, the reality that transformed the life of the woman caught in adultery and can transform yours as well, no matter how painfully broken you may feel.

It's what the woman realized when He told her to leave her life of sin: *Who Jesus is, dear friend, changes everything.*

He is truly the light of the world, who shines His revealing but healing ways on our darkest, most shameful secrets. Whose laser love can not only burn out our guilt and woundedness and restore us to health but also show us a whole new way to live. A whole new path to take of honesty, transparency, openness, where the inside you matches the outside you and you can freely love and be loved.

You see, the issue of sexual sin is absolutely about you. It's about who you were meant to be from the beginning and who you can become. Not defined by your own sins or victimized by another's. Not trapped in your shame or driven by your desires. But strong, confident, loving, forgiven, and free.

At the same time, it's not about you at all. It's really about Jesus. About the kind of life He died to bring to this twisted, perverted, broken world. It's about transforming grace . . . passion made pure . . . light that purifies.

And love, at last, gone right.

WORD OF GRACE FOR SEXUALLY BROKEN CHRISTIAN GIRLS

The only One who has a right to condemn you . . . doesn't.
You can leave your life of sin and follow Him into the light.

4

"You Can't Treat Me This Way!"

The Desolation of Family Violence and Abuse

My God is my rock, in whom I find protection.
He is my shield, the strength of my salvation, and my stronghold,
My high tower, my savior, the one who saves me from violence.
—2 Samuel 22:3 NLT

Lisa's mother used to call herself "the girl with the curl."

As in "When she was good, she was very, very good."

As in "When she was bad, she was horrid."

And Lisa's mother was right. Because those extremes of "good" and "horrid" defined Lisa's life as far back as Lisa can remember—which is only back to age seven or eight. That was her age when her father left home for good. It's when her mother got hooked on prescription medications following a traumatic mastectomy. It's when Lisa thinks that the "horrid" first showed itself . . . and the beatings began.

The attacks would come out of nowhere—slaps, punches, vicious kicks, hair pulling, curses, and insults that left Lisa crouched in terror. When the fury was finally spent, her mother would disappear into her bedroom for a while, then go out and buy Lisa some kind of treat. But she never apologized. She rarely even acknowledged what had happened—except to catalog the ways Lisa "made me do it" and to hiss, "You'd better not tell!"

Lisa never did. She was a strong girl, a responsible firstborn female who desperately wanted to please. So she joined in hiding her family's "horrid" reality, even as their home life deteriorated and even more secrets began to pile up. Such as the new boyfriend who lived with them for three years before marrying Lisa's mother. And the sexual abuse he started when Lisa was twelve. And the fact that her mother was rapidly becoming incapable of caring for the family. Increasingly, it fell to Lisa to clean the house, prepare the meals, care for eight younger siblings and stepsiblings, keep up with school, and care for her heavily medicated mother, who by now spent much of her time in bed.

At age fifteen, Lisa gave her life to Christ—a monumental and lifesaving event. For the first time in her life she felt chosen, special, blessed. She was certain God had a purpose for her, that He would show her the way, that He wanted her life to count for something. But how all that applied to her life at home, Lisa didn't know. Because though her mother and stepfather became Christians not long after she did, nothing much changed in the way they lived. The beatings continued. The molestation never stopped. Lisa still lived as Cinderella . . . with no glass slipper in sight.

Not that her life was *always* horrid. That was part of the problem. From the beginning, there were times when tension waned and the family would be almost happy. Her mother was especially encouraging. She'd say, "Lisa, you're my shining star." "Lisa, you can do anything, and I'm going to help you." Even her stepfather had his good moments, and Lisa's little brothers and sisters adored her. She loved them all too. And though this love brought her strength, it also worked to keep her trapped.

So Lisa let her mother sabotage her relationship with boys and talk her out of going to college. She did her best to stay away from her stepfather when he got "that look." She took on far more responsibility than she could be expected to handle. But the pain and pressure grew . . . until something finally gave way inside.

That was the day Lisa packed her bags, slipped out of the house, and disappeared—another good Christian girl who just couldn't take it anymore.

> *Violence is everyone's problem.*
> *It is an issue that is not going away.*
> *It is prevalent in our churches and*
> *in the communities our churches serve.*
> *We need to crawl out from under the church carpet and*
> *admit that we have been hiding from the problem, sometimes*
> *contributing to it, and not very committed*
> *to being part of its solution.*
>
> —CATHERINE CLARK KROEGER AND NANCY NASON-CLARK[1]

SO MANY ABUSE STORIES

I wish I could tell you my friend Lisa's story is unique. It breaks my heart that I can't. But the truth is that far too many "good" Christian homes are sources of pain and even outright danger to the most vulnerable people who live there.[2]

It happens every day. Christian husbands batter Christian wives. Christian wives abuse their husbands. Christian parents mistreat their children, and adult children mistreat their parents. Older, stronger brothers and sisters beat or molest younger ones. And Christian pastors, teachers, and other authority figures threaten, manipulate, browbeat, or twist God's truth to control their flocks . . . for abuse happens in the family of God as well as in good Christian homes.

And by abuse, I don't mean temper tantrums or impassioned arguments or even the occasional hostile act. I'm talking about a *pattern* of behavior in which one person uses any means possible to get his own way at another person's expense.

Such abuse may be *physical*—involving actual bodily pain or damage. It may be *verbal*—insults, belittling, sarcasm. It may be *psychological*—threats, mind games, social isolation, or forced financial dependence, or symbolic acts such as destroying property or hurting pets. Some abuse is *sexual*—ranging from indecent exposure to coerced sexual acts. Abuse can be *spiritual* as well—when authority is misused and biblical truths twisted to justify one person hurting another.

It hurts just to talk about it, to think of one person treating another that way. But if abuse has touched your life, you know the reality is far more hurtful.

Like Lisa, you may be an adult victim of childhood abuse. Normal discipline may have turned to vicious beatings. People who were supposed to love you insisted you would never amount to anything. Cuddling and closeness turned into something sexual and shaming. Sibling rivalry became a campaign of name calling, pinching, and whispered threats. And though these traumatic events are behind you now, you may still struggle with lingering fear, depression, and feelings of worthlessness.

But perhaps the abuse is *not* behind you yet. You may live with someone who punches, kicks, slaps, cuts, or sexually humiliates you.

You may walk on eggshells most of the time, never knowing what will set off the other person. Conversation at home often consists of insults and put-downs. You're forced to account for every penny you spend, every moment you're away from home. You may be confused, wondering if what you're experiencing is normal, whether it's really abuse, whether it's really your fault. Perhaps you've become so fearful and isolated that you have no idea what to think or where to turn. You can't even ask for help, because the thought of anyone knowing what your life is like makes you cringe with shame.

There's a chance you may be an abuser as well. You've lost control and disciplined your children too harshly. Or let loose verbally with wounding "zingers." Or even gotten physically violent with your husband—kicking, biting, or throwing things.[3] Maybe you've done things that scare you or flood you with guilt . . . or simply read the statistics and realized they could apply to you.

Even if none of these scenarios is true, you may be a witness to abuse. If you've ever worried about your spouse's methods of discipline, cringed when your grown child's spouse (or your own child) yelled at your grandchildren, or worried about the way your daughter's boyfriend treats her, you know how painful such secondhand violence can be. Perhaps as a child you watched one parent beat or browbeat the other. Perhaps you were aware a sibling was being molested but didn't know what to do. Or perhaps, like me, you live with someone whose childhood abuse affects your current relationship today. Any of these secondhand scenarios may haunt you with guilt and questions: *What should I have done? Why was I spared? Why does nothing I do seem to help?*

Even if you're blessed enough to avoid these "horrid" realities, chances are it's happening to someone you know. A neighbor. A friend of your children. A colleague or fellow church member. Someone you see every day could be struggling with the pain and shame and isolation of being an abused or abusing good Christian girl.

> *Abuse, like sin, is serious business. But sin, in God's scheme of things, never has the last word.*
>
> —JULIE ANN BARNHILL[4]

And that's the bad news—that God's people can do such things to those they claim to love. That good Christian families endure the trauma of abuse, some of it done in the name of God. It has to break the Father's heart—the way His children warp His good gifts and turn them to curses, the many ways we hurt one another.

WHY ABUSE?

Why in the world would one person—especially a Christian—abuse another person? And why would anybody *let* it happen to him or her?

You know the short answer: *sin.*

Like all sin, abuse is a twisted perversion of what God made good. He created us with a need for intimate relationships, for security, for sexual expression. He gave us families and gender roles and even spiritual hierarchies for our support and our security and protection. And because we are fallen, because we are wounded, because we are selfish, we inevitably end up misusing these good gifts.

Instead of holding each other tenderly, we cling to each other too tightly. Instead of protecting one another, we take out our pain and frustrations on the closest vulnerable person. Instead of building each other up, we desperately try to push ourselves to the top of the heap. Instead of doing what is right, we get it all wrong—and isn't that the very definition of sin?

But the issue of *control* is what distinguishes abuse from generic sin and selfishness. Abuse is essentially a power play—an attempt to dominate or coerce another person. This is so important to understand, because it's so often misunderstood.

You see, abuse isn't an anger issue, although abusers often use rage as a weapon or an excuse. It's not a relationship issue, although it can devastate a relationship. It's not a sexual issue, though abuse often plays itself out in sexual ways. And it's not a drug or alcohol or mental-health issue, although addictions and mental illness are often involved, or a class issue, although poor or uneducated families are subject to pressures that make the problems worse.

While any of these factors may be involved in an abuse situation or contribute to it, the underlying motive will always be *control*. Simply put, abusers act out of a desire or need to control their environment by controlling the people closest to them.

Behind this urge to control, of course, is fear, insecurity, need—a need to feel less vulnerable, to be on top, to not feel pain or loss. People who feel weak or out of control tend to tighten their grip wherever they can and take out their frustration on those who are weaker. Those who have been hurt or wounded attempt to make themselves feel less vulnerable by lashing out against those who can't fight back. And some people . . . well, some people just want to get their own way, no matter what. Sadly, it's human nature for those who fear weakness to prey on those who are even weaker, just as those who have been sinned against will almost always be tempted to sin.

Misguided assumptions and belief structures—or just plain ignorance—may also contribute to abuse. Julie Ann Barnhill, who describes her own struggle with abusive tendencies in a book called *She's Gonna Blow*,[5] believes this was a major factor in her interaction with her children. Her maternal frustration levels rose because she didn't fully understand how children develop. Normal, age-appropriate behavior seemed like willful defiance to her, so she lashed out at her children in an angry attempt to keep them in line.

In a similar way, an abusive husband may become frustrated if his wife doesn't act the way he thinks a wife is supposed to act. He may believe it's his right or his responsibility as head of the home to dictate and control everything that goes on and enforce that control by any means necessary. All too often, he is bolstered in this belief by the norms of his culture or the teachings of his church, although as we'll see, such teachings distort the biblical message.

Yet another contributor to abuse is past experience—because abuse is learned behavior. Abusers typically resort to violence and control of others because that's what they experienced or witnessed in their families of origin. Which means that if you've experienced violence in your family as a child—either as a victim or an onlooker—your chances of being involved in an abusive situation as an adult are much greater.[6] Even if you hated the violence and vowed never to fall into it, you may find yourself lashing out in times of stress or frustration. And even if you swore never to let yourself be abused, you may end up in another abusive relationship simply because it feels familiar.

And added to all this is the reality that, in the short term, at least, abuse works. Abusers *do* get their own way, at least in the short run. And abuse can be *cathartic*. That is, it actually feels good to the abuser, because violent outbursts serve to relieve pent-up tension.

This cathartic "payoff" helps explain why abuse in relationships often runs in cycles—and why it's so hard to stop. Immediately after an episode of abuse, the abuser typically feels calmer and acts more reasonable. He may be remorseful and apologetic, promising sincerely that the abuse will never happen again. For a while, he may be genuinely nice and kind and helpful, trying hard to atone for the trouble he's caused. But over time the tension builds again . . . along with the urge to relieve it by acting out toward someone close.

The whole process works almost like an addiction, and it can be fully as destructive. According to a report by the U.S. Surgeon General, domestic violence accounts "for more emergency room visits than traffic accidents, muggings and rape combined."[7] That's not even to mention the ongoing emotional trauma,[8] the physical and emotional isolation and loneliness, the mental-health issues, substance abuse, erosion of self, and destruction of faith and the ability to trust. As we've seen, abuse also creates abusers, passing along the pain and shame from generation to generation.

And abuse hurts abusers as well as their victims. For although the abuse usually "works"—it achieves its purpose of control and releases tension—it can never satisfy the underlying need that drives it. So the underlying anxiety continues, heightened by the guilt and shame of having harmed a loved one, the fear of being found out, and the fear of losing the very relationship the abuser tried so hard to control. For Christian abusers, there's a significant spiritual fallout as well. For the Bible stresses not only that this kind of violence is wrong, but that it hinders the prayers of an abuser (see Isa. 58:4; 1 Pet. 3:7).

WHY DO THEY TAKE IT?

If abuse is so damaging, why don't abuse victims stand up to their abusers and fight . . . or just run away? Many do—eventually. But many others put up with the abuse for years on end, even when it steadily grows worse. Catherine Clark Kroeger and Nancy Nason-Clark suggest three "F-words" to explain why this may happen.[9]

First, they may *fear* what will happen if they leave—further abuse (which is likely), rejection or ridicule, living without a man, or simply the unknown.

Financial concerns may also tie women to their abusers—they may lack the skills to support themselves and their children, or the abuser may keep such tight financial control that she can't accumulate the funds to escape.

And *fantasy* keeps abuse victims in dangerous relationships as well. Like Lisa, they may live in a world that is both "horrid" and "very, very good." They love their abuser and want the relationship to continue—they just want the abuse to stop. And sadly, that's not likely—unless something changes significantly.

> *There is a time for self-sacrifice—for the sake of the gospel, to save the life of another, to remain faithful to Christ—but surely not to enable the misbehavior of another. The seventh commandment implies that believers should take all possible steps to prevent murder rather than to implement it.*
>
> —CATHERINE CLARK KROEGER AND NANCY NASON-CLARK[10]

Fear, finances, and fantasy—those are three potent *F*s that hold back abuse victims from escaping their pain, and I would add two more. One is *fiction*—meaning lies. Abusers, like addicts, can be slick and masterful deceivers. They'll say almost anything to keep another person under their thumb. Abuse victims also lie to themselves, insisting, "It's not really that bad" or "It's all my fault." Both victims and abusers can become adept at lying to outsiders about what's really going on. And until the lies are challenged, there's little chance of any real change.

And the final *F,* which can be especially dangerous to good Christian girls, is *faith.* Not faith in itself, but faith combined with confused emotions, misreading of the Bible, and mistaken ideas about what God expects. Thus a sincerely faithful woman may put up with abuse because she wants to please God—and because she believes God wants her to submit to anything her husband dishes out . . . or she hopes her suffering will redeem him . . . or she has prayed for him to change and expects her prayers to be answered. She may be convinced it's God's will for families to stay intact no matter what or that she should forgive wrongs again and again.

That's not to say that biblical teachings on headship, suffering, prayer, families, and forgiveness are lies! But these teachings can easily be taken out of context and used to justify behavior that God would never sanction. That, in itself, is a form of spiritual abuse—the very opposite of what God wants for His children.

Nothing New

Sadly, abuse is nothing new. Families have been hurting each other throughout history. And that's true of God's family too. Some of the most prominent families in biblical history experienced episodes of "horrid" abuse.

Take, for instance, the sad story of King David's daughter Tamar, as told in 2 Samuel 13–14. Beautiful, wealthy, and privileged, this girl was a true princess. She was also quick-thinking, courageous, and resourceful. And none of these qualities was enough to save her from vicious abuse at the hands of her own half brother, Amnon, who developed a "thing" for her and hatched a plan to seduce her. He pretended to be sick and begged their father to send Tamar to care for him.

Talk about being set up! Tamar must have known something was wrong—it was such a strange request. But Tamar had orders from her father, the king. So she pushed back the long sleeves on her beautiful embroidered gown and set to work doing what she was told, baking bread for her "sick" brother in his chambers. But Amnon sent everyone else away and attempted to seduce his sister. Amazingly, Tamar kept her head and tried to talk her way out of her predicament, but Amnon wouldn't listen to reason. And when he realized he wouldn't be able to sweet-talk his half sister into bed, he simply pushed her down and raped her. Then he called for a servant and had her thrown—still protesting—from his chambers.

Violated and betrayed, Tamar ended up in a heap outside the door as the bolt slammed shut behind her. She looked down at her beautiful embroidered gown and acted appropriately: She wept! She tore her dress. She smeared ashes on her face. Then she ran home and told her brother Absalom . . . who was absolutely no help. He acted as if the abuse had been done to *him*—making light of Tamar's pain even while he made plans to avenge the rape by killing Amnon.

Their father, David, was also less than helpful. Though furious with Amnon, he did nothing to comfort his daughter or punish his son. He just let Tamar remain in Absalom's house—as the Bible tells it, "a desolate woman" (2 Sam. 13:20).

And that's almost the last word we have about Tamar—because as far as we know, there was no happily-ever-after for her. No redemption, no reconciliation, just bitter desolation. Absalom had Amnon murdered, then later rebelled against his father and was killed too. David struggled with overwhelming grief for his children and the knowledge that he had failed his God once more.

> *We must be very clear about the Bible's condemnation of violence and abuse. There are more than one hundred Biblical passages addressing battering, violence, rape, incest, stalking, lying in wait, twisting the words of another, threats, and intimidation. Since the Word of God condemns violence and abuse, the Church must be faithful in teaching this truth. How seldom is that message preached from the pulpit; and how powerful and life changing it could be!*
>
> —WORLD EVANGELICAL FELLOWSHIP TASK FORCE
> TO STOP ABUSE AGAINST WOMEN[11]

A sad outcome for a tragic tale—though I'm tempted to imagine it didn't really end there. I like to think Tamar did manage to move beyond her desolation. Maybe she followed her father's lead and turned to God, letting her bitterness and grief be gradually transformed. Maybe she made a place for herself in Absalom's household as the wise woman everyone turned to for help. Maybe she found a man who was willing to put up with a little disgrace to marry a beautiful, wealthy, and resourceful princess.

But again, we don't know. What we do know is that Tamar's desolation wasn't the very last word in her story. The last word is that Tamar wasn't forgotten—and that's something for all us hurting good Christian girls to take to heart.

For one thing, we are told that Absalom named a daughter after her and that this little Tamar became a beautiful woman (2 Sam. 14:27). No doubt this namesake grew up remembering her aunt. I like to think that David remembered Tamar too. For while David the king could sin with the best of them, he also was capable of true repentance, which is the one ingredient that can redeem abuse and change the direction of a family. I hope David rethought his part in Tamar's situation and did what he could to make amends to his daughter.

And yes, this is all speculation. Maybe it's wishful thinking. But the one thing we know for sure is that *God* remembered Tamar. That's why her story is in the Bible for us to ponder, a powerful example of how families are *not* supposed to treat each other. It's a warning for good Christian girls and good Christian boys as well—that abuse results in nothing but desolation.

So we remember Tamar as well. We *should* remember her. But when we do, I hope we also remember another member of God's family whose tale of abuse (told in Genesis 16 and 21) had a completely different ending.

HAGAR AND GRACE

How much more of this can I take? I see Hagar leaning awkwardly against a stunted palm, cheek pressed against the rough bark, tears splashing down onto her very pregnant belly, and Sarai's spiteful words still ringing in her ears. How could her mistress treat her this way?

Well, maybe she *had* flaunted her pregnancy a little. She knew Sarai was sensitive about being too old to bear children. But this whole situation was Sarai's idea! She was the one who hatched the plan to send Hagar to sleep with Abram, hoping her maid would bear a son for his aging father. Hagar, a servant, had no choice in the matter. So she'd done what her mistress ordered and submitted to the old man's embrace and conceived a child as instructed. And ever since, Sarai had treated her with nothing but contempt. Unreasonable demands. Hourly scoldings. And more and more work, though Hagar was nearing her time and tired easily.

I can't take much more! Do You hear me, God? At first it had struck her as strange to pray to a single deity when she'd had so many to choose from back home in Egypt. But she'd lived with Abram and Sarai a long time and grown accustomed to their God. Besides, this Yahweh was making her part of His plans—or so Sarai claimed. *I'm obviously too old to have children, but Yahweh promised Abram would be father to many. So maybe He's going to work through you . . .*

Hagar felt the child in her womb kick hard and allowed herself a little smile. A lively one, this child of hers—surely strong enough to father a nation. *No wonder Sarai is jeal—*

"Aren't you finished with the bread yet?" Sarai's petulant voice pierced through Hagar's thoughts. "There's still the stew to make, and I need you to do some spinning, and then I want you to sweep the carpets again. If you'd just get moving . . ."

Hagar groaned but answered as reasonably as she could. "The coals are almost ready; I just had to take a rest." She braced her back with a fist as she pushed away from the palm. "You just don't know what it's—ow!"

Hagar heard the *whoosh* of Sarai's walking stick almost the same instant she felt its stoutness on her shoulders. Not that hard a blow—Sarai was an old woman, after all—but hard enough to be painful. And humiliating. And frightening. Because as unreasonable as Sarai could be, she had never actually hit Hagar before. Was this the shape of things to come?

Another blow—and that's when Hagar ran. Holding on to her

belly, stretched-out ligaments creaking, Sarai's angry voice following her all the way to the edge of their clearing and beyond. Out into the desert, straight toward the setting sun. She didn't get far, but it was far enough to be dangerous. Hagar realized that as the moon rose and the temperature dropped and she heard the sounds of wild beasts in the darkness. But she couldn't go back. Not back to a mistress who hated her and a master who was content to use her for his own purposes.

She spotted a green spot near the road she was traveling—a little spring trickling from a pile of boulders. There she sat down heavily in the twilight, her stomach growling, wondering where in the world she could go.

And that's when she saw the angel.

A beautiful bright being who actually knew her name!

"Hagar, servant of Sarai, where have you come from, and where are you going?" the being asked (Gen. 16:7).

She thought that was obvious. "I'm running away from my mistress Sarai."

"You need to go back," he said. But just as she was opening her mouth to argue, he gave her a promise that was fully as wonderful as the promise Yahweh had made to Abram and Sarai. "I will so increase your descendants that they will be too numerous to count." He told her the baby would be a boy and that she should name him Ishmael, which means "God hears"—"for the LORD has heard of your misery" (vv. 9–11).

There was more, but Hagar could barely take it in. She was too amazed by the realization that Abram and Sarai's God had actually noticed her and her plight. That He was her God, too, not just the God of Abram and Sarai. That He cared about her and the baby and wanted to provide for them.

"You *see* me," she murmured in wonder. "You are the God who sees me. I have now seen the One who sees me" (v. 13).

That wasn't the end of Hagar's story. It wasn't even the end of her ill treatment at the hands of Abram and Sarai. But it was the beginning of Hagar's promised future, the first sign of God's amazing grace and her eventual liberation. Because Hagar obeyed the angel and went back home to Sarai and Abram. She bore her son, named him Ishmael, and raised him in relative peace for the next twelve years or so. Until, against all odds, Sarai bore Isaac—and the old rivalry between the two women was stirred up again.

We don't know exactly what happened. We're just told that Sarai (now renamed Sarah) took offense at the way Ishmael treated her son and convinced Abram (now Abraham) to send both Hagar and Ishmael away (Gen. 21:9–10). So Abraham banished his adolescent son and his mother into the wilderness with only a little food and a single skin of water. Hagar and her son almost died of thirst. But God not only took care of them in the wilderness, He also renewed His promise that Ishmael as well as Isaac would be the founder of a great nation.

Hagar never had to return to a life of abuse and servitude. In fact, God gave her a whole new life. The last we see of her in Genesis 21, she is raising her son in the wilderness and arranging a marriage for her Ishmael, who would become the father of the Arab race.

THE REAL MESSAGE OF THE BIBLE

What do these two stories—one sad, one more hopeful—tell us about abuse?

One is that abuse has serious consequences. Even when it's not fatal—and it can be!—abuse ruins lives and destroys souls. It can truly desolate an individual or a family, and the conflict it generates is readily passed from one generation to another.

And abuse can happen to anyone—not just the weak, not just the poor, not just the unchurched. It can ruin the lives of princesses or servants. Smart, beautiful, resourceful people can be abused and become abusers. So can Christians. So can people from intact, happy homes. I'm living proof of this. Though I grew up in a healthy, loving, supportive environment, one of my adult relationships was marked by vicious verbal abuse and even physical threats. Those who have been abused in the past may be statistically more likely to abuse others or submit to abuse. But the only real qualification for becoming acquainted with abuse is being human.

> *God does not call us to be content. . . .*
> *God does not call us to live in peace and harmony, at all costs. . . .*
> *God calls us to grow closer to God, to put our trust in God and to live in God's promise for us.*
>
> —KATE DUNN[12]

Being human, of course, also means not being perfect. That's another reality these two stories highlight—that abuse is never the victim's fault, even if the victim makes mistakes or acts badly. This is so important to recognize because blaming the victim is a common tactic for rationalizing abuse. "If you just kept the house better," a husband may claim, "I wouldn't have to get rough with you." Or a parent may tell a child, "It's your fault I hit you—you wouldn't behave."

But Hagar's story, especially, shows that a badly behaving victim is still a victim. Hagar's behavior toward Sarai after she got pregnant was thoughtless if not cruel, and Sarai's ill temper was understandable. But the Bible never indicates that Hagar's mistreatment was anything other than Sarai's responsibility—and Hagar's less-than-stellar behavior didn't prevent the Lord from caring for her.

Here's another thing to note in the stories of Tamar and Hagar and most other abuse scenarios: they involve not only an abuser and a victim, but also someone like David or Abraham who lets the abuse happen. Only rarely can abuse continue over any length of time without an enabler of some kind—a friend, a family member, a pastor or teacher—who knows or suspects what is going on but does nothing to stop it.

A given situation, in fact, may have more than one enabler—some fearful, some busy or distracted, some unsure what to do, some simply uncaring. And every good Christian girl is in danger of filling this role at one time or another. Every time we give glib or shallow advice to someone who is hurting, every time we notice a bruise but decide it's none of our business, every time we decide not to call a friend who has become withdrawn or defensive, we could be helping an abuser continue his or her reign of terror.

Does this mean we should all commit ourselves to rescuing abuse victims? Not necessarily. Without specific training and support, we can end up not only causing further harm but actually endangering ourselves and others. Yet I believe there are times when the Lord may bring an abuse situation to our attention specifically so that we can be catalysts for change in that situation. At the very least, we can act as a friend. We can listen and pray and research sources of professional help. Most important, we can reinforce the central message behind Tamar and Hagar's story, not to mention the rest of the Bible.

What is that message? It's summarized in Hagar's words: "You have seen me. I have seen the God who sees me."

THE GOD WHO SEES YOUR SUFFERING

The God who sees—that's the God of the Bible, the God we worship. He's the God who hears our cries of pain, who knows what we are going through, and who suffers when we suffer.

And He doesn't just watch and acknowledge; He *cares*! God is our refuge, the One who provides for us in our weakness and shelters us in our fear.

This powerful message echoes through Hagar's story and lingers behind the scenes in Tamar's. God hates the wicked things we do to one another, especially the evil we do in His name. He has a special concern for the powerless, the oppressed, the rejected, the victims of violence . . . the abused. And though the tendency to abuse one another seems entrenched in our fallen human nature, God is always at work to redeem us from our abusive tendencies and to rescue those who bear the brunt of this kind of sin.

But as we see in Hagar's story (and many others), God's help often comes in unexpected ways. The first time Hagar fled from Sarai, God actually sent her back into the abusive situation. (She would never have survived as a pregnant woman in the desert.) Her provision at that time was the secret confidence that God knew what she was going through and wanted to bless her. Then, many years later, God showed His grace to Hagar by helping her build a life away from Abram and Sarai. And Tamar was given the opportunity to live in safety in Absalom's house, far away from her abuser.

This brings us to another surprising implication of these two stories of abuse, which was that God eventually resolved them by separating the abuser from the abused. This is worth noting because a common Christian response to many present-day abuse scenarios is

> *Christians sometimes idealize the family. . . . The pretense of being a happy Christian family only confuses and compounds the tragedy of abuse against women. To deny, minimize or ignore the problem obstructs the work of the Holy Spirit. The Scriptures offer the hope of healing for troubled families, but it requires honesty, faith, hard work, and the support of the believing community.*
>
> —World Evangelical Fellowship Task Force to Stop Abuse Against Women[13]

to insist that keeping the family together has to take highest priority. But these stories and other passages in the Bible indicate that the preservation and restoration of a particular human relationship or even a family unit is not always God's primary concern (see, for example, Matt.10:35–37; Luke 9:57–62).

Yes, God values families—after all, He invented them. Whenever possible, God desires relationships to remain strong. But in the Bible, God never rates family loyalty higher than truth. He never ranks a human relationship higher than following Him or obeying His will. And when relationships break, when we continually fail each other, when we just can't live together in love and integrity, when one person insists on abusing another, God often provides a way of escape, a way to build a new life. In such cases even the breakup of a family, though tragic, can be seen as an act of mercy and grace.

Forgiveness, Reconciliation, and Healing

But what about forgiveness? Doesn't the Bible tell us to forgive? Absolutely!

Christians talk a lot about forgiveness. That's no accident, because Jesus told us to forgive. He said we need to forgive if we want to be forgiven. And He not only commanded forgiveness, but He modeled it, forgiving His own abusers even as He hung on the cross.

Both spiritually and psychologically, forgiveness is what makes reconciliation and healing possible in relationships. So forgiveness is obviously a big issue when it comes to abuse in Christian families—and it should be. Which means it's vital for abuse victims to forgive their abusers . . . right?

Well, yes and no.

Yes because forgiveness is important for healing.

But no because forgiveness is far from the *first* thing an abuse victim needs to do. And because far too many good Christian girls have been counseled to "forgive" too quickly, too easily, and then return to their abusers without assurance that anything has changed. They are pressured to forgive when what they really need to do is face the reality of what is happening, get themselves to a safe place, mourn the loss of the relationship they wanted, and begin to rebuild their lives.

It's absolutely true that at some point an abused person needs to choose forgiveness, to let go of the right to be bitter or to seek revenge. Such a choice is essential for healing. But forgiveness takes time. It's a process. And it's not easy. It's not *supposed* to be easy. Because God cares about justice, because He cares about the wounds of the oppressed, because He values real growth, He would never short-circuit the process of healing with cheap or superficial forgiveness.

And even more important, forgiveness isn't the same as excusing a wrong, allowing the abuse to continue, or even reconciling with an abuser. Though some would argue with me, I'm convinced there is absolutely nothing in the Bible that indicates that someone who is being beaten, sexually molested, threatened, or habitually browbeaten—in her own family, by someone whose responsibility is to love and support her—is bound by Scripture to remain in such a situation, forgive what has happened with no guarantee that it won't happen again, and continue to suffer the abuse.

Do the arguments spring up in your mind when you hear that? Are you thinking about the biblical pronouncements about divorce or the recommendations that wives should submit to their husbands or children obey their parents? Or the passage that suggests a woman can bring her husband to faith by doing what he wants?

All those arguments have been used both by abusers and misguided pastors, teachers, and counselors—sometimes with deadly consequences. And that's a shame, because when you look at these teachings in the context of the whole biblical message, God's intention shines diamond clear. God's intention is *never* for us to hurt each other or get our way at another person's expense, especially in a family.

As I indicate in a later chapter, when Jesus condemned divorce, He was upholding the sacred nature of the marriage covenant and the sin of those who break it—including those who break their vows to love and cherish a spouse.

And the biblical admonitions about submitting to authority are *always* balanced by orders to the person in authority. Yes, wives are to submit to husbands . . . while husbands are to love their wives the way they love their own bodies. And yes, children are to obey parents . . . but parents are also to avoid angering their children (Eph. 5:22, 28; 6:1, 4).

And as for "spare the rod and spoil the child," a catchphrase based on Proverbs 13:24, I can't find any serious commentary that interprets that proverb to mean parents are justified in beating, molesting, taunting, or threatening their children! Even that controversial proverb, in context, is a reminder that parents have a responsibility to guide and discipline children, not to dominate and control them.

The truth is, we're not called to dominate or control anyone. One of the themes of Jesus's entire mission on earth, in fact, was to overturn our basic human understanding of power—and remember, abuse is primarily a misuse of power.

The standard human use of power is to wield it at someone else's expense. Jesus repeatedly resisted that temptation, saying no to Satan's offer of earthly power (Matt. 4:1–11), correcting the disciples when they wanted to call down fire on a village who mistreated them (Luke 9:54–55), and rebuking them when they got into power struggles among themselves (Mark 9:33–37). He stressed that in God's kingdom the first will be last (Mark 10:31), the meek will inherit the earth (Matt. 5:5), and that helpless little children have an edge on finding favor with God (Matt. 18:3–5).

Jesus also showed us a different way to respond to an abuse

God is not only the God of the sufferers, but the God who suffers. The pain and fallenness of humanity have entered into his heart. Through the prism of my tears I have seen a suffering God. And great mystery: to redeem our brokenness, the God who suffers with us did not strike some mighty blow of power, but sent his beloved Son to suffer like us, through his suffering to redeem us from suffering and evil. Instead of explaining our suffering, God shares it.

—NICHOLAS WOLTERSTORFF[14]

of power. Our standard human response is to either fight back or knuckle under. Jesus modeled a third possibility—to stand strong and hold out for truth while avoiding revenge and retaliation. Think of Him cleansing the temple or standing up to the lawyers and Pharisees who tested Him. He taught us to forgive abuse, not to give in to it. To be salt and light, not punching bags.

And while He challenged us to have so much love we would give up our lives for our friends (John 15:13) or the sake of the gospel (Mark 8:35), He never suggested we should give up our lives for the sake of someone else's power trip. He certainly never called us to save anyone through our sacrifice. Dying for someone's sins is His job, and He's already taken care of that!

So am I saying that abusive family relationships are doomed and that reconciliation isn't possible?

Again, absolutely not.

I'm just saying that in an abuse situation, forgiveness and reconciliation cannot come first.

What comes first is truth—naming the abuse for what it is, without excuses or cover-up. Another top priority is safety—doing whatever is necessary to stop the abuse and break the cycle, even if it means leaving in the middle of the night and living apart. So is seeking help from God and others and accepting help in whatever form it takes, even secular ones. There will almost certainly need to be a period of healing and restoration for the victim, a time when the abuser works through old issues and learns new ways of living with others. And forgiveness will almost certainly play a part in this healing, but it may take awhile, and forgiveness won't necessarily mean restoring the relationship. Reconciliation can only follow true repentance—which involves real change over a period of time and a slow rebuilding of trust.

Keep in mind that repentance is not the same thing as remorse. It's common for abusers to feel remorse, apologize profusely to those they have hurt, and have sincere intentions for change—only to fall back into the abusive behavior. As with an addiction, the best intentions are often not enough, even when abusers claim God has changed them. That's not to say abusers *can't* change, but it rarely happens easily or quickly. The process involves true repentance and a deep commitment to stop all abusive behavior. It also requires the help and support of other people, the establishment of new patterns and habits, and—I believe—an ongoing, supernatural infusion of grace.

What Grace Can Do

Only time will confirm whether change is both real and lasting. Only time will show whether reconciliation is really possible. But even if an abuser never repents, God's grace can still work at transforming an abusive situation.

He did it for Hagar . . . and for Sarai and Abram.

I don't know if (or how) He did it for Tamar—though the fact that Jesus came out of David's family might suggest some clues.

And God definitely did it for my friend Lisa as well, though echoes of her abusive childhood continued to haunt her long after she left home. (After many attempts at reconciliation, she remains estranged from her still-abusive mother to this day.)

When I think about the long saga of pain in Lisa's life—and in the lives of so many good Christian girls—I'm almost overwhelmed. Yet when I ask Lisa whether she has experienced the grace of God in her personal abuse story, she is quick to answer. "God protected me," she insists. "He has been with me from the beginning. I have seen so many amazing things."

And it's true. Because God's fingerprints really are all over the story of Lisa's life, the evidence of His grace as overwhelming as the pain.

Maybe the biggest miracle is the fact that she emerged from her home of origin relatively intact and healthy—and that God repeatedly put her in places of safety where she could rest and heal and grow stronger. For a while she lived in a big city, surrounded by supportive friends. She married a childhood sweetheart who offered her love and support. Later God made it possible for her family to move to Europe, where she helped plant a church and raise their three children an ocean away from her abusive past.

Lisa sees her relationship with her three children as one of the most tangible evidences of God's gracious protection. She knew the

> *Our Great High Priest, Jesus himself is familiar with abuse. Take another look at his crucifixion. See how he was stripped naked, taunted, spit on, beaten, abandoned by his friends. He knows our pain intimately. And he has the resources that we need for our own journey.*
>
> —BONNIE NICHOLAS[15]

statistics about victims becoming abusers and feared her own capacity to lose control and harm her little ones. But except for one terrifying incident when her daughter was two, she has found ways to back off from the abusive impulse. She learned to lean into God's help, entrust her children to Him, and establish an atmosphere of openness and transparency with her children.

The story of Lisa's relationship with her stepfather is an even more amazing testimony to the power of grace in the life of both abuser and abused. This was a man, an elder in his church, who for decades led a secret sexual life. He cheated on his wife. He visited prostitutes. He molested young girls. Even when one of his victims brought him to court, he persisted in denial, even inviting God to strike him dead if he was lying.

The interesting thing is that he did drop dead several years later—but not before having a complete change of heart. He finally faced the reality of what he had done and threw himself on God's mercy. His repentance was deep and real, and he worked hard to make amends to those he had hurt, including Lisa. In later days, she remembers, "I actually had a better relationship with him than I ever did with my mom."

So Lisa lives in hope, although what happened to her should never have to happen to any of God's children.

If abuse is part of your life, please know there is hope for you too.

Because God sees you. He hears your cries. And He is working right now, at this moment, not only to bring you to safety but to give you a brighter future.

It won't happen automatically. It might not happen the way you think or turn out the way you would have chosen. You will probably have to seek help and make some hard choices. You may have some times when desolation seems to stalk you, when the wilderness stretches wide before you.

But there is a future for you. There is safety and freedom. You *will* see the God who sees you.

And this God is always very, very good.

WORD OF GRACE FOR DESOLATE CHRISTIAN GIRLS

The Lord is your refuge, your source of safety and freedom.
Open your heart to His provision.

5

"It Should Have Been Forever"

The Heartbreak of Divorce and Failed Relationships

They will come with weeping;
they will pray as I bring them back.
I will lead them beside streams of water
on a level path where they will not stumble.
—Jeremiah 31:9

It's over."

I don't know about you, but I wince when I hear those words—because they almost always announce a breakup, a failed love.

"It's over. I can't pretend anymore."

"It's over. I want someone else."

"It's over. I'm leaving."

"It's over. I just don't love you."

And so often, for growing numbers of good Christian girls, those words mean something more.

They mean, "This marriage is over. I want a divorce."

That's what my good friend Connie heard when her husband of ten years announced he didn't love her anymore and didn't want to be married to her. The words shocked her to the depth of her being. She loved her husband and their boys and had just given birth to her fourth son. She was happily and productively plugged in to her local church and growing in her faith. And she really thought her marriage was working. After the painful demise of her marriage to a drug addict, determined not to make the same mistake again, she had been drawn to Nick's stability, his family values, his work ethic. She thought they got along well. And though she had known her husband was under stress at work, she had no inkling he'd been confiding his troubles to a woman at work—the woman he would later marry.

Once Nick made the unilateral decision to end the marriage, however, there was no going back. He agreed to go to counseling with Connie but refused to do any of the real work. Eventually he filed for what would become an ugly divorce, with his whole family rallying behind him to make sure the settlement weighed heavily on his side.

Within a year, completely against her will, Connie became a divorce statistic. A good Christian single mom with four little boys to raise and two failed marriages under her belt.

And Connie's not alone. Divorce is becoming more and more common in the church, just as it is in the general population. You've probably heard the statistics: anywhere from 25 to 50 percent of first marriages end in divorce. The specific numbers vary according to state, age, and other factors. But statistically speaking, I'm sad to report, the church doesn't seem any different from the general population when it comes to the dissolution of marriages.[1] If anything, the divorce rate is higher among conservative Christians and in the Bible Belt than it is among atheists and agnostics and the more "secular" areas of the country. And while this may be because Christians are more likely to marry (and thus divorce) rather than simply live together, a look at almost any congregation these days will reveal plenty of members who know the brokenness of divorce. I know that's true in my church, in my work with women's ministries, and among my friends.

I think of Nancy, whose husband of twenty years grew more and more distant and unaffectionate despite her efforts to spice things up and rekindle the romance. That marriage ended not long after their twelve-year-old daughter discovered a compromising e-mail between her husband and a colleague.

Then there's Trish, whose fighter-pilot husband informed her he didn't want to be married. They had just been married a year or two and were stationed in Panama at the time. Trish went home to the States, expecting him to follow so they could work on their problems. He didn't follow. In fact, she never saw her husband again.

There's Georgia, who loves her charming, artistic husband but just can't live with him anymore. For years, she gladly supported his performing career . . . until his chronic financial irresponsibility and massive tax debt—he just never filed!—wore her down. She's finally decided she can't go on living with "Peter Pan." As of this writing, with deep regret, she has filed for separation.

And there's my friend Elise, who has chosen to stay with her husband for the time being . . . but has been so worn down by his chronic negativity and depression and his inability to support their family that she can only survive by living a more or less separate life. (Even without divorce, a marriage relationship can falter and fail, and living with that can be as painful in its own way as a legal breakup.)

Every failed relationship tells a different story; all of them are sad. I know women who have finally left a husband after years of physical, emotional, or verbal abuse . . . and women who have given up after decades of trying to connect with an emotionally distant stranger. I know women whose marriages ended on "biblical grounds," and those whose marriages just ended. Women who have endured one unhappy marriage and never tried again, and women who have married and remarried several times.

And I think of myself as well. I am a woman who has been divorced once, as a young woman, after just two years of marriage. And as of this writing, I am legally separated from my husband of more than twenty years. The details of this situation are still too fresh for me to disclose, especially because they involve the privacy of others besides myself. And I still don't know what the outcome will be, though I trust we'll be able to keep our family intact. I would love to be able to report in a postscript or another book that we were able to be reconciled. But if I am honest with myself, I have to face the fact that another divorce is possible for me.

> *One truth about God which I continue to discover anew is that He has more for us than we can imagine. His plans far exceed our plans, and His grace makes possible so much more than we can envision.*
>
> —NANCY PICKERING ACREE[2]

I debated long and hard before revealing that. It wasn't the impetus of this book. But I want you to know from the outset that I know firsthand the pain of this kind of brokenness. I am living it at this moment. I am depending utterly on God's mercy in this situation. And day by day, I am learning His mercy is enough to carry me. Day by day, I am being cleansed and renewed and empowered by the Holy Spirit. And that is what I want to share with you in this chapter about failed relationships. I've seen Him do amazing things in my life despite my relational brokenness. Maybe, in a way, because of my brokenness.

Because Jesus, remember, does His best work with broken people. I am staking my life these days on the belief that God's mercy is limitless, that His grace flows freely to anyone who comes to Him.

Anyone.

Even those whose most intimate relationships fail.

Not a Good Thing

Please understand—I am not claiming divorce is a good thing. Even non-Christians will usually admit that divorce is regrettable. And the good Christian girls I know whose lives have been touched by divorce will tell you it was among the worst experiences of their lives and counsel those who are still married to pull out all the stops to avoid divorce.

Because divorce is incredibly hard. It's painful. It's a bereavement, the loss of something once cherished—but without the closure or finality of death. For most people, it's a deep, deep disappointment, one of those "I'll nevers" come true. Often it involves rejection or deception. There's almost always guilt, especially for Christians. And divorce often dovetails with other problems—alcoholism, abuse, depression, sexual addiction, financial difficulties—that increase the pain exponentially.

Divorce is also expensive—especially for women, who still are most likely to retain primary responsibility for children and whose earning power is usually less. Living expenses double at a time when energy and attention may be curtailed. Legal fees can take a big bite out of any pocketbook. Connie's lawyer told her quite frankly that five years after a divorce, a husband's financial situation is usually back to predivorce levels. The wife's financial situation typically continues to deteriorate.

Even today divorce still carries a painful stigma, especially for good Christian girls. Other people feel compelled to pass judgment, to decide who is right and who is wrong, to debate whether the church should condone the divorce . . . and people tend to treat divorced Christians differently than they treat others.

And yes, this picture is changing—definitely in society at large, where divorce seems to be accepted as a given, but even in conservative evangelical churches that once judged any divorce quite harshly.

When I divorced at age twenty-two and remarried several years later, I was treated as an outcast by many fellow Christians, including some of my own extended family. One person literally did not talk to me for ten years. Others made it clear that God was totally disgusted with me and that I was an embarrassment to the body of Christ.

And yes, there were issues of my own sin involved as well as my husband's sin. No, I did not have a clue at the time of the fallout of my choices. But did the way I was treated by other Christians move me toward repentance and healing and new life? To be honest, I don't believe so. If anything, it added to my shame and made it harder for me to face up to my own sin and find forgiveness.

Fortunately, such harsh judgment seems to be a thing of the past in most churches today. Divorce carries less of an overt stigma, although divorced Christian women (like many singles) still have difficulty finding a place in many couples-oriented churches. And as my friend Connie will testify, those who have been divorced more than once still face considerable suspicion. Christians seem to be allowed one marital failure but judged harshly for multiple divorces—as if God turns His back on anyone who has sinned more than once.

In addition to the issues of pain and guilt and finances and stigma in church and society, a divorce brings on an onslaught of difficult and painful issues. There's worry over children, the stress of coping with the legal system, the overwhelming responsibility of single parenting, questions about dating or remarriage, the challenge of handling everyday issues such as home repairs and yard work, and making a living.

And beyond it all, above it all, is the almost overwhelming sense of failure. For me and so many women I know, this is the most painful aspect of divorce. There's an old saying: "Love is for men a thing apart; 'tis woman's whole existence." And while that might not be entirely true in this day and age, there's still a lot of truth in it. Because most women I know tend to judge their success in life according to their success in relationships.

We want to be loved. We want to be in love. We want our marriages to be happy, our relationships successful and fulfilling. And most women I know, especially good Christian girls, are willing to absolutely knock themselves out to make it happen. It's usually women who buy the self-help books (and nag men to read them). And it's usually women who keep on trying harder when things aren't working well, though what we try may not be what is needed. And when divorce happens, for one reason or another, it's women who often feel the sense of relational failure most acutely. Divorced or divorcing women often feel they have failed themselves, failed their former spouses, failed their children, and failed society—a huge burden of failure for one person to carry.

And, of course, we're acutely aware of failing God.

Because there's no way around the reality that divorce is a sin.

What Jesus Didn't Do

I have no intention of going over the many different theological evaluations of which divorces are more acceptable than others, which divorce situations are more sinful than others. For one thing, you can read all that in other books. For another, that's exactly the kind of approach that adds pain to lives of those who are already hurting.

And Jesus refused to do that. Not even when the Pharisees quizzed Him repeatedly on that very subject.

Jesus stressed a high view of marriage—that it's a sacred union, a divine joining of a man and a woman that humans shouldn't dare to pull apart (Matt. 19:5–7). But He refused to quibble over the what-ifs of marriage and divorce the way the Pharisees in their day and many church people in ours tend to do. The Pharisees posed a lot of questions about "bills of divorcement" and widows marrying their husband's brothers—usually to trap Jesus into making a theological mistake. Church people in our day tend to do the same about whether there are biblical grounds for a divorce (usually adultery), whether abuse or addiction changes the picture, whether a divorced person can remarry, whether a marriage can be annulled or a remarriage allowed after divorce. The conclusions vary according to church, denomination, biblical translation, and individual interpretation.

In His day, Jesus cut through all the wrangling by stressing the hard truth: all divorce is sin. It's all wrong—a sure sign of hardened hearts. It's a big mess. It hurts people and tears apart families. It shouldn't happen. God never intended us to do to one another the kinds of things we do in divorce.

And you know what? As a divorced Christian woman, I absolutely agree with that assessment. Most divorcées I know, especially Christians, would agree. Divorce is a sin. It results from sin. It involves at least two sinners—maybe not equally, but both partners inevitably contribute to a failed relationship. And it generally causes pain that causes more sin.

But what the quibblers fail to face, I think, is not the reality of sin in divorce, but the way Jesus responds to sinners.

Which, of course, is the whole point of this book. And also the heart of a remarkable scene in which Jesus came face to face with a woman whose marital history was one big disaster.

We read her story in the fourth chapter of John. We don't know her name; she's usually called "the woman at the well" or "the woman of Samaria." But we could also call her "the woman of failed relationships" because she had gone through five—count 'em, five!—husbands. Possibly she had been widowed five times, though that seems unlikely. Perhaps she had been issued a bill of divorcement by one or more husbands—a formal arrangement that made it possible for her to marry again.

> *In heaven's eyes, you are not half of something broken. . . . You have been made whole.*
>
> —KARI WEST AND NOELLE QUINN[3]

She may have simply been abandoned or "sent away" to fend for herself, as sometimes happened to married women who displeased their husbands. We know she was currently living with a man who was not her husband, but whether she offered him sex or he merely offered her protection is an open question. We just don't know.

So what else can we guess about this woman? The way she spoke to Jesus hints that she had at least a rudimentary theological education. She was quick-witted and intelligent and wasn't afraid to talk to men, though her wariness toward Jesus hints that these very characteristics had gotten her in trouble before. The fact that she visited the well in the heat of the day hints that she was an outcast, especially among the women of the town. As a Samaritan, she was also an object of contempt for most Jews.

This woman, in other words, was a poster child for messed-up relationships.

And a poster child for how Jesus treats our most dismal failures . . .

THE WOMAN WHO HAD FAILED

Another day. Another empty water jar. Another trip to Jacob's well.

And today was going to be just as hot as yesterday.

She must have sighed as she ventured from the dimness of the shabby house into the blazing noonday sun and hoisted the empty pot to her shoulder.

This was definitely not the life she expected. Not the life she had hoped for. But you did what you had to do to survive. Ever since that spoiled little boy, her first husband, put her out, she'd had to make survival her first order of business.[4]

She shifted the pot on her shoulder and squinted into the brightness. As hard as it was to face the daily chore in the hot sun of noonday, it was better than the alternative—walking the evening gauntlet of women at the village well.

Women with husbands. Women whose lives had been easier. Women who were all too quick to pass judgment, if only out of fear that what happened to her might happen to them. (And no one knew better than she how precarious their lives could become if their husbands found fault with them.)

If only . . . She squared her shoulders, pushing back the memories. She usually avoided looking back over her life—there was too much she'd rather forget. But today's trip out to Jacob's well seemed to bring it all rushing back.

Memories of her father, who used to teach her Scripture and history and discuss her people's faith and traditions with her. And of her mother, who used to gently scold him for talking to her as if she were a boy. "You'll ruin that girl for sure. No one wants an argumentative woman."

Obviously, her mother was right. But today the thought of those long-ago conversations with her father made her blink back tears. Since he died, no one had bothered to talk to her with real fondness and respect for her intelligence.

Certainly not the village men—talking to them was out of the question these days. Not the women, either, for the most part. The few who would speak to her had little to say. It was all just idle chat about their children and their families and their husbands and who sold the best water jars. As if she could afford a new water jar. As if she would ever have children. As if a decent husband would ever want her.

Though she often craved company and sometimes even braved their disapproval, she tired quickly of their company. That's why she mostly kept to herself. When she wasn't cleaning that pitiful little house. Or hauling water. Or cooking meals. Or sleeping with a man who wasn't her husband in order to have a roof over her head. Or doing any of the thousand little humiliations that made up her days.

You did what you had to do, but there were limits. Which was why she'd decided to walk all the way out to Jacob's well. The water was better anyway—clean and clear. There was always a little corner of shade where she could rest and enjoy a deep, refreshing drink before trudging back home. And Jacob's well was usually deserted at this time of day, which suited her just fine.

But it wasn't deserted. Not today. She grunted with irritation when she saw the stranger. A man. Even worse, a Jew.

Being judged by the village women and the local rabbis was bad enough. But to give up her precious solitude for someone who would despise her for being Samaritan and might compromise her reputation even more . . .

She sighed. Sometimes you just couldn't win. But you did what you had to do—which, in this case, was just to ignore the stranger.

She approached the stone lip of the well, fiddled with the ropes, and lowered her water jar—carefully, because it was the only one she had that didn't leak. But she almost dropped the pot when she heard the voice behind her.

Was He actually speaking to her—this man who by His own traditions wasn't even supposed to speak to a woman in public, much less a Samaritan woman?

Was He really asking her for a drink?

Stranger still, was He standing there without a cup or a bucket and offering to give her water?

It was too much. In confusion, she blurted out something inane about water jars and her ancestor Jacob, who built the well. And that's how the conversation started—a dialogue that frightened yet thrilled her. It was the kind of talk she used to have with her father, one thoughtful person to another. Just a friendly debate about Samaritans and Jews and the right place to worship. About wells and sheep and water jars.

For a while, she was actually enjoying herself. But then He wanted to talk about her. And that was just too much.

How did this man know that she had been married five times? That she had long ago given up on the possibility of a legitimate relationship with a man? That she was so thirsty for company and conversation, she'd fall into one with a strange Jewish man at the well?

And what in the world did He mean when He said He'd give her living water?

It was such an odd thing to say that she misunderstood Him at first. She thought He was offering her some new kind of well or water system, some way of avoiding the daily trudge to the well. A lovely thought, though obviously impossible. She almost laughed, just thinking about it.

And then she stopped laughing. Because when His real meaning began to soak in, she could barely wrap her mind around it.

For He wasn't talking about a new well, but God's own mercy. A dependable source of cleansing and refreshment from the inside out, like this deep well bubbling up in the desert. A fresh start for a life that was going nowhere, a heart that had shriveled and hardened.

But how could a sweaty Jew with a tired face and worn sandals dare offer such a thing? And what was He thinking, offering it to her? Didn't He know who she was, what she had done?

But He did know—that was obvious—and it didn't even faze Him. He knew all about her and still promised forgiveness. And who could do that but . . .

Her heart grasped the astounding truth before her mind could begin to comprehend. Even then, she couldn't actually get the words out.

"I know . . . the Messiah . . . will come," she stammered, watching His reaction. "When He comes, He will explain everything . . ."

And then He admitted it—the impossible truth that made all the rest possible. "I am the Messiah," He told her (John 4:25–26 NLT). She drank in the words like a cold draft of water from the deepest well. And felt something come alive deep inside of her, in all those hard, shriveled, dried-up places.

A trickle of wonder.

Then a bubbling up of hope.

And finally a rushing flow of possibility so powerful that she hardly noticed the arrival of the man's friends and their disapproving glances. She even forgot her water jar in her rush to get back to the village and all the people she usually avoided.

She had to tell them what she knew.

That she had met One who knew everything—even her sin. That He had changed everything—even her cynical, hardened heart. And that His offer of bubbling, cleansing, refreshing living water was for real.

Not just for Jews, but for Samaritans.

Not just for men, but for women as well.

And not just for people who did everything right, but for people like her—who somehow managed to get it all wrong.

WHAT JESUS SAYS TO OUR FAILURES AND MULTIPLE SINS

Don't you just love that story? It's such a vivid picture of the way Christ deals with all our intimate mistakes, our secret and not-so-secret shame, our relational failures. Even the pain and shame and sin of a broken marriage. Or two broken marriages. Or three.

> God . . . does not hold in his hand a list of my failures. He is not waiting to judge me. He is waiting to be with me. He is waiting to embrace me and welcome me home.
>
> —RUTH GRAHAM[5]

He doesn't gloss over our failures or minimize our mistakes. But He also doesn't spend a lot of time wrangling over who's right and who's wrong, who has sinned and who hasn't, who should do what and get what. Not at first, anyway.

What He does is call every one of us to turn our attention away from our failures and toward Him.

Oh dear sister in Christ, please pay attention here. Because I believe Jesus's answer to your current relational failures is exactly the same as His answer to any of your sins. It's the same answer He gave to the woman at the well.

His answer is *truth*—you are called to face the truth about the sin in your life.

His answer is *forgiveness*—you can repent of your sin and start over without condemnation.

But most of all, His answer is *Himself.*

You see, God isn't nearly as obsessed with our sins and our failures as we usually are. He's not worried about assigning blame and determining who's at fault. He knows all that anyway.

His to-do list for us at the point of our failures has only one starred item: "Turn to Me. Give Me your attention. And then open your life to what I have to offer."

You see, the gift of living water is available to you.

Yes, you. No matter what you've done. No matter how many relational failures you have under your belt. Whether you're single and struggling with dating, married and wrestling with intimacy issues, contemplating divorce or trying desperately to avoid it, languishing in an unhappy marriage, slogging through the legal system, or fighting to heal from a breakup. Even if you've been divorced more times than Elizabeth Taylor. Even if your parents divorced when you were little and now you're terrified of even trying.

No matter who you are or how you've lived, you're still eligible for living water. It's there for the asking. All you have to do is open up to that trickle of wonder, that bubbling up of hope, that rush of possibility.

It really is that simple. But simple doesn't always mean easy, because we're all still living in a fallen world. Because all sin—and especially relational sin—still has long-lasting, real-life consequences.

Because in this world we have trouble, which means that even with Jesus we'll face times when we don't know what to do or we can't bring ourselves to do what is right.

But that's exactly the point of living water. Because water is never a one-time gift but a flowing, ever-fresh source of cleansing . . . of refreshment . . . and power.

What Living Water Can Do for You

What does all that mean specifically? It means that living water is the answer for all the ways you've messed up your relationships, failing yourself and failing your partner.

And you've done it, you know. So have I. Even if your divorce or estrangement is not your fault. Even if you've been cheated on, lied to, totally mistreated. Even if you've done everything you know to save your marriage—the truth is, you're a sinner too. You've also contributed to the pain, the loneliness, the anger, or the isolation.

But Jesus's living water is there to cleanse you of all that. When you open your life to its cleansing flow, you offer your mistakes and failings to the One whose blood can wash you truly clean. Just as He did with the Samaritan woman at the well, Jesus offers you forgiveness for the times you turned away, the times you hardened your heart, the times you lashed out in anger, the times you were too caught up in your selfish needs to consider the needs of your partner. And in the process, He makes it possible for you to begin forgiving others. Even the person who turned away from you, hardened his heart, lashed out cruelly, or ignored your needs in favor of his own. Even, in time, yourself.

And remember, this isn't limited forgiveness. You're not given a one-time ticket to the bathhouse but condemned to live dirty after that. Living water is the original renewable resource—it can't be used up. As long as you're willing to drag your dirty self and your dirty laundry to the Source, the cleansing power of living water will be available for your relationships. And this cleansing flow can also make new love possible, because living water is a source of refreshment and possibility as well as cleansing.

Jesus said to the Pharisees that divorce had been allowed because "your hearts were hard" (Matt. 19:8). I think that's still true today. When we are hurt and rejected and shamed, our natural response is to protect ourselves, to toughen up, to dry up, to pull in on ourselves. No matter how hard we try to "be a good person" and "do the right thing," we can't help getting defensive, cynical, selfish . . . hard.

But opening ourselves to the refreshing living water of Jesus's love is like soaking a sponge in a glass of water—our dried-up hearts unfold before our eyes. What was shriveled and hard becomes soft and alive and full.

When our hearts are hydrated, refreshed by living water, we can grow into new possibilities, new relationships, new hope for a failing marriage, or eventually a new, healthier marriage. Even better, we're given the strength to do the hard work of learning new ways of relating. Because the flow of living water is a source of power as well as cleansing and refreshment.

Anyone who has tried to swim against a current knows there's power in the flow of water. That's true of living water too. When you swim downstream—with the flow—everything seems easier. You still have to swim, to do the work, but you have that little extra boost that takes you farther.

That's the power of living water for your life. It offers possibility when you've exhausted your own, when you've given everything you have to give, when you're used up and out of gas. Jesus's living water can give you the strength to bite your tongue instead of lashing out with a cutting remark. The strength to speak up when you need something. The strength to get your kids out of an abusive home. To find a better counselor. Sometimes, on bad days, it's the strength you need just to get out of bed. Or to walk into church with your head held high when everything in you wants to stay home and lick your wounds.

But again, the power of living water can only help you when you're going with its flow—living in obedience to the Holy Spirit. The more you learn to relax into its flow, the more dependably it will carry you along. Because the power that Jesus offers you is not the power to do things your own way but the power to answer His call on your life.

Where Living Water Can Take You

What is God calling us to do and be? First, of course, God calls us to love. And not just vague, theoretical love but deep wholesome intimacy—with Him first and then with others. He's made us with a deep thirst for intimate, loving relationships. But one of the most deadly consequences of the Fall is the tendency to warp and misuse this desire.

A famous philosopher once told a parable about porcupines on a cold night. Drawn together for warmth, they end up pricking and poking each other so painfully that they have to pull back into polite (but chilly) distance.[6] Isn't that an accurate picture of the way we often live together—that endless cycle of hurting and being hurt and protecting ourselves by hurting others again?

Relationship failures like that are almost inevitable given the kind of pain life deals out to most of us—the abuse that warps us, the mistakes that haunt us, the events that traumatize us, the guilt and shame that warp us.

And of course it's why we need Jesus—to call us to truth about ourselves and show us a different way to be. We need living water flowing through us to be able to manage any kind of healthy intimacy with God or with another person.

We also need living water to be faithful—and that's another call of God on our lives. I'm not just talking about sexual faithfulness, though that's part of it. God wants us to be loyal, to keep our promises to ourselves, to each other, to Him. He wants us to live in love and integrity. And again, human selfishness makes faithlessness the norm. But the gift of living water means that He is faithful even when we're not. He keeps His promises to us even when we break ours. More important, as He heals us, He gives us the strength to be faithful like Him.

Even before that, He gives us the strength to be honest and open. And that's so necessary for any kind of intimate relationships. Not just honest in the sense of not lying, but also open-eyed about our needs and our failings. Willing to admit our weaknesses and our vulnerabilities. Willing to open our lives to God and to one another and to face our sins instead of covering them up and denying them.

Which brings us, of course, to repentance—a crucial part of our cleansing and refreshing and empowerment. God doesn't want us making the same mistakes over and over again. He calls us to confess our failures, to obtain forgiveness for our sins and healing for our hurts, and to do better in the future. But as I've mentioned, God doesn't give out a set number of "repentance" tickets either. We're not told, "You can have so many mistakes and that's it." Jesus counseled His disciplines to forgive "seventy times seven" times (Matt. 18:22 NLT)—or again and again . . . because that's the kind of forgiveness our heavenly Father offers us when we come to Him in repentance.

God calls us to try again, even when we've failed. Even more important, He calls us to take our eyes off our failures and concentrate on following Him. For the longer I live with my own failures, the more I am convinced that God's primary interest in us is not our success but our reliance on Him. He's even more concerned about our growth than our goodness. And He wants us to rely on Him, going with the flow of His living water instead of trying to succeed on our own.

> *Repentance consists not so much in flagellating ourselves over our "failures" as in courageously and painstakingly reorienting our priorities, unlearning old patterns, turning our faces, like the sunflower, toward the dawning of the light of God.*
>
> —WENDY M. WRIGHT[7]

And this, in a sense, gives us a whole new definition of failure. Because I believe that from God's perspective, the only true failure is to not avail ourselves of the Source of living water. All other failures—even multiple failures—can be Christ's opportunity if we listen and don't cut Him off. Which means even the most painful divorce is a perfect opportunity for living water.

But living water is only powerful when it's allowed to flow. And that's something else God calls us to. We're meant to be channels of His grace, conduits for His love, pipelines for His living water.

The word Jesus uses for "living water" in John 4 could also mean "running water."[8] In fact, that's what the woman at the well thought He meant at first. No wonder she was excited. The thought of having water come to her instead of trudging to the well for it—she could definitely go for that.

But when the Samaritan woman finally understood what Jesus's gift really was—the cleansing and refreshing and power He was offering her—she absolutely flipped out. She was so excited that she left her water jar by the well. And leaving something as valuable as a water jar was unheard of—almost like leaving her purse or her cell phone!

But she did just that. She left her jar sitting by the well and rushed into town to share the news about Jesus with all the people who had shunned her . . . the people she had shunned as well. Once she opened herself up to the flow of living water, you literally couldn't shut her up about what Jesus had done for her.

And that's the final gift of living water, the answer of Christ to our relational failures. The answer to our botched attempts at intimacy is . . . a new kind of intimacy. A new way of relating. A connection with others that depends on the flow of the Holy Spirit. And a commitment to reaching out and loving others instead of condemning them, sharing with them Jesus's good gifts of cleansing and refreshment and power.

Jesus's Last Word on Sin and Relationships

One of the scriptures commonly quoted in Christian circles when discussing divorce is a simple one from Malachi 2:16: God hates divorce.[9]

And it's true.

Of course God hates divorce. He hates all sin. All the terrible things our fallen natures get us into—like physical illness and death and war and the terrible things we do to one another. Like the way we stigmatize and ostracize and ignore and fail to care for those who are hurting in our midst. Like the cruel or thoughtless ways the church sometimes treats those who have been divorced.

God created marriage as a sacred institution, so divorce is a

> *God loves the divorced but hates divorce.*
> *Oh, how we tend to go from one extreme to the other.*
> *On one hand we preach the anger of God toward those who fail*
> *and elevate divorce as the sin above sins (which it's not).*
> *The result is a battered and bruised people wondering if God ever*
> *has a place for them again.*
> *Or, in our efforts to be compassionate toward the battered and*
> *bruised, we go overboard . . . Observers note this compassion and*
> *think "If divorce is that easy, then why stay married?"*
> *But the tension must remain tense. God hates divorce.*
> *He hates it because it destroys the children whom he loves.*
> *But let us be equally loud and clear and state that God loves the*
> *divorced, that it is not a sin among sins. The same God who will*
> *forgive your bad attitude or bad temper can*
> *forgive a bad decision in marriage.*
>
> —MAX LUCADO[10]

serious sin, with serious consequences. Yet with Jesus, sin is never the last word. That's the whole point of living water. God's remedy for sin is just as available for those in failed relationships as it is for other sinners. It's repentance. It's forgiveness—and accepting that we're forgiven. It's being cleansed and refreshed and given the strength to move on in newness of life.

Which doesn't always mean our failed relationships will be restored.

Yes, God heals marriages, just as He heals people of illness. I've seen it happen, and it's beautiful.

But even in cases of illness, God doesn't heal everyone the same way. He doesn't restore every body to health here on this fallen earth. For some people who are sick, even good Christian girls, the healing is spiritual or emotional rather than physical. Sometimes it comes after death. And practically speaking, I believe that's true of some marriages.

Restoration is certainly possible. And if you're struggling in your marriage, the cleansing, restorative power of living water is available for that process. And it's so important to try. Whatever it takes—counseling, prayer, apologies, forbearance, date nights, communication skills. Whatever.

But as Connie and Nancy and Trish and Leanna and I will testify, sometimes you can try and try and things just don't work out. Because of sin. Because of hardness of heart. Because the pain of a mismatched relationship or a traumatic event or an ongoing, intolerable situation can be too much for a fallible human to bear. I absolutely believe that only the Holy Spirit can tell you when it's time to let go . . . but that there are times when the Holy Spirit does tell you that it's time—that a divorce may be the least damaging of a group of bad options.

And when that happens, when we who have failed in relationship manage to peer out of our pain just enough to turn to Jesus, He'll still be standing there, offering His gift of living water. I absolutely believe that. As I said, I'm staking my life on it.

Jesus is there, right by the well. Standing ready to cleanse us, refresh us, strengthen us, guide us.

He offers no condemnation, just a cleansing, refreshing, powerful flow.

And that is absolutely His answer to "It's over."

Jesus's final words on the Cross, after all, were not "It's over" but "It is finished" (John 19:30). And if we hear the message of Jesus to the woman with five husbands—really hear His words of loving grace—we know those words apply to us as well.

He doesn't say, "It's over."

He says, "For you, it's just beginning."

He doesn't say, "You're a failure."

He says, "I am the Messiah. The Christ."

He doesn't say, "You've messed up; now suffer the consequences." (Though of course we do.)

He says, "I know all you are and all you've done. I know your fears and your failures. And I've come to change all that."

You see, "It is finished" really means "I've done it—it's all taken care of."

Shame soothed. Brokenness healed. Sins forgiven. Failures fixed. Thirst slaked. Our faithlessness redeemed by the One who is ever faithful. Our sins and failures washed away. Our dry, hardened hearts softened and plumped up. Our inner deadness brought to life. Our defeated lives put to use for His glory.

Indeed the time is coming, as Jesus promised the Samaritan woman at the well, "when the true worshipers will worship the Father in spirit and truth" (John 4:23). When we'll live in healthy relationship with both God and other people. Whether we are single or married or divorced, failures or successes, thirsty or filled, we can depend on that.

Because when our Lord Jesus is calling the shots, regardless of who we are and what we've done, it's never over until He's finished.

WORD OF GRACE FOR HEARTBROKEN CHRISTIAN GIRLS

The Lord knows everything you've ever done . . .
and He wants to give you everything you'll ever need.

6

"I Never Meant to Go There"

The Treacherous Trap of Addiction

If we claim to be without sin,
we deceive ourselves, and the truth is not in us.
If we confess our sins, he is faithful and just,
and will forgive our sins
and purify us from all unrighteousness.
—1 John 1:8–9

Don't even go there!"

When did people start using that expression? I don't remember saying it as a kid, but it's pretty entrenched in my vocabulary now. And wherever it came from, it expresses a reality I believe can save us . . . or ruin us.

How can it save us? Because there are places in life that we're better off not visiting. Experiences it's safer not to have. Activities we're wise to avoid. Extremes of even good things that can bring us grief if we carry them too far. So we're warned by our parents, our pastors, our teachers and counselors, "Don't even go there."

But all too often, we go there anyway.

Because we're bored . . . or curious . . . or angry . . . or hurting.

Because a friend entices us or a family member shows us how it's done.

Because we really can't tell when we've gone too far with a good thing.

And because we all have this human tendency to get attached to stuff we take and things we do and people we care about . . . in ways that just aren't good for anyone.

Every human being you have ever met, in other words, is susceptible to developing an addiction. And many of us do. We go there. We make a choice that gives us a feeling we like—at least at first. Then, at some point, we get trapped. Dependent on a substance or an activity or a relationship to get us through the day or the night. Needing more and more to get the desired effect. And unable to get ourselves unattached, no matter how hard we try.

It happens to more good Christian girls than any of us want to admit.

Some were raised by addicts, and their childhood still haunts them. Some agonize over children who develop drug problems or spouses who gamble. Some have been injured by drunk drivers, robbed by drug-addicted thieves, or been bankrupted by a family member's compulsive spending.

And some of us, of course, have become addicts ourselves.

We are alcoholics, defending our "freedom" to enjoy wine "like Jesus did" but unable to relax without at least a couple of glasses. We are drug addicts, doctor shopping or Net surfing to maintain our supply of prescription pills. We are shopping addicts, hooked on credit cards or eBay . . . sex addicts, driven by the stimulation of masturbation or pornography or affairs . . . or compulsive gamblers, hooked on the thrill of getting something for nothing in a casino or the lottery.

We smoke, though in certain circles we'd never admit it. We are emotional overeaters, reaching for the chips or the ice cream whenever we have an emotion and unable to stop until we finish the bag or the carton. Or we may turn our food compulsions a different way and become anorexic or bulimic, attempting to manage our pain or fear by obsessing over what passes our lips.[1]

And if you're looking at these examples and thinking, *Oh, I'd never go there,* consider that addiction can wear respectable faces too. It emerges as codependency, sometimes described as an addiction to approval. Or workaholism that swaps health and relationships for hard-driving success. And a surprising number of Christian girls are religious addicts, dependent on a constant supply of Bible studies and worship services and Christian books—as opposed to a vital relationship with Christ—to make us feel all right.

The Voice of Addiction

Am I implying that Bible studies and tortilla chips are as dangerous as cocaine or crystal meth? Absolutely not. I'm also not saying that going to church or eating snacks or being in a relationship are bad things in themselves. You can go to church a lot or eat way too much salt and sugar and still not be an addict.

And yet . . . we all have the capacity to get attached to something in our lives in a way that destroys our freedom, that harms ourselves and others. Don't be deceived: addiction to *anything* can be a treacherous trap. Addictions wreck families and friendships. (An addiction counselor once told me that every addiction affects a minimum of ten other

> *Few of us, if any, can say, "It could never happen to me."*
> —Anderson Spickard Jr. and Barbara R. Thompson[2]

lives.) They drain bank accounts and ruin careers. They damage bodies and minds and wreak havoc with spirits. They contribute to suicide and sexual sins and abuse and divorces and almost every other kind of brokenness that affects good Christian girls. Even a socially acceptable addiction like workaholism or religious addiction can wreak long-term havoc in the life of an addict and those who love her.

No wonder we're warned not even to go there. I sincerely wish I'd never even gone close.

But I have.

This chapter, in fact, is one of the most painful for me to write, because the brokenness of addiction has been part of my life for many years.

Someone close to me is an alcoholic—a good Christian girl who continues drinking despite repeated stints at rehab. Friends and family members have tried to intervene, but nothing seems to stick. We all hold out hope for recovery, but change still seems very far away—and this person's life is well on the way to falling apart. Though she's been able to function productively for years in spite of her addiction—she's truly a brilliant and able person—the alcoholism recently cost her a high-profile job. Her health has started to fail. Her long-term marriage is faltering, and her husband recently filed for separation. Her children love her, but they're confused and hurting deeply. Though she continues to show up for church most Sundays, she's really just going through the motions. And through it all, she refuses to recognize that something is very wrong with her life or take steps to recover.

The whole situation is heartbreaking—unbelievably painful. I get frustrated and angry every time I think about it. I hurt for her husband. I ache for those kids. I get furious with my friend for what she's doing to herself and her family and her friends—the lies, the broken promises, the refusal or inability to face up to what her life has become. But even on days when my patience runs thin with her, I have to look at my own life and see the places where I tend toward addiction as well.

And no, I'm not an alcoholic. I've never shot up heroin or methamphetamines or snorted cocaine. Gambling isn't my thing, and I've never been much of an overeater. And yet there have been lonely evenings when my husband was out of town and one glass of wine "to relax me" stretched into another and maybe another. And there have been seasons when those relaxing glasses became a daily habit. During a particularly rough stretch, my friends even confronted me about those glasses of wine. And so far, by the grace of God, I've been able to retrace my steps before I developed a serious problem. But it could easily have gone the other way. According to my research, it is possible to drink socially or be totally abstinent for a number of years and then, at some point, cross over into addiction.[3] I can easily see how that could happen to me, especially in times of pain and stress.

And shopping—now there's an addiction I can relate to! I've always loved the challenge of finding just the right item, the fun of stockpiling gifts, the camaraderie of shopping with friends, the satisfaction of finding just the right shoes to go with my new outfit. I have shopped to celebrate, shopped for fun, shopped to bond with my friends or my children. And when I was feeling bad, there was nothing like a little "retail therapy" to raise my spirits. I'd think, *I've had a really awful week, so I'm going to go reward myself with a new outfit.* Or, *I'm going to go reward myself with a new piece of jewelry. I deserve it. I've put up with a lot.*

My shopaholic tendencies even became a joke with my kids. They would see me wearing something new and ask, "Well, Mom, did you reward yourself today?" We would all laugh, of course. My shopping was a big joke even to me . . . until I realized I was spending money I didn't have, making just the minimum payment on my credit cards, creating tension with my husband. Yet there always seemed to be something else I "needed." Just one more item to cross off my shopping list.

In this tendency too—most definitely by the grace of God—I've been able to back off into sanity before I got really trapped. But I'm acutely aware of how easily my shopping could slide into a full-fledged addiction. That happened to a friend of mine, whose shopping habits almost plunged her well-heeled family into bankruptcy.

So far, I've been able to budget my purchases and pay most of the bills. I've also been working hard on turning to the Lord instead of to Visa or to *vino* when I'm feeling lonely or angry or bored or frustrated. Yet I still have to fight that persistent little inner voice that whispers, "Just one more time . . ."

You've heard that voice, haven't you—whispering in your own head or in the words of someone you care about?

It's the one that whispers, "Just one more"—though it's almost never just one.

Or "Just a little won't hurt"—though it's not really a little, and it usually does hurt somebody.

Or, famously, "I can stop this anytime I want"—when it's just not true.

The voice that keeps telling us, against all reason, that we really *need* to go where we want to go . . . and that other people might get trapped, but we won't.

That's the voice that, under the right conditions, any one of us can start listening to.

The lying, persistent, deadly voice of addiction.

> *There are many sources of pain in this life—some come from relationships, some of it is physical, some comes from the trio of guilt, shame, and worthlessness. Wherever it comes from, the tragic mistake is to take a good gift of God and misuse it to bury pain and find some pleasure. Using those gifts correctly, however, not only undercuts addiction but also unleashes the heart to truly enjoy.*
>
> —DAVID ECKMAN[4]

SARA'S STORY

I recently spent time with a woman who knows even better than I do about what happens when we listen to that voice. Her name is Sara. She's a sixty-one-year-old grandmother, a clinical psychologist. She's been a Christian for almost forty years. And for all that time, she's also been an active or recovering alcoholic and drug addict. Even though it's now been twenty years since her last drink and even longer since she took her last prescription pill, she still says, "I could get addicted to green M&Ms if you give me enough time."

How does a good Christian girl become an addict like that? I've already hinted at some of the reasons—boredom, curiosity, anger, desire, family history. And pain . . . especially pain. Pain that life dealt her, and the pain of her own choices as well.

Sara grew up as the middle of three girls in a relatively well-to-do family. Her father was a doctor from an Irish Catholic background. Her mother was a Jewish musician who also happened to be an alcoholic and addicted to diet pills. Sara herself started drinking at age twelve and began taking pain pills after she broke her back in a horse-riding accident at fourteen. During college and early graduate school, like many of her peers, Sara experimented with various "recreational" drugs and developed a three-pack-a-day nicotine habit.

But looking back, Sara doesn't think she'd crossed the line into addiction at that point. Because when she became a Christian at age twenty-three, she stopped—just like that. She was converted through the influence of some Young Life leaders who lived in the apartment across the hall. Something about the way they lived attracted her, and she wanted to live the way they did. So she gave up drinking, gave up smoking, gave up drugs. It wasn't hard at all . . . or so she thought.

Then Sara made a mistake many young Christians make. "I kept my eyes on the people who led me to the Lord rather than the Lord they led me to. And I was disappointed by them. They were human! They hurt me." So she decided to run away from her friends and from God. "I thought, 'Well, okay, God won't find me in New York City. He's not there, so He's not going to look for me there.'" Sara moved to New York, found a job in advertising . . . and fell back into the drinking and the drugs. It wasn't long until her behavior was completely out of control.

She drank heavily, snorted cocaine, popped prescription pills, whatever she could secure—"cough medicine with codeine; it didn't matter. I was willing to do almost anything." The pattern of destructive choices led to other problems, including a painful relational breakup, a pregnancy, an abortion. The pain and guilt drove her to more substances in an effort to numb her disappointment and guilt and fear and loneliness.

After several years, partly through the influence of a praying Christian friend, Sara found her way back to the Lord. But by that point she was a full-fledged addict, dependent on alcohol and especially prescription pills. She became proficient at obtaining them—going from clinic to clinic with various vague complaints, asking her father for meds, exploring various mail-order channels. (Today, she would be shopping on the Internet.) And she managed to compartmentalize her life so she could continue to drink and do drugs while living as an active Christian. She was no longer partying and carousing, just ingesting enough substances, mostly prescription medications, to let her function "normally." In the self-deception common to all addicts, she even told herself the pills weren't a problem—after all, they were *prescriptions.*

God, of course, was not deceived. A very few praying friends knew what was going on in Sara's life as well. And deep down, under her denial, Sara knew too. She finally reached a point when she looked at the pills in her hand and realized what they were doing to her. She was an addict. More traumatically, she was just like her mother.

That realization was motive enough to get her off drugs. She did it cold turkey—just stopped using. She also decided to move to another city and start a new life. And all went well over the next few years. She married and began a family. She worked awhile and then stayed home with her boys. When her children were older, she started a clinical practice in psychology from her home. And she carefully stayed away from drugs during all that time.

The trouble is, she didn't stay away from alcohol.

> *Becoming free is not an easy process, nor is it always an enjoyable one. Notwithstanding those facts, there is no greater reason for living. The process is the only thing that gives our lives substance and value.*
>
> —Luci Swindoll[5]

After all, she reasoned—more self-deception—she was a drug addict, not an alcoholic. She functioned quite well without the pills. And her drinking didn't really interfere with her life. She and her husband were active in their church. She was known as intelligent, energetic, efficient; unlike her mother, she never indulged in binges. The fact that she depended on a daily ration of alcohol to manage her feelings was a carefully guarded secret, even from her husband and her two younger boys, who don't remember ever seeing her drink.

It took another decade or so for Sara to face the reality that she was an alcoholic. Even when she had her last drink—"twenty years ago, on Labor Day"—she wasn't ready to tell the world. She told herself and others she wanted to lose weight and "get healthy." Only a month or so later did she admit to a close friend—and to herself—what the real problem was. She finally said the words: "I'm an alcoholic."

At that point Sara started to realize what her addictions had done to her. A physical revealed that her liver had basically stopped functioning. Her memory was spotty, with occasional full blackouts. Her relationship with God had long gone flat and stale. Although she had always been a high-functioning addict, she was definitely not functioning well.

And so Sara got serious. She went into therapy. She began attending Alcoholics Anonymous meetings several times a week. She started keeping a journal. She asked her Christian friends for prayer and support. She told everyone she could think of what her problem was and asked them to hold her accountable. She visited local restaurants and begged them not to sell her drinks. She told her doctors and dentists not to prescribe pills for her. She even chose to forgo Novocain at her dental appointments and pain medication after surgery.

And somehow, by the grace of God, Sara managed to stay sober. Step by step, day by day, she's managed to stay that way. It's now been twenty years since her last drink, thirty-two years since her last prescription pill. As for her last green M&M, she won't say, except to insist that her freedom still depends on daily doses of God's grace.

She's still an addict, in other words.

But she's living free and she's helping others—a powerful testimony to what God can do with even the most stubborn addictions. But her story is also a vivid reminder that addictions are powerful and complex . . . and that simply knowing Christ will not necessarily be enough to prevent good Christian girls and those they love from "going there" or to rescue them from the trap of their own attachments.

A Sin and a Sickness

Does it shock you that I would say that knowing Christ isn't enough to prevent you from addiction?

It shouldn't.

After all, just knowing Christ isn't enough to keep any of us from sinning! It isn't enough to stop us from betraying the people we love or acting out sexually or failing in our marriages or messing our lives up in a number of different ways. As we've seen again and again, none of us is immune from the fallout of living in a fallen world. And that means we can all choose to take God's good gifts and use them in destructive ways.

You see, addiction has a million specific causes, but almost all of them stem from the human desire to experience pleasure and escape pain. God made us with these desires and He made them good. He wanted us to be able to enjoy His creation (pleasure) and to avoid what isn't good for us (pain). He also made us with the capacity to develop habits and become attached to people and objects. Habits save us energy by allowing us to put some of our life on "autopilot," doing some activities without conscious thought. And attachments are crucial to our ability to develop loving, interdependent relationships with God and other people. All these things—pleasure, pain, habits, and attachments—are given to us as blessings for our lives.

But as is so often true with God's gift, we fallen people tend to misuse them. So in our drive to find pleasure and escape pain, we turn to objects that are inadequate, dangerous, or both. Instead of rejoicing and finding pleasure in God's goodness and the beauty of creation, we enjoy the sparkle of champagne, the "rush" of cocaine, the exhilaration of finding just the right ring to go with a new skirt, the thrill of sex with a stranger. Instead of coming to God with our pain or leaving the source of pain behind us, we seek to numb the feelings with a cocktail or distract ourselves with Internet porn. If we like the experience, we do it again . . . and again . . . until the behavior takes on a life of its own. A habit is born. We become physically, emotionally, and spiritually attached to whatever we're taking or doing. If the process is allowed to continue, we reach the point where we simply can't stop on our own. We become addicted.

Another way of saying all this is that addiction is sin. It's a misuse of God's gifts, a "missing of the mark" (the literal meaning of *sin*) as Romans 3:23 describes. It's also a form of idolatry, in that something or someone other than God—booze, money, pills, shopping, power—becomes the essential center of your universe. No matter what you profess with your lips or even think with your mind, if you're addicted you are essentially worshipping the object of your addiction.

And addiction is intertwined with sin in so many other ways. It involves behavior that hurts ourselves and others and gets in the way of our relationship with God—lies and deception, drunkenness, sexual immorality, abuse, even murder. Some addictive pursuits (such as extramarital sex) are sinful in themselves. And one person's sin can push another person toward addiction. Thus an alcoholic father's abuse influences a child to numb the pain by taking drugs. Or a wife of a sex addict may begin shopping excessively to cope with the pain and to get back at her husband.

Addiction is a sin problem—there's no way around it. But simply addressing the sin element in addiction tends to be ineffective because addiction is also a sickness, a complicated disease that affects the whole person—body, mind, emotions, and spirit. Alcohol and drug dependency and some other addictions are actually listed as such by the American Medical Association, and almost all addictions fit the basic description of a chronic disease. There is some evidence that susceptibility to certain addictions is genetic. There is a clear and predictable progression of symptoms. The attachment is chronic; it doesn't go away on its own. It's also progressive; it gets worse without treatment. It's treatable, though relapses are common. And if not treated, addiction leads to added complications and even death.

Do not destroy your life over a big lie. You feel hopeless because you have been using your own power, not because there is no hope. You feel hopeless because you have been headed in the wrong direction, not because there is no hope. You feel hopeless because you have cut yourself off from others who could help you and guide you, not because there is no hope. . . . You are not hopeless because there is not hope. There is hope for you, if you will just persevere long enough to find it.

—STEPHEN ARTERBURN[6]

Some Christians object to describing addiction as disease because they believe it excuses an addict of responsibility. "You can say you're sick," they charge, "and that means you just couldn't help it—it's an excuse to sin." But I have absolutely no problem with thinking of addiction as both a sin and a sickness. In fact, I think recovery is more likely if we think that way.

After all, there are plenty of purely physical illnesses that are at least partially caused or spread by human sin and irresponsibility—lung cancer from smoking, heart attacks from overeating, STDs from illicit sex, colds spread by not covering the mouth and not washing hands. And treatment of any disease calls for responsibility on the part of the victim—taking medications, eating right, exercising, physical or mental therapy, whatever the doctor orders.

More to the point, I absolutely believe that God is the ultimate source of all healing—for physical illnesses such as cancer and for "biopsychosocialspiritual" diseases such as addiction.[7] He is also the remedy for sin in our lives. He is always working to bring us to physical and mental and emotional and spiritual health in ways that are both well mapped out (in the Bible) and entirely mysterious.

Sometimes He heals us outright, and sometimes He makes us wait. Sometimes the healing is primarily physical; more often it is emotional and spiritual as well. He often involves other people as agents of healing—professionals such as physicians and pastors as well as praying and supportive friends and family.

And God *always* requires our cooperation in the process of our own healing. He asks us to repent, accept forgiveness and forgive others to be "healed" of sin. He requires us to adjust our lifestyles and cooperate with doctors to be healed of physical illness. He wants us to look at ourselves honestly and kindly—to examine our hearts and understand our emotions and forgive ourselves to be healed of emotional disease. And when we find ourselves trapped in addictions, all of the above apply.

Thinking of addiction as both sin and disease doesn't excuse us from responsibility. In fact, it asks a lot of us.

Not more than we can do—though when we're trapped in an addiction, that's really hard to believe.

And definitely not more than God can do—if we let Him.

But that's a big *if*. . . because the very nature of addiction works to keep us addicted.

THE NATURE OF THE DISEASE

"No one *wants* to be an addict." That's something Sara tries to explain to the spouses of those who come to her for help with addictions. No one enjoys the experience of being trapped or the practical fallout of addiction—health problems, relationship failures, financial struggle, shame, guilt. (It goes without saying that no one likes being married to an addict . . . or being the parent or child or friend or coworker of one.) But while he or she may not want to be addicted, the addict desperately wants to do the addictive *behavior*—to experience the alcohol or the drugs or the shopping or the gambling or whatever. Once a person has crossed the line into addiction, that wanting feels like irresistible need . . . a need that grows stronger as time goes on.

Addiction, you see, is sneaky and relentless. It's a progressive disease, which means it doesn't get better on its own. The addict builds up a tolerance to the substance or behavior and requires more and more to achieve the desired pleasure or relief. More beer to get to sleep. More food to feel satisfied. More and kinkier sex to get the same thrill. Tolerance happens because the brain actually adjusts to the presence of the substance or the behavior and achieves a new kind of equilibrium—the body is fooled into thinking the present level of involvement is "normal." So the addict needs more and more to feel better—and "more" translates into more and more addicted.

Addiction is not only relentless in moving forward, but it also resists going backward. Because the addiction sets up a new balance of brain and body chemistry, any attempt to discontinue the addictive behavior usually sets off withdrawal. The addict may feel antsy or irritable or experience a rebound reaction of symptoms opposite to those the addictive behavior creates. Withdrawing from severe alcohol or drug addiction may cause a violent physical reaction—nausea, chills, pain, hallucinations, and more.

Even when withdrawal symptoms are relatively mild, an attempt to stop an addiction usually results in persistent obsessive thoughts . . . because addiction inevitably hijacks the addict's attention. She may not necessarily think about booze or pills or eating all the time. But if for some reason she *can't* satisfy her addiction right away, she can't think of anything else. Addicts can be astonishingly single-minded, setting aside all other interests and relationships when they're focused on satisfying their addiction. When an alcoholic craves a drink, she obsesses about getting one, and there's no room in her mind for love or loyalty or anything else. In the same way, a compulsive overeater obsesses about chocolate and a porn addict obsesses about getting alone so he can log on to his favorite Web site.

And the addict can't simply decide to stop indulging in the addiction. That's because it's the nature of addiction to sap the will. Once the addiction has taken hold, ordinary willpower just doesn't apply. The addict may be able to give up the substance or behavior for a while, but she will inevitably give in again at some point. In the language of Alcoholics Anonymous and other "twelve-step" groups, an addict is out of control, powerless over the addiction. In biblical language, she has been "given over" to the sin of addiction (see Ps. 81:12; Acts 7:42; Rom. 1:24–28). Her only choice for recovery is to admit the truth about her powerlessness, confess that she's trapped, and rely on God for release.

> *Strong determination is no defense against addiction. I have watched more than one stubborn, strong-willed person involuntarily drink him- or herself to death, and the only significant difference I have ever noticed between seemingly strong and weak personalities is that strong-willed alcoholics pursue their drinking more aggressively.*
>
> —ANDERSON SPICKARD JR.[8]

But that's one of the trickiest aspects of addiction, because addicts find it notoriously difficult to face reality or even recognize truth. That's because addiction, like Satan, is a consummate liar, and *self-deception* lurks at the very heart of any addiction. All addiction, as far as I can tell, is built on shifting sand—fake, unreliable, chaotic reality. Lies like "I can handle it." Or "I can quit whenever I want to." Deceptions about where we've gone and where we're going, what we want and what we're going to do.

No wonder recovering from addiction is so hard. How can you find healing for a disease when the disease itself convinces you that nothing's wrong?

The saving grace in all of this, as far as I see, is the fact that grace sometimes does break through. Sometimes, in quiet moments, we can see through the deception. Sometimes another person helps us see through them. Sometimes a crisis—a job loss, a car accident, a credit-card refusal—shocks us into reality for an instant. And those rare moments of honesty hold the promise of hope. For in those brief instances we have a chance to look at ourselves and the addictions that control us and see what a crock the whole thing is.

That's our window of opportunity, our instant of possibility. And if we can stay in those moments long enough to make the smallest of decisions, we have a chance to sidestep the relentless, resistant, obsessive, and deceptive nature of addiction.

Where We Need to Go

The good news is that really does happen. Addicts do get better. With help, quite a few good Christian addicts manage to move toward freedom and healing and to lead fruitful lives.

Which is not to say the healing is easy or quick.

The sin-disease of addiction may be one of the trickiest afflictions we humans encounter in this fallen world. There are questions of heredity and environment, brain chemistry and spiritual connection, what we can do and what we can't do, release and relapse. Every day, it seems, someone discovers something new about how addiction works and offers a new idea about how it can be treated. And even with treatment and improvement, addiction is never really cured. Neither is sin, for that matter. Just as all good Christian girls remain sinners, addicts remain addicts all their lives—their brains permanently altered to respond to the addictive substance or behavior. An addict can live free as long as she is able to stay away from the addictive substance or behavior. But she is always a few steps away from falling into the trap once more.

So the subject is complicated as well as heartbreaking. And I'm certainly not in a position to unravel it all for you. I'm not a therapist or a pastor or an addiction counselor—just a good Christian girl whose life has been darkened by the pain of addiction. Even if I were an expert and I had all the answers, I wouldn't try to squeeze them into a simplistic, zipped-up version that fits in a single chapter of a book.

More to the point, there are already plenty of programs out there to help people recover from addictions—excellent counseling centers and organizations, superb rehab setups, and community-based groups such as the time-tested, spiritually based, and highly practical programs based on the twelve steps of Alcoholics Anonymous. (I've listed some of these in Appendix B on p. 259.) There are good books to give you information, supportive groups to encourage you, and plenty (though not enough) wise and savvy pastors and Christian counselors to help you as you struggle to recover or find help for a loved one.

So I have no intention of using this chapter to outline the healing process.

But I do have a suggestion about where it has to start.

For a good Christian girl to find freedom from the treacherous trap of addiction, she needs to say no to just one pervasive lie of addiction.

It's the lie of "don't even go there."

Remember I said at the beginning of this chapter that "don't go there" could save us or ruin us? It can save us by warning us away from attachments that can enslave us. If we never choose to dabble in alcohol or cigarettes or porn or toxic religion, we can save ourselves a lot of grief.

But once we're there—once we're addicted or involved with an addict—"don't go there" becomes a problem. Because even when we've ignored the warning, it stays in our hearts and our heads. But now it's twisted, because addiction twists and distorts everything. When we're trapped in our own desires and controlled by our attachments, the "don't go there" in our hearts keeps warning us away from the places we *need* to go.

Away from the truth about our sin and brokenness.

Away from the reality that we are no longer in control of our lives.

Away from the Truth that really can set us free.

Until we say no to "don't go there," we'll never get where we need to be. But when by God's grace we do say no, when we resist just one of addiction's relentless lies, we have a stab at freedom.

More to the point, as a woman in the seventh chapter of Luke discovered, we have a chance to walk with the One who sets us free.

A Still, Small Decision

We don't know that she was an addict, although she might have been. Given the mess she had made of her life, I wouldn't be surprised if she also tipped a few wineskins to get her through the night.

What we know about this woman is that she was notorious in her community. Luke 7:37 tells us she "had lived a sinful life"—probably sexually promiscuous. She may even have been the village prostitute. At any rate, the upright citizens of her community had written her off as a lost cause. Maybe she had written herself off too.

I see that woman as living a little like the Samaritan woman at the well—on the fringes of society. Well known and yet set apart, avoiding respectable citizens whenever she could. Trapped in her life of sin but perhaps pushing that awareness to the back of her mind so she could get through the day.

> *Medically speaking, alcoholism is most often a progressive disease. If left to run its course, it gets worse, not better. At any given time, the alcoholic may appear to be holding her own or even recovering, but the overall direction of her life remains the same—downhill. Driven by an overwhelming craving and blinded by denial, she slides into spiritual, psychological, physical, and social devastation. Each aspect of her disease reinforces the others, and she is trapped in a cage that seldom opens from the inside.*
>
> —ANDERSON SPICKARD JR. AND BARBARA R. THOMPSON[9]

But I wonder . . . how many times had she tried to give it all up? And how many times had she failed?

How many mornings did she wake up bleary-eyed and count her money, telling herself she had no choice but to do what she did? That it was who she was and there was no way out? (Her society surely offered few options for a single woman with a bad reputation.)

How many evenings did she dread the knock on the door . . . yet fear the day when no one would knock?

Did she wonder about what she would do when her fading beauty was completely gone and no one wanted to pay for her services? Did she finger her little alabaster jar of perfume, an expensive gift from a past admirer, and wonder if the time would come when she had to sell it? Could she bear to part with her most treasured possession? And what would she do then?

The more I think of it, the more I'm convinced that woman hit the wineskins pretty regularly.

But then something happened that changed everything. This

sinful woman heard of Jesus and took in His message of grace and forgiveness. We don't know when or how it happened. Maybe she heard about Jesus from a talkative "client." Maybe she followed a crowd and heard Him preach in the marketplace or overheard one of His conversations with the disciples. Maybe their paths crossed and they actually had a conversation—Jesus was known for doing that kind of thing.

However they met, He must have said something that stuck in the woman's mind and haunted her heart. Words that spoke to her spirit until something finally clicked deep inside her. A shifting of values. A transfer of treasure. A still, small decision almost below the level of her will.

She didn't think of it as changing her life. She wasn't sure that was possible.

She just knew she had to go to Him.

I'm convinced that by the time that woman went to see Jesus, she had already put all her eggs in His basket. And that's what gave her the courage to go someplace she would never have set foot before . . . to the house of a Pharisee named Simon, who had invited Jesus to dinner. A house full of judgmental people who considered her lower than dirt.

Can't you see that poor woman standing outside the house in the shadows, swallowing hard, working up the courage for what she knows she has to do? She's not even sure why she's there, what she expects. But somehow she knows her very existence depends on it.

She stands there clutching her little jar of perfume, the alabaster cool beneath her fingers. Watching the door. Does she dare? She waits in the shadows, working up the nerve . . . compelled to go in, yet terrified of what she knows will happen.

She'll be accused of so much . . . and it's all true! She's done everything they think she has, plus some things most of them can't imagine. She sees her sin so clearly now. All the excuses she's relied on over the years—that the townspeople are self-righteous hypocrites, that she performs a valuable service, that she actually *likes* her life of sin—dissolves as she ponders what she heard the Teacher say, what she saw in His eyes. For the first time in many years, she's facing it all—the filth, the shame, the sordid pursuits that are making her old before her time.

She's facing it all because of Him. Because of what her encounter with the Lord has given her.

A glimmer of grace.

A window of possibility.

Enough hope to grab on to.

Just enough faith to go where she needs to go.

So she pushes past the servant who answered the door. She ignores the man's whispered protests as she follows the sound of voices to the well-lit dining chamber. She lurches into the room . . . then gulps as she steps through the doorway.

Every shocked face—the men at the table, the women serving them—throws her shame back in her face.

Every outraged murmur reminds her how far she has fallen, how hopelessly trapped she's been.

Every step she takes toward Jesus feels like an echoing mile.

But she's going there anyway.

And that's the place we have to start when it comes to escaping the treacherous trap of our addictions.

We have to go there.

We have to walk past all the lies and the self-deceptions, past all the whispers that we can't do it and we don't want to. We have to take a step out of the trap even when we're convinced there's nothing out there for us.

And then we have to take another step. And another . . . in the direction of Truth.

She scans the room until she finds Him. His eyes meet hers and He nods. Then she walks toward Him, step by step . . . past the stares of scorn, the whispers of accusation, the pain and the shame of her own awareness.

Step by step, her eyes locked on His.

And by the time she gets there, she knows that she's going to be free.

Because she's gone to the place of her deepest shame and found the One who could make her whole.

No wonder she falls down at His feet in gratitude and exhaustion. No wonder she weeps so freely that her tears fall down and soak His toes. No wonder she's willing to pour out her treasured perfume on those feet and use her own long hair to dry them off.

For the first time in so many years, she's free to let down her defenses and really cry. Free to open her hands and give instead of worrying if she'll have enough. Free to live without the shame and regret that trapped her as surely as the norms of society did. Free to experience honest gratitude and true hope.

Free at last to make herself free.

And Jesus understood. He knew what had happened—saw it in her face the minute she had entered the room. She had already opened her heart to the possibilities of forgiveness and grace and faith.

In the very act of stepping toward reality, that woman had begun her journey to health. All that remained was sorting out the details . . . like explaining to the shocked Pharisees what had happened: "She was forgiven many sins, so she is very, very grateful."

And confirming to the woman what made the difference: "Your faith has saved you. Go in peace."

For that, too, is the Lord's word to all good Christian girls trapped in addiction.

Your faith really can save you.

But it has to be faith that's deeper than belief, more active than intellectual assent. It has to be faith that is willing to step out of the trap and go to the place of your deepest shame. To give up the treasures you clutch so tightly—the attachments that get you through the day. To take a first step forward into what feels like nothing but shame and the pain and emptiness . . . the place where you'll find your Savior.

How do you get that kind of faith?

Not through willpower . . . because the very nature of an addiction disables the will.

Not through insight and honesty . . . because an addict lives by self-deception.

Not because of other people's rejection or your own shame or fear

---

Looking back (isn't hindsight amazing?), I can clearly see that the more I trusted God, the more trustworthy I found Him. The harder I leaned on Him, the more support He supplied. It wasn't trust, in and of itself, that brought me peace. It was the One in whom I trusted. . . . The more I sensed his nearness, the easier it was for me to let go of self-reliance. . . . The more I focused on God's capability, the less overwhelmed I felt by my inabilities. The more I reminded myself of God's sovereign power, the less intimidated I was by the things I couldn't control.

—PAM VREDEVELT[10]

. . . because those painful feelings can just as easily drive you deeper into the addiction.

No, I'm convinced it can only happen with a click in your heart. With a glimmer of grace.

With a still, small decision to grab on to hope and start walking toward freedom.

From Reality to Recovery

As far as what comes next—well, that's complicated. I'm sure it was complicated for the Luke 7 woman. Because once she left that house, she still had a lot to work out in her life. She had to make a whole new life for herself that fit the new freedom in her heart. And for a woman with a reputation in that particular day and age, that couldn't have been easy. How would she support herself and her children? How would she find new friends? How could she live with the knowledge of what she had done with her life? And how could she resist the temptation to fall back into her old, familiar ways?

How indeed?

How does an alcoholic get through the day without a drink? Or a shopaholic cut up her credit cards? How does a gambler live without gambling, a compulsive overeater or an anorexic rely on balanced, healthy meals? How does a religious addict find a healthy balance or a control freak loosen the reins on her family and friends?

And how do any of us whose lives have been touched by addictions figure out the true implications of the famous Serenity Prayer—coming to terms with what we can control and what we can't control, what's our responsibility and what belongs to someone else . . . or to God?

It's hard. It's a daily battle, complete with relapses. But that's what the ongoing work of recovery is like. Interestingly, enough, it's also the basic work of living well in the world. In fact, I've come to see the entire Christian walk as a form of recovery from sin of some sort. Choosing again and again to go with Christ to the places of our deepest shame. Facing our sin as honestly as we can. Cleansing our bodies and souls from the toxins left by years of misuse and neglect. Learning to enjoy pleasure without overindulgence, to avoid unnecessary pain but welcome the suffering that helps us grow. Growing to love what is truly lovable and to depend on what is truly dependable.

It truly takes a lifetime to sort it all out.

And doing it is both profoundly simple and practically impossible . . . without a higher power, that is.

But the beauty of it all is that our higher power isn't just across the room, calling us to Him.

He's walking with us too.

It's His grace that makes it possible for us to go where we just can't go. His hope that generates the first little click. His faith that lets us trust what we can't see. His love that pulls us out of our self-centered selves. His truth that first and finally sets us free.

If we're good Christian girls, of course, we have a name for our higher power.

His name is Jesus.

And even when we're walking the line, struggling day by day and moment and moment, He's matching us step by step.

And step by step, one day at a time . . . if we let Him . . . He will make something beautiful out of lives that are both sinful and sick.

Jesus's "Dirty" Little Secret

The longer I live, you see, the more pain and brokenness I've seen on this earth, the more I'm convinced of two things:

First, life would really be better if we could somehow manage not to sin. Sin is ugly. Evil is painful. I sincerely wish that Adam and Eve had never "gone there" and touched that fruit in the garden!

But they did. The result has been century after century of pain and brokenness and sin and life-destroying experiences like addiction.

And yet . . .

The second thing I'm convinced of is that our gracious and loving and amazingly creative God can turn our broken, sinful lives into something far more beautiful than we can imagine. He's been doing it from the beginning, working to clean up our messes and transform our lives. He sent His Son to provide the ultimate remedy for our sin. Even now, His healing, redemptive grace continues to flow into the messy areas of our lives, the corners we've painted ourselves into. He offers us possibility where we see only pain.

And God doesn't just work around the pain. He *uses* the pain. When we dare to bring Him our brokenness, our impossibilities—when we dare

Many of us are tempted to think that if we suffer, the only important thing is to be relieved of our pain. We want to flee it at all costs. But when we learn to move through suffering, rather than avoid it, then we greet it differently. We become willing to let it teach us. We even begin to see how God can use it for some larger end. Suffering becomes something other than a nuisance or curse to be evaded at all costs, but a way into deeper fulfillment. Ultimately mourning means facing what wounds us in the presence of One who can heal.

—Henri Nouwen[11]

to meet Him at our point of deepest shame—that's when He really begins to shine. That's when He starts making something completely new.

That's the secret reality that shines from the story of the Luke 7 woman. When Jesus's Pharisee host Simon spotted this scandalous woman in his dining room, he immediately said to himself, "If this man were a prophet, he would know who is touching him and what kind of woman she is—that she is a sinner" (v. 9). The Greek word he used for "what kind of" is actually derived from two Greek words—*poios,* meaning "what" and *dapedon,* meaning "soil."[12] He was implying that Jesus didn't clearly comprehend just how dirty this woman was. He was essentially calling her a soiled woman, claiming she was filth—manure, even worse. (At that point in her life, after she'd faced the reality of who she was, the woman probably agreed with him.)

But when you think of it, a little dirt isn't such a bad thing. It may be ugly. It may be full of bugs and old roots. It may be laced with manure and decayed garbage . . . or worse. But dirt is the best possible medium for growing something new and beautiful. If it's handled right—if it's nurtured and enriched and cared for by the right Gardener—soil nurtures life.

I've seen this in the lives of so many recovering addicts like Sara, who have chosen to trust their desires to God. Something beautiful grows from the soil of their brokenness. Something better, more loving, more humble, more compassionate.

Something more Christlike.

But it wasn't just their pain that did it. That's important to recognize.

Remember it was pain and their sinful response to it that started the whole problem. They chose to go there, and that dark sojourn brought nothing but more brokenness. Their lives were barren soil, shifting sand—their whole existence stuck in the muck . . . and worse.

It was only when they chose to go where Jesus was—to make the small step or the giant leap into reality, release, and recovery—that the soil of their lives began to bear fruit. It was then that the pain, the shame, the brokenness was gradually plowed under, turned over like compost, and put into service for life.

"You don't know what kind of woman this is."

But Jesus knows.

He knows the hunger for beauty and happiness that drives you to seek pleasure. He put it there, remember?

He knows the pain that drives you to latch on to any source of relief. The Bible makes it clear that He's acquainted with grief.

He understands the deceptive call of misplaced attachments, the forces that cause us to "go there" and then trap us in our sin and selfishness. The Bible says Jesus was "tempted in every way" (Heb. 4:15), which must mean He was tempted to misuse.

Most important, He knows how to use the muck and manure of your life—addictions included—to grow you into something He can be proud of.

He knows who you are.

He knows who you can be.

All you have to do—and it's simple but not easy—is make a still, small decision . . . to go where He is.

❧ WORD OF GRACE FOR TRAPPED CHRISTIAN GIRLS ❧

The way to peace and true freedom is open to you.
Go there.

7

"Can God Hear a Crazy Woman?"

That is why we never give up.
Though our bodies are dying,
Our spirits are being renewed every day.
—2 Corinthians 4:16 NLT

It afflicts one in ten of the world's people[1]—one in six in the United States.[2]

At its best, it hinders productivity and makes life more difficult.

At its worst, it can be fatal.

Practically no one wants to admit to having it—and those who do are often shunned and feared.

It destroys marriages, pulls families apart, drives people to drink and drugs and despair.

If you hadn't read the title of this chapter, you might assume I'm talking about AIDS. But of course I'm talking about mental illness. And mental illness can be fully as devastating, especially for good Christian girls.

After all, we've been raised on the Great Commandment: "Love the Lord your God with all your heart and with all your soul and with all your mind and with all your strength" (Mark 12:30).

But what happens when your heart is torn and your soul is on a roller coaster? When your strength is sapped by worry or sadness? When your mind just won't work the way it was meant to?

More specifically, what happens when a *mood disorder* such as depression or bipolar disease sends your emotions soaring to delirious heights or plunging to unfathomable lows? Or a *psychotic disorder* such as schizophrenia taunts you with delusional visions and voices? Or an *anxiety disorder* such as obsessive-compulsive disorder or posttraumatic stress disorder leaves you paralyzed with fear or imprisoned by your own behaviors and obsessional beliefs? When a *developmental disorder* such as autism makes it hard for you to learn or relate to others? Or a form of *dementia* such as Alzheimer's disease eats holes in your memory and changes your very personality?

How do you love God then? How do you connect with Him or with anyone else when your dependable tools for connecting— memory, thought, perception, emotions, energy, will—are on the fritz? When your thoughts and emotions betray you, how do you even know who you are?

And that's not even to mention the way the world—and the church!—treats those who suffer from mental illness. The fearful or uneasy glances. The tendency to steer clear of you, as though your illness might be contagious. The reluctance to hire you or trust you. The spoken or unspoken suspicion that you must be faking . . . or dangerous . . . or morally compromised . . . or spiritually deficient . . . or possessed by demons . . . or just plain self-indulgent.

How do you live with that kind of stigma? And how do you cope when someone you love—a husband, parent, sibling, child, or friend—can't seem to function normally . . . or doesn't seem to be "in there" at all?

No Easy Answers

You're probably tired of all these questions, but I've asked them on purpose. Because for good Christian girls whose lives have been touched by mental illness, life itself can feel like a series of questions . . . with few answers in sight.

Let me be quick to add that *I* don't have a lot of answers either. I even hesitated to include this chapter because there's so much about mental illness that I don't understand. (As far as I can tell, there's a lot that even the experts don't understand either.)

> *While we don't know how to cure mental illness for the most part, we do know that those who are mentally ill can be healed and made whole in a way that we cannot understand, but in the way that God does. . . . Healing is about becoming awake to the fact that we are loved. Loved by God and called to be loved by our brothers and sisters in Christ. Healing is about being made whole in God's healing embrace even if we are not cured. . . . Jesus did not promise to fix everything we encounter in this mortal life, but he said to his disciples, "And remember, I am with you always, even to the end of the age."*
>
> —Judith Davis[3]

But I do know a little about what mental illness can mean in the life of a good Christian girl. I know what it's like to slog through the muck of severe depression—by far the most common form of mental illness.[4] I'm very close to a woman whose life has been turned upside down by her evangelist husband's bipolar disease. A terrifying, hereditary, brain-destroying disease has struck down several members of my extended family. A dear friend has struggled with obsessive-compulsive disorder since she was a child, and one of my own children has experienced severe anxiety issues. I've experienced the heartache of watching a loved one suffer from age-related dementia, prayed with victims of posttraumatic stress disorder, counseled with parents of autistic children, interviewed many others whose lives have been touched by mental illness.

And then, of course, there's Sherry, whose story both breaks my heart and deeply inspires me. To me, Sherry and her family put a living face on the chronic pain and frustration of living with mental and emotional disease . . . but also showcase what God's grace can do in even the most desperate situations. But before I tell you her story—because mental illness is so often misunderstood—I'd like to touch on just a few of the things that make this issue so problematic both for good Christian girls and their non-Christian sisters.

WHEN GOOD BRAINS GO WRONG

When I speak of mental illness, I'm referring to a disruption of thought or emotion that results from something going wrong in the brain—the physical organ that produces and regulates thought, memory, emotions, sensory perception, communication, and decision making. But this is where things get really complicated, especially for Christians—because Christians believe we are *more* than physical beings. The Bible clearly states that we are spiritual beings as well, made in God's image and capable of communicating with Him in our spirits, and that this spiritual reality is also tied in with our thoughts, memories, emotions, perceptions, communication, and decision making.

Christians are not the only ones who believe this, of course. Although some scientists and philosophers have adopted the materialistic view that human beings are nothing more than an intricate collection of electrical impulses and chemical reactions, many others have argued a reality that seems intuitive to most of us—that we are something more than the sum of our physical parts.

Just exactly what that "more" means has been debated for centuries—with words like *body, spirit, soul, mind, will,* and *consciousness*—and I can't claim to have it all sorted out. But when it comes to mental illness and good Christian girls, a few basic realities stand out to me.

> *The Word of God pierces to the place that life and spirit meet joints and marrow. . . . Mental illness can only be partially addressed until it comes to a place where the biochemical meets the spiritual. . . . We understand that while in the realm of the merely human things may appear hopeless, with God, everything is possible.*
>
> —Jackson H. Day[5]

First, even if we are more than just bodies, we *live* in our bodies. More to the point, we use our bodies to communicate, to think, to function, to make our way through the world. Our brains are part of our bodies. And because of the Fall, which introduced disease into the world, our physical brains can malfunction—just as the heart, bone, liver, or pancreas can.

They can be physically injured, as in the case of head trauma or stroke. They can become diseased, as in the case of Alzheimer's or Huntington's disease. Or they can become chemically or electrically unbalanced, as in the case of depression or bipolar disorder. And just as medical treatments like insulin can work wonders with diseases like diabetes, medical treatments can make a dramatic difference with diseases like depression, schizophrenia, or obsessive-compulsive disorder. I believe such treatments can truly be a gift of God to His suffering people.

However, just as our physical bodies can become diseased, our spiritual beings are subject to malfunction, usually because of our individual choices, but also because we are influenced by the fallen world around us. Such spiritual "disease," which disrupts our relationship with God, is the essence of what we call sin. It's the state of separation from God that causes us to rebel against Him and break His laws with our physical bodies. And sin, too, has an influence on what happens to our minds and emotions. It can drive us to abuse our bodies with substances that eventually damage our brains. It can create guilt that weighs down our minds. It can cause trauma to others that endangers their sanity.

The intricate relationship between body, mind, emotions, will, spirit, and consciousness is mysterious and hasn't been completely explained, much less agreed on. Neither has the connection between spiritual sin and physical illness. But it's fairly clear that physical disease can affect the spirit, that sin can affect the body, and that body, mind, emotions, will, spirit, and consciousness can be disrupted by both physical and spiritual breakdowns.

WHY DOES IT HAPPEN?

Although mental illness is by definition a malfunction of the brain, in fact, it can have a number of different causes.[6] It can be self-inflicted, the result of unhealthy personal choices such as drug or alcohol abuse. It can be triggered by physiological or neurological abnormalities that affect the brain—a brain tumor, a weakness in a blood vessel that causes a stroke, a malfunction in glands that produce important chemicals that help brain cells "talk" to one another. (There is evidence that some of these circumstances can be hereditary.) Extreme stress or trauma such as rape, abuse, or wartime experience can generate certain kinds of mental illness—people really can "crack" under the strain of what life does to them. And although I believe some Christians overemphasize the work of demons, there are certainly cases where mental illness symptoms can be linked directly with demonic activity. (I'll talk a little more about this later in the chapter.)

Understanding this distinction between the *causes* and the *experience* of mental illness can be helpful because it shows how complex the situation can be. But I also believe we need to be careful about focusing too much on what caused a given mental illness.

In the first place, it's often hard to pinpoint a specific cause, because an illness may involve several different factors. More to the point, putting too much emphasis on the cause of a given mental illness can easily contribute to the pain and stigma that haunt the mentally ill in our society. It can bring us to the dangerous place of blaming a sick person for her illness.

It's undeniably true that all people—sick people included—are sinners. All of us—sick people included—fall short of the glory of God! All of us—sick people included—stand in need of grace and redemption. And it's arguably true that many (but not all) sick people contributed to their own illness in some way. And yet we can't look at a mentally ill person and conclude she "brought it all on herself." The mysteries of body and spirit are such that it's almost impossible for one person to sort out the sins of another and to determine what (if any) sin caused what dysfunction.

What's more, the Bible warns us specifically against this kind of thinking. Stories like that of Job and Jesus's healing of the man who had been blind from birth (John 9) show that there isn't always a clear cause-and-effect between sin and human affliction. They make it clear that God's redemptive purposes may be at work right in the middle of painful, baffling affliction.

> *The stigma associated with mental illness can stop the work of Christ dead in its tracks. Stigma is "dis-evangelism." Stigma is a sin that all of us are guilty of at one time or another—judging others by surface aspects of appearance, ethnic background, education, economic achievement, or behavior. When we stigmatize we are saying, "God can judge people by what's in their hearts—but count me out!" Or we're saying, "Yes, I know God loves everyone—but as far as I'm concerned, God made a mistake."*
>
> —JACKSON H. DAY[7]

The message of the entire Bible, in fact, is that God's ultimate purpose for all His people is health—physical, spiritual, and relational. He created us for wholeness. And despite our sinful choices, despite the fact that we live on a fallen planet, despite the influence of Satan and his minions, He is continually in the process of healing and restoring us. He is truly making all things new for us—heart, soul, mind, and strength.

The sticking point, for most of us, is that God does this in His own way and on His own timetable. As long as we live on this fallen earth, in physical bodies, we will be subject to the pain and frustration of living with the results of the Fall—including souls that are tainted by sin. And bodies—including brains—that are susceptible to illness and malfunction. And healing that sometimes—even most of the time—takes a long, slow road . . . as it has for my friend Sherry.

A MOMENT-TO-MOMENT GOD

Sherry's problems began almost as soon as she was born, the fourth child in a severely dysfunctional family. Almost from infancy, she was sexually molested on a regular basis by both her alcoholic father and an older brother who was later diagnosed with schizophrenia.

But the sexual abuse was not the most painful aspect of family life for the quiet, sensitive Sherry. Even worse was the yelling, the screaming, the cursing, the fights. Everyone seemed to pick on everyone else, and the children never knew when their father would "go off" and begin beating everyone around him with his belt. Their mother, fearful of her husband and committed to not making waves, took care of the family's physical needs but did little to protect her children.

Sherry remembers her childhood as a search for peace and safety in a chaotic environment. Sometimes she would find solace in the woods nearby—until her brother and her friends took her to a little shack there, made her look at pornographic pictures, and then took turns raping her. She remembers closing her eyes during the worst of it and just going away in her mind.

Sometimes she would "lose" hours or days or even more. And sometimes she had a vague sense that something was not right with her. But how could she even know what was right when everything around her was obviously wrong?

Still, Sherry survived. She grew up, played with friends, went to school, even did well enough to be accepted at college. She chose a school as far from home as she could manage while still paying in-state tuition. And life got better for Sherry as soon as she closed the door of her home behind her.

She majored in special education and found she loved to teach. She found love at college too. Almost before she knew it, she was married and the mother of twin girls.

Sherry loved being a wife and a mother. She relished being part of her husband's close-knit family—the only functioning family she had ever known. And she was soon to join another family, the family of faith. A friend invited her to attend a meeting at a nearby church, where she joyfully responded to the invitation to accept Christ as her personal Savior.

That was the beginning of a deeply satisfying relationship with Jesus, one she would desperately need in the years to come. Because the psychological fallout from Sherry's horrific past was beginning to settle on her life.

The depression began even before her marriage fell apart. But the discovery of her husband's infidelity, an ill-timed pregnancy and subsequent miscarriage, and a civil but painful divorce combined to send her spiraling down—way down. The deep, debilitating moods would sometimes leave her crouched in a corner, unable to function. It was all she could do to take care of her girls. Sometimes she couldn't even do that.

A stay in the hospital helped. Sherry got better, but then the depression returned with a vengeance, so she was hospitalized again. The pattern of depression, hospitalization, stabilization, partial recovery, then relapse would continue over the next few decades.

Despite her illness—or because of it—Sherry clung tightly to her relationship with Jesus. And during that time, God gave her a gracious gift. Sherry fell in love with the son of one of her spiritual mentors, a divorced father who was also a Christian executive. She had met Steve years before, but their connection grew when he visited her in the hospital. Their courtship continued as she grew better. By the time they married and moved to the state where he lived, she was doing well emotionally.

They enjoyed about three months of health and happiness together before Sherry's symptoms returned with a vengeance. She had to send her children to live with their father because she simply couldn't care for them. Her moods swung violently from fury to despair to numbness to giddy joy and back to fury. Sometimes she would cut herself. She thought about suicide constantly and tried it more than once. Sherry was hospitalized again and again as doctor after doctor scrambled to treat her illness and Christian friends prayed fervently for her health.

Years went by, and diagnosis piled upon diagnosis. Sherry began treatment for bipolar disorder. And posttraumatic stress disorder. And borderline personality disorder. And then one doctor put a name to something that had been part of Sherry's reality for most of her life. The official diagnosis was dissociative identity disorder, or DID.

> *[Mental illness] can take one to a place of darkness. But darkness is also a place of yet to be formed possibilities, not an entirely bad place to be. . . . Life can be harsh. The paradox is, that life can also be trusted.*
>
> —ANN JOST, a painter who suffers from depression[8]

What is DID? It's what many people know as multiple personality disorder. It's usually classed as an anxiety disorder, and it commonly develops as a survival strategy in children who, like Sherry, experience severe and ongoing trauma. Essentially, DID involves an attempt to "dissociate" from the painful situation by developing multiple identities, each with a unique personality, awareness, and memories, and often with no awareness of one another. Over the course of treatment, Sherry and her doctors would eventually uncover at least twenty-five different identities—including several infants who remember being "touched," a four-year-old named Jessica who adored her abusive big brother, a violently angry teen named Teresa, and a functioning wife and mother named Jana.

Though DID is a somewhat controversial diagnosis, it rang true to Sherry and her husband. The description of typical symptoms—ranging from depression to blackouts to violence to a sense of emotional disconnection—felt eerily familiar, and they felt relieved to have a name for what was wrong. But naming the illness was not the same as being healed. Sherry continued her grueling cycle of hospitalization, improvement, then collapse. She tried different doctors, different facilities, with varying degrees of success. Then Sherry was referred to a well-known clinic several thousand miles from home that was doing cutting-edge work with people like her. She and Steve hesitated because of the distance but agreed to try the new place for six months.

Those six months stretched into six and a half years.

Six and a half years of living apart from her beloved husband, who faithfully visited, and her children, who still lived with their father.

Six and a half years of ever-changing medications, intensive therapy, room restrictions, suicide watches.

Six and a half years of learning to name the abuse that had contributed to her pain and working to integrate her fragmented personalities into one functioning person.

Six and a half years of learning to depend on God—a God she somehow continued to love and trust, even when her confused emotions and disordered thoughts made Him seem far away. (As she points out, such "desert times" happen even to Christians without emotional or mental problems.)

After several years of intensive treatment, Sherry improved enough to live with a local family and go to the clinic as an outpatient. Then, finally, she was allowed to go home—a completely different home than the one she left, because her husband's job had been transferred to a different city. She was even able to begin teaching again—for a while.

But the following years saw plenty of setbacks. There were more doctors, more changes of medication, even a series of ECT ("shock therapy") treatments—plus the discovery of a new personality named Rachel. Over the course of four years, she had to be hospitalized twenty-seven times.

Then finally, five or six years ago, Sherry seemed to turn a corner. Her meds seemed to be working. Her moods settled down. The cutting and the suicide threats subsided, and the periods between hospitalizations grew . . . until one year she realized it had been a year since she had been in the hospital.

Finally, Sherry was able to have a life. She reconnected with her now-grown children and several of her siblings. (Her parents and abusive brother had died.) She found fulfillment in visiting people in hospitals and nursing homes. Best of all, for the first time in their twenty-five years of marriage, Sherry and her husband began to enjoy a real life together—puttering around the house, going out with friends, traveling for his business or on vacations. When I spoke to her last, they had just come back from a cruise.

So today Sherry is doing better than ever.

Better, though not yet cured.

Functional, though not yet fully healed.

And deeply joyful that God has brought her to a place where she can enjoy life with the man who has loved her so faithfully, the children who have grown up to make her proud, the grandchildren who delight her, the God who has never left her side.

Sherry still takes daily medication for her bipolar disorder, resisting the temptation to discontinue it. Like many who suffer from bipolarity, she misses the manic symptoms, which make her feel powerful and confident. But she believes that taking her meds is part of her responsibility to her family and the God who has used doctors to bring her to this place in her life. She even quotes Charles Spurgeon, "Christ compels me," to explain the way she has come to see her medical compliance.

As far as her DID is concerned, Sherry has reached a place of partial

---

The Christian hope is not only for the individual Christian, nor only for the church itself, but for all of creation, which was bound in decay by that first sin. . . . All creation will be redeemed from pain and woe. Of course, for the mentally ill, this understanding of Christian hope gives comfort and encouragement. Sorrowing and sighing will be no more. Tears will be wiped away. Even fractious brains will be restored.

—KATHRYN GREENE-MCCREIGHT[9]

integration. She still thinks and speaks of her different identities by name and in the third person, still refers to herself sometimes as "we." But the "alters" are aware of each other now, and Sherry recognizes them all as aspects of herself. Teresa, the angry teenage identity who was responsible for Sherry's most violent and self-destructive episodes, seems to have become more peaceful. "I believe Teresa may have become a Christian," Sherry says.

Best of all, Sherry has reached what for her is an astounding milestone. "I've wanted to be dead for so many years," she says, "and it's just in the last two or three that I like being alive. And I think if God said, right now, 'Sherry, would you like to come home with Me, or will you stay on earth and let Me do My work through you?' I'd actually choose staying here.

"That was my Christmas present to my husband's family a few years back. I told them that I want to be alive now."

And Sherry has an earnest message she asked me to pass along to readers of this book: "Tell them it's possible to have emotional problems and mental problems and still be a good Christian. You can still love God and serve Him.

"And no matter what you think when you're having problems," she says, "He will never leave you or stop loving you. He's always been right there with me. He's never let me down.

"I call Him my moment-to-moment God."

The Pain of Mental Illness

I wish you could meet Sherry. Just talking to her and Steve bolsters my faith in a God who is bigger and more powerful than the most painful circumstances we can encounter. And this is so important to recognize, because mental illness is such a painful and problematic experience.

In some ways it's like any chronic illness. It disrupts family schedules. It drains emotional and financial resources. And because the symptoms come and go, it leaves victims and families nervous even during the good times, wondering when the other shoe will drop.

But mental illness also does its own distinctive damage. Because it alters behavior and personality, its toll on relationships can be especially heavy. Even with the best intentions, it's hard to maintain a connection with someone whose moods are erratic and unpredictable, whose behavior is changeable and sometimes destructive, and who sometimes just doesn't seem to be "there." And it's hard to handle the give-and-take of being a wife or mother or daughter or friend when you can barely manage to make it through the day. So mental illness easily tears families and friendships apart. It also costs people their jobs and their homes. (A large percentage of the homeless are mentally ill.) It drives them to "self-medicate" with drugs, alcohol, or addictive behavior like gambling or compulsive shopping. And mental illness can be physically dangerous—sometimes to others, but more often to its victims, who may endanger themselves through poor judgment or suicide attempts. Sadly, suicide is a common "side effect" of brain disease.

Through it all, mentally ill people and their families often struggle with an overpowering sense of shame, a painful sense of being different, defective, or out of control. They feel acutely the stigma of mental illness—the awareness of being judged, shunned, rejected, or ridiculed—and the frustration of being unable to handle everyday life. Guilt can be a significant factor as well. Victims feel guilty for what they've done or said during episodes of the disease, for being a burden, for complicating the lives of others. And caregivers often struggle with guilt for feeling angry with a sick person, for needing help with care or resorting to institutionalization, or for being unable to stay in the relationship.

For Christians, mental illness brings up troubling questions involving sin, morality, and personal responsibility. It's hard to sort out what a mentally ill person can control and what she can't. To what extent can a sick person be held responsible for decisions that caused or exacerbated her condition? And what about the way she acts because of her illness? Depressed people can be profoundly self-centered. Manic people can trample on the rights and feelings of others, spend money their families need, or act out sexually. Schizophrenics can be driven by voices to commit acts they would normally believe wrong. Dementia or anxiety disorders can trigger uncharacteristic, even hostile behavior.

Then there's the question of how a mentally ill person encounters God. Mental illness that skews our perceptions of reality can also skew our experience of the divine. Certain kinds of mental illness can result in heightened or abnormal experiences—visions and voices that may be interpreted as coming from God. Depressive illness, on the other hand, can seem to hide God behind a cloud of darkness.

And on top of all this is the traditional—and mutual—distrust between psychiatry and conservative Christianity. The pioneers of psychotherapy tended to be suspicious of religion and even blamed much mental illness on religious belief. Some psychiatric practitioners and researchers still hold this attitude. And some Christians have overreacted to this distrust and condemned life-changing forms of treatment, adding the stigma of seeking professional help to the stigma of mental illness. They hold that you can't be Christian and seek psychiatric help—a "throw the baby out with the bathwater" attitude that has condemned many a good Christian girl to unnecessary suffering.

THE BIBLE AND MENTAL ILLNESS

What does the Bible have to say about these troubling issues? Specifically, it doesn't say anything at all. There's not a single verse in the Bible about bipolar disease, Alzheimer's disease, obsessive-compulsive disorder, or schizophrenia. There's little direct comment on how to distinguish brain illness from spiritual malaise or on whether we should trust psychologists.

There are some clear instances in the Old Testament of behavior that could be symptomatic of mental illness. King Saul seemed to have mental problems that caused wild mood swings and erratic behavior that eventually led to his death. King David, more famously, apparently suffered from intense periodic depression, which he described in his psalms of lament. The prophet Elijah also seems to have suffered from a period of acute depression where he literally wanted to die.

The New Testament, of course, contains many instances where demons are blamed for behavior that resembles many mental illnesses. Jesus Himself healed many people who were said to be demon possessed—including a violent man who ran around naked and screaming among the tombs (Luke 8:26–39) and Mary Magdalene, who was said to have been delivered from seven demons (Luke 8:2).

Plenty of people, Christians included, believe that demon possession was merely an ancient explanation for what we now know as brain disorders. Others believe that demons were especially active and caused symptoms of mental illness in Jesus's day but have little to do with the mentally ill today. Still others tend to credit all "crazy" behavior with the direct work of demonic beings—and they contend that such demonic activity is behind much of today's mental illness as well.

My own belief lies somewhere in the middle. I believe many, if not most, of the healings Jesus performed involved real demons. He specifically gave His disciples the authority to drive out demons, and He actually talked to a number of the evil spirits that had occupied human beings. The demons knew who He was—they called Him by name. Sometimes they even tried to negotiate with Him, though in the end they had no choice but to obey His orders.

But note that this didn't happen in *every* instance of supposed demonic activity that Jesus encountered. Sometimes Jesus healed "possessed" people without specifically addressing a demon (see John 9:32). In cases like that, I believe it's possible that demons weren't involved at all. Jesus Himself was accused of being demon-possessed (John 9:48–52; 10:20), so we know that not every diagnosis of possession was correct. So I think it's reasonable to assume that at least some of the people Jesus healed of "demons" may have actually suffered from disorders of the brain such as depression or schizophrenia—just as many good Christian girls do today.

As to the work of demons today, I tend to believe that while Satan is ultimately behind all forms of human brokenness and is certainly capable of causing the miserable symptoms of mental illness, in our society he usually prefers to work in sneakier, less spectacular—but even more powerful—ways. Most of my Christian sources who have worked with the mentally ill confirm that they have encountered only a few cases that they believe to be demonically caused.

But no matter the cause of mental instability in the Bible or today, the outcome was—and is—the same. Jesus has compassion on those who are afflicted. His concern is always for their healing—body, mind, and spirit—regardless of what caused the illness. During His time on earth, He was quick to respond to almost all of these who sought His help for confusion of thought and careening emotions.

But note that I say *almost*.

Because Matthew (15:21–28) and Mark (7:24–30) tell a story in which Jesus wasn't quick at all to respond.

When He didn't seem concerned with healing at all!

What Was Jesus Thinking?

This isn't a story I like very much, to tell the truth—because it just doesn't sound like the Jesus I know. It's the troubling tale of His encounter with a determined woman who lived in the region of Phoenicia, near the cities of Tyre and Sidon.

Matthew calls the woman a Canaanite, probably referring to her ancestry and stressing she came from a race that had been defeated by the Jews. Mark calls her Syrophoenician, referring to where she lived, and Greek, probably indicating the language she spoke. The point of all these descriptions is that she was definitely not a Jew. And that's not surprising, since Jesus and His disciples were not in Jewish territory. They had traveled away from home to the town where the woman lived.

Maybe they were trying to find a place to rest away from the crowds. Maybe they just wanted to see a different part of the world. Whatever their purpose, they hardly expected to be stopped by a desperate pagan woman who had heard a little about Jesus and was absolutely bent on getting Him to help her.

"Lord, Son of David," she cried out to Him, "have mercy on me! My daughter is suffering terribly from demon-possession."

She may have been right about the demon, although this is

another case where Jesus never actually spoke to the demons. That worried mother might well have misdiagnosed a case of "ordinary" but very scary mental illness—autism, perhaps, or epilepsy. But she was obviously less worried about the specific cause than she was in her child's suffering . . . and her hope that maybe the traveling Jewish rabbi could make a difference. So she sought out Jesus, buttonholing Him in a house (according to Mark) or out on the street (according to Matthew), begging Him to heal her daughter.

How did Jesus respond to her pain? He didn't respond to her at all! He basically ignored her. And to me, as a woman, that's just infuriating. I can't stand the thought of pouring out my heart to Jesus and having Him just stand there and look at me. It feels like flat-out rejection. Why did Jesus treat her that way?

The disciples thought they knew—and they definitely approved. They thought the Canaanite woman was a foreigner and a nuisance, and their main desire was to get rid of her. So as their Lord's silence hung in the air, they added their rude two cents' worth. "Tell her to go away," they urged. "We're tired of her crying after us."

And Jesus didn't contradict them. He didn't come to the woman's defense. He just looked from one annoyed face to the other, then down at the woman. She must have been frustrated and hurt by this response. Wouldn't you be? But she didn't say anything. She didn't want to antagonize a possible Source of help.

Then Jesus made things worse—or at least it seems that way. He told the woman that healing her child wasn't in His job description. "I was sent only to the lost sheep of Israel," He said.

I find it so hard to believe that my compassionate, caring Jesus really said that! The disciples must have eaten up the words, which seemed to confirm their own assumptions. Can't you see them crowding around Jesus, punching His shoulder playfully, throwing a casual arm over His shoulder to lead Him away from this annoying woman?

But she wouldn't give up. Instead, she knelt at His feet, begging, "Master, help me."

Poor woman! The Jesus I know could surely not refuse such a plea.

But He did refuse her—and insulted her as well: "It is not right to take the children's bread and toss it to their dogs."

Even in today's Middle East, to call someone a dog is a serious put-down. Was Jesus really doing that to a frantic mother and her afflicted daughter?

But the gutsy Canaanite woman threw His own words right back at Him. "Yes," she answered quickly, looking up and daring to meet His eyes, "but even the dogs eat the crumbs that fall from their master's table."

In other words, "I'm not giving up. I'm not going away. No matter

> *As one who society and the church have always invited to the table, I hope those of you who at best have only received the crumbs will not wait for people like me to include or welcome you to the table. Take a chair. You are already there. Those who would deny you do not have the authority to exclude. It's not their table. Your uninvited presence points out the obvious. God reigns. You are the Gospel. Be cheeky. Live it with authority. We'll get used to it.*
>
> —CLAY NELSON[10]

what You say, how things seem, I'm going to keep pursuing health for my baby. I know You can help her. There has to be a way."

She spoke the words—and that's when everything changed . . .

The disciple's jaws must have dropped at what Jesus said next. Perhaps the Canaanite woman's jaw dropped too—the shift in His attitude was so sudden. It was the moment of a great perspective change.

I love the way *The Message* translation describes it: "Jesus gave in. 'Oh, woman,' he said, 'your faith is something else. What you want is what you get!' And the gutsy, persistent, desperate Canaanite woman ran home to learn it really was so."

What God Honors

Isn't that a strange story? Something about it bothers me whenever I read it.

It bothers scholars as well, because they're always scrambling to explain the words and actions that sound racist and rejecting, just not what we would expect from a compassionate Healer.

Some commentaries say Jesus knew all along that He would heal the girl, that His insulting words were a way of testing the woman's faith, pushing her to the next level. And frankly, that explanation doesn't help me much. Why would a loving Savior do that to a woman in such pain? Surely He could test her without insulting her.

Other scholars suggest that Jesus knew from the beginning how strong the woman's faith was and that He was simply using her to teach the disciples a lesson. According to this view, He conducted the whole dialogue with a twinkle in His eye, perhaps winking at her as He spoke, stringing the bigoted disciples along by agreeing with them and then rebuking their attitudes by agreeing to heal a Gentile woman's daughter.

Still others suggest that Jesus Himself, in His humanity, was on a learning curve about His mission. According to this view, the Canaanite woman actually changed His mind and heart with her quick-witted reply to His narrow-minded announcement. Her persistence, courage, and faith taught the Lord a lesson and helped Him grow into a deeper understanding of what He was supposed to accomplish.

What do I think? To be honest, I don't know. Even with all this explanation, the story still bothers me.

But maybe that's the whole point.

Maybe this story is in the Bible to remind us that the way God works, the way He heals us, the way He responds to our needs and our prayers, doesn't always conform to our expectations. That's certainly true for many I know who suffer from mental illness.

So often, as in Sherry's case, the process of healing is a slow, painful one-step-forward, one-step-back proposition. Sometimes we cry out for relief and God seems to be silent. Nothing gets better, as far as we can tell. Or we make progress, think we're improving, then relapse. A medication that is effective one day stops working the next. The troublesome thoughts or feelings or sensations return. And through it all, God may seem a distant or even a preposterous concept. We say our prayers, and we don't hear a thing.

Or sometimes, under certain conditions such as mania or schizophrenia, we experience Him in ways so extreme or bizarre or spectacular that an ordinary experience of God in more lucid moments almost seems like desertion. Sometimes heaven seems to be taunting us in our pain or laughing in our face. Sometimes we feel rejected, unheard, unwanted, let down. Even insulted.

In times like that, I think it may help to look again at the troubling story of the Canaanite woman. And I think we have to look *past* the mystery of how Jesus responded to her and focus on how the story turned out.

Because the focus of that whole encounter, as I see it, is not just that Jesus ended up healing the woman's daughter—though that's important—but that He honored her tactics.

He honored her persistence—that she just wouldn't give up in the face of obstacles. That she was willing to risk the annoyance of others and persevere in seeking help.

He honored her courage in reaching past stigma and prejudice. As a woman and a Gentile, she was not welcome to speak to a male Jewish stranger. But she braved the ingrained attitudes of the disciples and perhaps even those of Jesus Himself. She met Him in the street, according to Matthew. She collared Him in someone else's house, according to Mark. She had to have been afraid—afraid for her daughter, fearful for herself, worried about what would happen. But she was undeterred. Love compelled her to push past her fear. Love inspired her courage.

Jesus certainly honored the woman's humility—her willingness to kneel at His feet and not take offense at His words. To honestly admit her need and her lack. To seek help from someone who was a traditional enemy of her people.

Yet, at the same time, He honored the woman's dogged conviction

> *This nameless woman teaches us that persistence is a form of prayer. She teaches us that talking back to God isn't always a sin. Sometimes, when you're acting out of love and faith and not just out of anger, talking back to God is what you have to do to get the blessing you need.*
>
> —SUSAN PALWICK[11]

that she had a right to ask for what she needed and that God could be trusted to give it to her. That woman was downright presumptuous, at least as far as the disciples were concerned. She assumed she had a place at God's table (even if it was *under* the table). She assumed she had a right to ask God for what she needed—that Jesus should heal her daughter simply because He was God and because her daughter needed healing.

And how did Jesus respond, in the end, to the combination of persistence and courage and humility and conviction that so annoyed the disciples?

He called it faith! And He even indicated that her very attitude was what made her daughter's healing possible.

It makes sense when you think of it. For what is faith but a combination of persistence and courage and humility and conviction? What is faith but an unwillingness to give up because somewhere deep inside—perhaps even deeper than conscious thought—you believe that God wants to bless you?

That is the affirmation I believe we can find in the problematic story of the Canaanite woman, and it's a message of hope for those in the problematic grip of mental illness or any of the other difficult issues this book confronts.

I believe God calls each one of us to faith—but not the passive faith of believing the right things and belonging to the right groups. He calls us from a passive acceptance of whatever life hands us to a position of active, confident expectation. But He also calls us from expecting easy or final answers to a humble acceptance of the ways He chooses to work in our life. God calls us to trust in His love and grace, to cling to believing that He will accomplish His best in us, even when our thoughts and feelings and perceptions and memories betray us.

When You Can't Manage Faith

I have to tell you, some of the most persistent, courageous, humble . . . and faithful . . . people I know are good Christian girls who have wrestled with the frustration and the stigma of mental illness. In fact, it was in the very context of their illness that many of them developed a depth of faith that challenges and inspires me.

Sherry was right. It really is possible to have emotional problems and mental problems and still love God and serve Him.

But here's the rub. While the circumstances of mental illness can teach the kind of faith Jesus commended in the Canaanite woman . . . the illness itself can make that faith hard to come by. You can be too depressed to be persistent, too manic to be humble, too wracked with anxiety to be courageous, too confused to believe in anything with confidence. Or you may be a frustrated caregiver whose own faith falters under the strain of trying to stay connected with your mentally or emotionally challenged loved one.

That brings us back to the question we started with: How do we believe in God and serve Him and love Him with heart and soul and mind and strength when these very parts of us are compromised?

And here's the best answer I can manage—one that's straight from the Bible.

The answer, once again, is *grace.*

The answer is a loving, compassionate God who reaches down to us when we can't reach up to Him.

When we can't manage faith—and it happens more than many people want to admit—I truly believe we can trust God to make up the difference.

He knows our frames, remember. He remembers we are but dust (Ps. 103:14). He knows the limitations of our physical bodies, our sin-wracked souls. And His grace is sufficient to cover the ground between the best we can manage and the kind of fulfilling, purposeful life He wants for us.

A friend of mine reminded me of that comforting truth not long ago. This forty-something woman held a lucrative, high-profile job as a life coach. Her life was going great. But then she learned her mother had Alzheimer's disease. Year after year she watched her mother decline with every visit, to the point that her father could no longer cope. There were no siblings to share the load, and my friend considered a nursing home out of the question. So she chose to give up her job and care for her mother full time. She went to live with her parents. For the next year and a half, until her mother died, my friend fed her, bathed her, changed her diapers, turned her in bed, did whatever she could to make her mother comfortable.

> *Some will advise you to expect a miracle. Actually, you can do better than that. You can expect God to meet you at your point of need and walk with you every moment of life. Don't be discouraged. When all the platitudes fail and the quick fixes fade, Christ remains at your side to lift you up and see you through.*
>
> —LARRY KEEFAUVER[12]

"That must be so hard," I told her one day. "To give up your time, your independence—your whole life!—to care for a woman who doesn't even know who you are."

"You're right, Tammy," my friend said. "My mom doesn't know who I am. But *I know who she is.*"

And it's so true.

You see, we may not always understand what's happening to us.

We may not be able to manage much persistence or courage or humility or belief. We may have times when our hearts and souls and minds and strength simply let us down and we don't even know who God is.

But God knows who we are.

To Him, we are more than our mortal bodies, more than our malfunctioning brains, more than our confused and sinning souls, our divided minds, our faltering spirits.

We are His children. He made us. He sees our suffering. And He loves us just as fiercely as the Canaanite woman loved her child, just as tenderly as my friend loved her mother. Though His ways may sometimes baffle us, we can still trust in His loving heart, His gracious spirit, His healing power.

He walks beside us and shares our suffering, even when we feel confused and alone.

He tenderly provides the help we need, even when we don't recognize His caring face.

He is working right now to bring us to complete healing and wholeness—whether it's medication that helps us get through the day, friends who reach past fear to offer us love, or a whole new spiritual body (and brain!) in the life to come.

He is truly our moment-to-moment God.

And moment by moment, as we dare to come to Him and kneel at His feet, to give Him whatever we can of our heart and soul and mind and strength, He will pour out grace to do the rest.

Healing our broken hearts.

Giving rest to our tormented souls.

Renewing even our confused and broken minds and spirits.

Granting strength to walk through whatever the years will bring.

Moment by moment, in His grace, He is bringing us home to Him.

WORD OF GRACE FOR TORMENTED CHRISTIAN GIRLS

You are more than your mind, more than your brain.
You are God's child.
One way or another, He will bring you peace.

8

"No Matter What I Do, I'm Never Enough"

The Weariness of Constant Striving

And God is able to make all grace abound toward you,
that you, always having all sufficiency in all things,
may have an abundance for every good work.
—2 Corinthians 9:8 NKJV

My friend Donna is beautiful. And not just everyday beautiful. I'm talking supermodel gorgeous—tall, slim, amazing blue eyes, exotic cheekbones, a dazzling smile. She actually worked as a model at one point in her life.

Donna's successful, too, with a professional background in public relations and a new position as an analyst for a wireless broadband research firm. On the side, she's an independent consultant for a company that sells high-end clothing at home parties, which means she dresses extremely well. At a recent meeting, a supervisor pointed her out as a role model for "developing a personal style."

Donna lives with her husband and three little girls in a lovely house in a nice neighborhood with a spectacular view of the mountains. She's a dedicated Christian, a loving and committed wife and mother, a talented musician, a loyal friend.

In fact, if you met Donna, you'd be convinced she has it all—high energy, loads of talent, a sweet personality, truly an impressive woman. You'd never guess she struggles every day with the same issue that plagues so many good Christian girls I know . . . the feeling of never quite measuring up.

But she does struggle, every day of her life. No matter how hard she works—and she works *very* hard—she's haunted by the suspicion that she's doing her life all wrong.

On the job, she second-guesses herself on her decision to leave her PR career. She worries that her skills aren't adequate to be a top achiever in her new field. (She has a history of quitting any pursuit where she can't excel.) She worries that she and her husband don't make enough money, but also wonders if she's cheating her kids by not being a stay-at-home mom and not volunteering at their school more often. Whether she stays up late to bake cookies for a classroom party or grabs a box from the grocery store, she fears she's shortchanging someone or being judged by someone else.

At church, Donna worries about turning down an invitation to perform in a church musical. At home, though she prays every morning, she kicks herself for not studying or reading the Bible more.

In the neighborhood, she compares herself to the full-time moms and the working women who have household help. She's sure they're checking out her house and yard and children and her activities and judging her for her shortcomings.

As to being beautiful and fashionable and savvy, Donna just can't see it. She considers herself totally clueless when it comes to putting clothes together. In fact, she took on her clothing-consultant gig partly because she's insecure about what to wear. She liked the idea of being involved with a "collection" where every item went with something else. But she still spends a lot of extra time studying to develop a better fashion sense.

Donna admits she's "hyper-driven." She also admits she's weary of trying so hard and that her constant striving causes conflict with her family and friends. She knows she needs to learn to "rest in the Lord," and with counseling and lots of prayer she's learning to relax a little.

But even then, she worries that she's not relaxing enough . . .

DRIVEN CHRISTIAN GIRLS

Does any of this sound familiar?

If you're a good Christian girl, I'm almost certain it does.

That's why I've included this chapter in a book full of edgy issues like suicide and sexual brokenness and abuse and mental illness. Because feeling inadequate may not be as dramatic as being abused or having an addiction, but it can be fully as painful. And it's definitely more pervasive. Sometimes it seems like everyone I know suffers from some variation of this mind-set.

I see it in the frustrated tears of women who come to hear me speak.

> I can't expect *myself to always be a wise, patient, and attentive woman. I want to be, of course, but many times I fall short. When I'm tired, I snap at my kids. When I find twenty-five messages waiting for me on my voice mail, I want to run away from everything. Although I try very hard, I'm not always who or what I want to be.* But I can expect *God to pour grace over my weaknesses as I offer them to Him, and to provide strength and time to restore.*
>
> —PAM VREDEVELT[1]

I hear it in the weary voices of women I overhear in the coffee shop and the friends who join me there.

I also feel it in my own heart, especially when other painful issues of my life press in on me.

That's when I start comparing myself with the woman next door. Or thinking I need a new outfit for the occasion I'm going to. Or feeling guilty for flipping through a magazine when I could be starting dinner or reading my Bible. Or telling myself I need to accept more speaking gigs and write more books and be much more productive in all my work. Or reminding myself that one child or another needs more attention and time with me.

And yes, there's a reason Donna and I are friends. We're sisters in our insecurities, our restlessness, our sense that something might fall apart if we ever truly relaxed. (Given the way we've set up our lives, it might!) And we're like so many women I know. Women who wrestle with a constant sense of being inadequate or judged or not measuring up. And carry a burden of guilt because of our failures and inadequacies. And wear ourselves out with the effort of constantly improving ourselves—or feeling we're expected to.

We're both good Christian girls, of course. That's part of the problem. We *want* to be good Christian girls. We also want to be good wives and irresistible lovers and great moms and loving daughters and successful businesswomen and powerful prayer partners and loyal friends. We're programmed to meet needs and fulfill expectations, and we try so very hard to do just that. But we're still bombarded with messages from the inside and the outside that tell us we're just not _____ enough. (You fill in the blank!)

Not beautiful enough (or thin enough—that's a big one—or busty enough, sexy enough, old enough, or young enough) to get a man or keep a husband or wear the best clothes or impress a boss or fit in with our friends.

Not successful enough in business or marriage or school or friendship to be secure.

Not accomplished enough (educated enough, gifted enough, hardworking enough) to get respect.

Not woman enough to keep a man or get pregnant or carry a child to term.

Not a good enough mother to provide kids with the stimulation they need or keep them from making the wrong choices.

Not organized enough to keep the house clean or manage all the kids' stuff or say yes to the next project.

Not financially blessed enough to impress the neighbors or give our children what we want to give them or support the church the way we believe we should.

Not Christian enough (spiritual enough, prayerful enough, generous enough) to get into heaven or be looked up to in church or feel like God approves of us.

The specifics vary, but that constant familiar litany keeps on sounding in our ears, reminding us we've got to work harder.

In the inner chambers of your heart, God steps past all your talents and hard work—all that you would think he values. He goes straight for the messy, broken places in you.

—PAULA RINEHART[2]

And do better.

And keep trying.

And reach for excellence.

And meet others' needs and expectations.

And live up to our own high standards.

And not give up, no matter what.

I don't know about you, but just thinking about it makes me tired. Living it is enough to make me throw up my hands.

Christian Girls Who Live in the World of "Not Enough"

I can tell you so many "not enough" stories here.

I can tell you about Nan, my cute, outgoing, competent friend who grew up feeling dumpy and unattractive—her grandfather always called her his "little round girl." And though she became an actor, an award-winning playwright, and a TV producer, though she married and had children, she never could shake the feeling that she just wasn't as pretty as other women. How much that feeling contributed to difficulties in her marriage, Nancy doesn't know; there were other issues besides her looks. But her "little round girl" legacy came crashing in on her when her husband began having Internet flings and then decided he didn't want to be married. Nan actually cashed in retirement funds for plastic surgery at that point, and she's glad she did—the "nips and tucks" helped give her the confidence she needs in her new life. But she still struggles to come to terms with living as a short fifty-something woman with "roundness" tendencies in a culture that favors young and tall and thin.

I can also tell you about Barbara, who chose business college over a university because her prominent Southern family had suffered financial reverses. She went on to own her own business, teach in a private school, run a church youth program, organize a profitable charitable auction, and raise a beautiful, college-bound daughter. She is well spoken, intelligent, well informed, and deeply thoughtful. Yet her chronic concern is that people will discover she is "uneducated" and think less of her.

I could tell you about Tracy, whose anorexic mother goaded her about her weight and whose early sexual activity left her with a severe case of pelvic inflammatory disease. Tracy became a Christian, married a wonderful man . . . and then learned that the disease had made pregnancy almost impossible. Six long years of grueling and expensive fertility treatments finally resulted in the birth of triplets! But the sense of falling short, of being unable to do what comes naturally to most women, hurt her as deeply as her mother's accusations of being fat.

Then there's Janice, who finally had to find a day job because the novels she worked so hard to write were just not selling. And Natalie, who put all her energies into raising her sons right, only to lose her eldest to a homosexual lifestyle and to struggle with drug issues in the lives of the two younger ones. And Nadine, who discovered her husband's affair and worked very hard to heal their shaky marriage, only to discover her only daughter was severely anorexic.

All of them good Christian girls.

All of them loving, idealistic, full of the best intentions.

All of them faced with that awful sense that their best was not enough.

And their problem isn't new. It goes all the way back to Genesis 29–31, where we find the story of a woman whose looks and love just weren't enough for the man who married her.

Good Biblical Girls Who Didn't Measure Up

She would never forget the look on Jacob's face when morning came—or the humiliation she felt when she saw it.

Leah had begged her father, Laban, not to follow through with his plan to make her wear her sister's veil and enter the marriage tent in place of Rachel. But Laban was intent on marrying off two of his daughters at once and keeping a hardworking son-in-law in the family. He'd seen the looks Jacob threw his younger daughter, knew his love for Rachel was strong enough to keep him around for seven more years.

Leah had seen it too. Her eyes were a little weak,[3] but she knew love when she saw it.

And when a man had no eyes for her . . . she knew that too. That's why she begged and pleaded when she heard Laban's plan. But eventually she gave in . . . because a girl had to obey her father. And because she, like her sister, had fallen in love with her kinsman from a foreign land. She admired his handsome face, his hardworking hands, his strong spirit, his devotion to his God.

So in the end, despite her misgivings, she put on the veil and went to him.

She told herself it would all work out. That she could prove her love in the marriage tent. That in their intimacy he would come to love her, though she wasn't as spectacularly beautiful as Rachel.

But all those arguments fell flat in the morning light when Jacob realized he had been tricked. His fury and disgust wedged in her heart like a splinter. She knew he blamed her as well as Laban, and she couldn't really disagree with him. The poor man had worked like a slave for seven years . . . for Rachel, not Leah.

Jacob stormed out of the tent in search of Laban and came back sulking because, as Leah well knew, the deed couldn't be undone. At least he didn't take out his anger on her by beating her or simply leave, as some men would have done. That in itself said something about his character.

So Leah held on to hope—because, after all, she had seven years before Jacob could bring Rachel home to be her rival. Seven years to concentrate on being such a good wife that Jacob would have to love her. And she'd do her part. She would work hard at home and, when needed, in the fields. She would do her best to please him in bed—he was a man, after all, and she didn't think he'd refuse her. She'd increase his wealth and bear him sons.

And as for the loving, longing glances he threw her sister—those she would simply overlook.

Leah had time on her side . . . surely time enough to win her husband's love.

It was certainly worth a try.

The trouble is, it didn't work.

> *It is in the bad moments of my life that I must choose to learn the opportunity that hides at its deepest center. When my inadequacies rise, rebelling against my carefully constructed external persona, then— then—God can get my attention.*
>
> —Karen Burton Mains[4]

Leah did bear Jacob son after son—tangible signs that the Lord had blessed her. Again and again, as she named each baby, she told herself, "Surely now my husband will love me." But though Jacob loved his sons, his preference didn't seem to change. Even when Rachel joined the family and produced no children, Jacob still had eyes only for the beautiful one, the golden girl, the sister so irresistible that a man was willing to invest fourteen years of unpaid labor just to marry her . . . when he already had a wife! No matter how Leah tried, no matter what a good wife and mother she was, no matter how richly God blessed her—for children were considered a sign of God's blessing—she just couldn't seem to move past that humiliating reality.

Such a sad story! Any woman who has ever been rejected or devalued by a man can feel her pain, her desperate and fading hope, her growing disappointment as circumstances wore her down. She just couldn't win!

But that didn't stop Leah from trying . . . even when Jacob completed his second seven years' labor for Rachel's hand, married her, and brought her home. Even when Rachel flaunted her status as favored wife.[5] Even when Rachel's infertility turned her golden-girl smugness to bitter jealousy and their rivalry to a pitched battle.

For Rachel, too, faced her own "never enough" issue. Because even though beautiful and beloved, she had difficulty conceiving—in those days a sure sign that she was a deficient and unblessed female. By the time Rachel finally had a child and Leah temporarily stopped bearing children, the whole household was in an uproar . . . all because of that awful experience of trying and trying and just not being enough.

THE CULTURE OF NOT ENOUGH

Aren't you glad that good Christian girls today don't have to worry about being married to their sister's husband? We have enough problems as it is. Almost from the time we are born, we're assailed by contradictory voices that seem to agree on only one point—that we need to be more and better, and we must meet someone else's standards if we want to be happy and loved.

If the story of Leah and Rachel is any indication, that feeling may be a built-in aspect of the human condition. But surely our current materialistic, looks-obsessed culture makes things worse, dictating in no uncertain terms the parameters of what we are to be. We take it in through so many sources—television, movies, magazines, the Internet. And the standards for what it means to be "enough" are almost unreachable. In the looks department, we're to be beautiful and sexy, impossibly thin and yet muscular and physically fit, full breasted, eternally young and yet classy, and with a fresh, natural beauty. We must be bright but not intimidatingly so, hard driving yet accessible. We must strive for excellence and do everything possible to win, but we should be friendly and approachable too. We women should maintain a successful career but also take the time to nurture superior kids and decorate our own large, expensive, and well-organized homes. While we're at it, both our white clothes and our teeth must be whiter than white, and the food we offer to our families must be gourmet quality. (Have you ever noticed that women's magazines tend to offer food ads and weight-loss articles right next to one another?)

As the mother of young women, I often cringe at the "not enough" messages our culture sends them. A recent article in the *San Francisco Chronicle* reports that girls are more stressed than ever about their weight, grades, and sex, according to three new studies by Girls Inc. Calling it the "supergirl dilemma," researchers found that girls still feel pressure to please everyone and look perfect while also trying to seize opportunities their grandmothers might not have had, such as attending college and pursuing careers.

"One girl said, 'The problem is I can never be thin enough, I can never be pretty enough, and I can never be good enough.' . . . Nationally,

60 percent of girls reported that they often feel stressed, and 33 percent of girls said they often feel sad and unhappy. Even in elementary school, nearly half of respondents said they feel stressed."[6]

Who knows how many of those "stressed" children and teenagers will end up being tomorrow's frantic and driven Christian women?

The People Who Judge Us

But it's not just a generalized "out there" culture that pressures girls and women to do better and better, to meet impossible standards. Specific people in our life—influenced by the culture as well and by their own insecurities and warped perceptions—set the "enough" bar impossibly high. The people in our past—peers, siblings, and especially our parents—wield an especially powerful influence. What they say to us and the way they treat us during childhood and adolescence tend to stick deep in our minds.

That's easy to see in my friend Donna's case. She was the youngest child of older parents who both had trouble with alcohol. Her mother cycled in and out of mental hospitals when Donna was a child and eventually abandoned the family to, in her words, "make a new life for herself." After an eye injury grounded her father from his pilot job, he moved his younger daughters from town to town looking for work, usually unsuccessfully. Then he was institutionalized with early-onset Alzheimer's and died three years later, when Donna was just sixteen. She spent her adolescence being cared for (and bossed) by older sisters, her college years scrambling for scholarships and working long hours to put herself through school.

No wonder Donna is driven. From her early experience, she internalized a load of "not enough" messages: *I'm not normal . . .*

People will let me down . . . I'm the little sister no one respects . . . I'll never have enough money . . . I don't know how to dress . . . I've got to be the very best or I'm nothing . . . If I ever let down my guard, life will fall apart.

My friend Trish, too, struggles with memories that shape her feelings of "not enough." Trish's anorexic mother prided herself in being slim and nagged her normal-sized daughter about being fat. For many years, Trish resisted the message. Then, after her first husband left her, she plunged into a full-blown eating disorder—first anorexia, then bulimia—that wrecked her health and almost cost her much more. A grace-filled meeting with another bulimic who happened to be recovering proved to be a lifesaver for Trish. After years in recovery, she is now happily remarried and the mother of two. But to this day she can never look in a mirror and think, *I look pretty good.* In fact, she can't visually tell if she's a size two or fourteen. Her brain just echoes her mother's litany of "not thin enough"—and she has to consciously remind herself where the truth lies.

> *The first of three problems with comparison is that we usually compare our weakness with another's strength—leading us to a skewed apples/oranges conclusion. Second, what we believe we see in someone else might not be reality! We tend to exaggerate and overestimate the strength of others. Finally—and please hear this—* our wounds and weaknesses, though painful, carry secret treasures and strengths that could be gained no other way. *Our wounds do not make us inferior, but too often they cause us to feel inferior.*
>
> —STEVE STEPHENS[7]

The voices of our past can echo loudly in our hearts and minds, but people in our present fuel our "not enough" feelings as well. Competitive colleagues and bosses, critical (older) parents and siblings, high-achieving friends and neighbors and school parents, pastors and church friends, even our own husbands and children dish out the message that we've got to try harder to be loved and accepted.

Aline, for instance, grew up in a family where she was constantly loved and affirmed, the apple of her parents' eyes. Though she struggled with weight like the rest of her family, she also grew up feeling she was beautiful and worthy of love. But she married a fitness-conscious man who began to lose sexual interest in her when she put on a few pounds. Aline was mortified. In her mind, she was still a worthy and desirable woman, and she had a hard time accepting the reality that her husband didn't feel that way.

Aline and her husband love each other. Over time, they were able to communicate and work out some of their problems. But Aline still lives with that huffing-and-puffing sense of "not enough"—that feeling that if she doesn't keep the weight at bay, she will lose everything she cares about. Now she's beginning to worry about the signs of aging.

She's living with the painful reality that, for any of us, success is a moving target—and often it's other people, driven by their own issues and insecurities, who keep it moving.

Who Says We're Not Enough?

It's easy enough—and accurate enough—to blame our drivenness, our "not enough" mentality, on outside forces such as culture and the expectations of others. It really isn't "all in our head." People *do* judge us. Society judges us. Other Christians judge us, and often quite harshly.

At the same time, if we're really honest, we driven Christian girls will have to admit that often the person who puts the biggest "not enough" pressure on us is . . . *us*.

We experience rejection and resolve to be nicer so it won't happen again.

We fall on our face and pick ourselves up and vow to run faster next time.

We look at our successful friends and neighbors and colleagues and conclude we're woefully inadequate and need to try harder.

We grow up in chaos and feel the need to tighten our grip.

We read the Bible (parts of it), and decide we'd better get busy winning people to Christ.

But what's really driving us, much of the time, is not what happened to us or what other people or even God expects of us. What's driving us is what *we think* has happened or is expected. Or, more to the point, what we think will ease our pain or boost our egos or make us feel better.

It's not always a conscious process. It's hard to sort out our own motivations and easy to get confused about what has happened to us and what it means. Our faulty thinking and mistaken conclusions fuel our sense of inadequacy. So before we know it, we're huffing and puffing through life. Working longer hours. Juggling priorities and scheduling every minute and getting up early and staying up late. Doing everything we can to measure up to our own view of what we're supposed to accomplish. Worrying we still won't be able to get it all done.

And interestingly enough, we often do very well . . . for a while. We do good work. We help others. Our efforts seem to bring glory to God and bring us confidence and a healthy sense of accomplishment—until we finally run headfirst into our own limitations.

Then we get sick from the stress. Or develop addictions and compulsions, obsessing with feeling better about ourselves, leaning on substances like alcohol or tobacco or caffeine to give us a boost and help us keep at it. We may throw up our hands and give up . . . or grow depressed . . . or stop correcting our faults and call that "accepting ourselves." We may demand that the world adjust to us and grow bitter and frustrated when it doesn't. Or pretend to be good enough, sacrificing honesty in the interest of cleaning up well and looking happy.

THE TRUTH ABOUT OUR INADEQUACIES

Actually, most of us do all of the above at one time or the other—or at the same time, in different areas of our lives. And no matter which response we choose, the seeds of "not enough" grow into a bitter harvest.

We may end up weary and frustrated. Resentful of others' needs and expectations. Judgmental of their weaknesses. Envious of their possessions or talents. We may be angry with God (whether we know it or not) for not giving us what we want. Angry with ourselves and sure that our inadequacies are to blame for the bad things that have happened to us. So caught up in our own problems that we have trouble seeing anybody else. And unable to appreciate or even see the abundant blessings God has laced through our lives.

And "enough" still remains a moving target . . . always out there ahead of us.

Always out of reach.

Because the truth is we will *never* be enough.

We're mortal. We have limited physical endurance and emotional strength and intellectual capability. We're fallible and make mistakes. We need help and encouragement.

We feel inadequate, in other words, because we *are* inadequate. God's made us that way.

God created us for relationship, to depend on one another. He gave us different, complementary gifts that are supposed to work together like the parts of the body do (see 1 Cor. 12:12–31). He called us to love each other, to support each other, to encourage each other, to carry each other's burdens—to be an interdependent community, not a universe of independent superstars. And He calls us into fellowship with Him too. It's part of our nature to feel restless and incomplete if we're not connecting to God and depending on Him.

So in the economy of God, "not enough" is not really an issue.

What is an issue is our skewed thinking about who we are and what's expected of us—our stubborn insistence on more, more, more. When we let the contradictory messages of culture and the unhappy voices of people we know and our own inclinations turn our "not enough" reality into frantic attempts at self-sufficiency.

And that's where we really get ourselves in trouble.

Because that's where "not enough" and "try harder" start sounding a lot like sin.

Sinful Drivenness

I'm not saying it's a sin to feel inadequate or even to feel driven. I don't think any feeling is a sin—because we don't really have control over how we feel. (We do have control on how we respond to our feelings, but that's a different issue.)

I certainly don't believe it's a sin to work hard or improve ourselves.

There's nothing inherently wrong with losing weight or wearing makeup or even having a tummy tuck. I generally applaud women who make a success of their businesses or put a lot of effort into being a good mom or feel compelled to throw themselves into Christian service. Jesus never called us to be lazy, ineffective slobs!

At the same time, drivenness is a danger issue. It's very easy for "not enough" to shift into sinful thinking and "try harder" to morph into sinful behavior.

Pride is a common downfall for driven Christian girls, for example. We tell ourselves we just have high standards, but secretly we're just trying to be better than everyone else. Or we take on more responsibility because we secretly feel that we should be in charge. "I'm never enough" can really translate into "It's all about me—I'm responsible for everything that happens in the world."

And drivenness easily morphs into hypocrisy and self-righteousness, the sins that Jesus judged most harshly. The more we push ourselves toward our own view of perfection, the harder we try to be enough on our own, the more likely we are to either pretend that all is well when it isn't or to point our fingers at others' inadequacies.

It's so painful to me to remember a time in my own life when I did just this. We adopted a beautiful daughter, Tatiana, from Russia. And like many children who spent their earliest years in an orphanage, Tatiana was a special-needs child. We spent a lot of time in hospital waiting rooms and counselors' offices, trying to find our way around her attachment issues and multiple physical ailments. Though I loved this little girl with all my heart and believed passionately in the international adoption (I still do), I also struggled daily with the fear that my good intentions and efforts would not be enough to make things right with Tatiana.

Then I heard that another couple in our small care group, wonderful Christian people with two other children who were in the process of adopting a little girl like Tatiana, had decided not to go through with the adoption. They just didn't think they could handle the challenge.

To say I wasn't gracious to these people is an understatement. I raked them over the coals: "How could you get that child's hopes up?" "Are you going to throw away your other kids too?" Basically, I destroyed our relationship. And it took me more than a decade to realize my reaction to them was a sinful response to my own sense of inadequacy. I was prideful, self-righteous, and cruel, not to mention unfair. And though I've long ago confessed my sin and accepted God's forgiveness, it still pains me to remember the way I acted, the things I've said. And though I've written the couple, apologized, and asked for their forgiveness, I have never heard from them again.

I do want to add, though, that God's grace has worked powerfully in Tatiana's life. Today she is a thriving and beautiful nineteen-year-old who just came back from a year of studying Bible abroad and is working as a nanny for a wonderful Christian family. I couldn't be prouder of her. Now I pray God's grace will work just as powerfully in the life of the family I so offended.

Have you ever thought that drivenness can be a form of lust? How many times do we tell ourselves "I'm not enough" when what we really mean is "I want more"? That desire for more and more of a good thing is a built-in part of our sinful nature. So is the kind of self-deceit that tries to cover the desire with a more socially acceptable insecurity.

In the same way, "I'm not enough" thinking can hide a very basic failure of faith—what we're really feeling is "God is not enough for me" or "I can't depend on God." Our striving may reflect our perpetual dissatisfaction with what we have been given and our desire for different blessings than what God has chosen to bestow. (Could that have been part of Leah's problem?)

Whenever good Christian girls are driven and striving and hurting and unhappy, I think it's fair to assume that sin is inevitably involved. But that shouldn't surprise us. As I've mentioned again and again, we live in a fallen world. That means we will sin, and we will be sinned against, and all this sin is likely to fuel our "not enough" drivenness.

But driven Christian girls who are not enough have Jesus . . . who *is* enough.

That really does make all the difference.

Or at least it gives us a place to start.

WHAT WE REALLY NEED

You see, the big question for driven Christian girls is not whether God can help us. We know He can—we're good Christian girls, remember? We know He forgives our sins and saves our souls. We've tasted His goodness, experienced His grace. What we haven't been able to do is open ourselves to His rest. We can't seem to let go of our "not enough" fears and desires that keep us so insecure and exhausted.

To gain a new perspective, our questions must be simple and profound.
What is important?
Who is important?
What are we going to do about it?

—DON OSGOOD[8]

Most of us, I'd guess, have told ourselves to lighten up, only to fall back into our old driven thinking. We've tried and failed to heed the message of Psalm 37:7 and Matthew 11:28—to rest in the Lord and to come to Him for rest. We've accepted the good news that Jesus is all we need, and we really believe that. But we can't seem to stop feeling driven and needy.

So we wonder if we need therapy. (That's a possibility. I strongly encourage broken people to seek out Christian therapy . . . it has literally changed my life.)

Or in-depth Bible study. (That's always a good idea.)

Or prayer and meditation. (It's a powerful source of help.)

Or the support of friends, pastors, and teachers. (Definitely a must—because we're *not* enough, remember?)

But in the long run, the Lord's word of grace to those of us who are harried and hassled and driven and striving, those of us who can't shake the voice of "I'm not enough," starts with the word He gave to another harried and hassled and driven woman who happened to be one of His favorite people—Martha of Bethany. The one who fussed and fretted about throwing a perfect dinner party for Jesus and His friends and got upset because her sister Mary didn't help.

I've given a lot of dinner parties, and I can picture the scene so clearly. There's Martha ladling sauce into a bowl or folding a cloth for the bread basket, assuming her sister is right there with her. She says something like, "Could you bring me the basket from the window ledge?" No answer. So she turns around, realizes she's alone, and blows her top. She goes storming into the room where Jesus sits, disciples all around Him, Mary at His feet. And the sight of them all just sitting there just makes things worse.

"Lord," she whines, "I'm doing all this stuff to make You welcome, and Mary's just sitting there. Don't You care? Make her come help me!"

I've always wondered what Mary did at that moment. Maybe she felt guilty and started to get up. Maybe she just rolled her eyes and looked at Jesus with an expression that said, *My crazy sister is at it again.* Maybe she went over and hugged Martha because she knew the pain that drove her sibling to be such a perfectionist.

We don't know what Mary did.

We just know what Jesus said—and His word for us driven Christian girls is just as gentle, just as full of grace as His words to Martha that day.

"Martha, Martha," He told her softly, "You are worried and concerned with many things, but *only one thing is needed.*"

The Voice to Listen To

"Only one thing." I hope those words were enough to calm Martha's driven heart, to slow her hands, to change her perspective. (They help me a lot when I can wrap my mind around them.)

I hope she heard what He was really saying, which was not, "Don't serve, don't work, don't try" . . . but, "First things first."

What He was telling her, with exquisite love and tenderness, was, "You need Me most of all. And here I am—so you can relax!"

Isn't that the word that all of us need to hear, the word that can not only calm our hearts but also, over time, change them?

We are worried about so many things.

So much occupies our attention and drives us to work and work, try and try again, or give up in frustration.

So many voices conspire to tell us that we're not up to snuff, that our efforts are insufficient, that we ought to be ashamed because something serious is wrong with us.

So many voices urge us to work harder, try harder, get busier, not let up . . . because if we ever did, everything might fall apart.

But in the midst of it all, there's just one thing we need to do.

We need to put down our spoons and dishrags and planners and to-do lists and focus in on the One who loves us best. The One who whispers, *Listen to Me first. Not to the expectations of others. Not to the pain from your past or your fears of the future. Let My voice be the one that guides you.*

Let Me show you what it means to sit at My feet and rest.

The Unexpected Miracle

Sound like a miracle?

If you're someone who has been hurt by others' expectations and your own, if you've fallen into the habit of constant striving, actually being able to relax can sound like a miracle. It can also sound as likely as a rosebush in Death Valley. Because it's one thing to believe in miracles and something else to expect a miracle right in the middle of your driving and striving.

But Jesus, of course, is in the miracle business.

And sometimes the greatest miracle He grants us is a changed perspective.

I think that's exactly what He was offering Martha that day in Bethany. It's what He offers us as well when we turn to Him for help with our drivenness, our "not enough" anxiety.

For as we choose to focus on Him . . . to keep listening for His voice . . . He starts changing the way we look at ourselves and Him. And as that happens, we start to settle down. Our driven impatience gives way to contentment. (Yes, it really can happen.) Our dissatisfaction relaxes into gratitude. It's all part of what Paul calls the renewing of our minds (Rom. 12:2). We think differently. Our perspective changes. And gradually we realize that we're different, less driven people.

Practically speaking, it happens as we set aside time to come to Him. As we talk to Him over the course of the day. As we listen to Him in His Word and the silence of our hearts. As we consciously choose to trust Him. To practice waiting for His timing. And deliberately giving thanks for His blessings.

> *Thinking too highly of ourselves. Thinking too low. Both are dangerous pastimes for a believer in Jesus Christ. Perhaps that is why Romans 12:3 advises us to "think of yourself with sober judgment, in accordance with the measure of faith God has given you." This sober judgment—this clear-eyed self-analysis—helps us look at ourselves honestly. It enables us to step back and make an objective evaluation of our gifts and our callings, our weaknesses as well as our strengths. And it never forgets to factor in God. For only in faith, with sober judgment and reliance on the Holy Spirit, can we ever manage to see ourselves as we really are.*
>
> —JOANNA WEAVER[9]

But I'm *not* telling you the way to get over your drivenness and compulsiveness is to work harder on prayer and Bible study, to try more diligently to be content and thankful. That would be a typical driven Christian girl response—to hear just another "not enough" message on top of all the other issues. And that's not what Jesus is saying. It's not what He asks of us.

What He wants is our attention. Our listening ears. Our willingness to turn to Him, to expose our thoughts and feelings to His influence.

And most of all, to open our hearts to the truth of what God thinks about us.

How God Sees Us

The entire message of the Bible, as I see it, has to do with how God sees us. And the Bible has both good news and bad news about that.

The truth is we're not enough . . . because we're incomplete and imperfect and weak.

Because we're sinful and rebellious.

Because we're supposed to work together and we just can't get along.

Because we need God desperately and we forget that reality on an hourly basis.

We're so inadequate, in fact, that it's downright pitiful. And that's the bad news.

But here's the good news—and it's amazingly good.

Even in the midst of our inadequate, lying, sinning reality, God loves us passionately. Tenderly. Enthusiastically. With a Father's care and tenderness. He sees so much potential. He wants so much for us. For thousands of years He's been pursuing us, making it possible for us to draw near to Him. He even sent His Son to save us—not because of our efforts, but simply because we're His.

That's hard to understand, I know. Believe me—I know! I still struggle with my compulsive, workaholic tendencies. I still wrestle with the pain my inadequacies cause me and those I love. I'm still ashamed to be not enough, and I keep bustling around to rectify the situation when what I really need to be doing is turning to Jesus.

But I'm gradually beginning to understand. God's grace is teaching me. Being a mother is teaching me too. And a conversation I had with my daughter Mackenzie a few years back gave me one of my most powerful lessons.

> *Repentance is not necessarily the gloomy and self-loathing practice it is sometimes made out to be. To repent is not to be confirmed in what that little voice keeps whispering: that you are no good, that everything bad that happens to you is your own fault, that if only others knew what you were really like, they would cease to care for or be interested in you. No. True repentance begins with the felt knowledge that we are loved by God. . . . If we cannot find ourselves there then perhaps our preparation might consist of the prayer that we might know ourselves as beloved, that the divine lover might reach down into our self-hatred . . . and touch us.*
>
> —WENDY M. WRIGHT[10]

Mackenzie is my wonderful firstborn, a child who seemed to come out of the womb responsible and has almost seemed to raise herself. She's just one of those "good kids"—well behaved, thoughtful, hardworking, fun, a true delight.

When Mackenzie was seventeen, though, she embarked on a dating relationship that worried us a little. The young man was good-looking, charismatic, significantly older than she was, and my husband and I felt a little red flag go up. My husband even had a little talk with him about honoring our daughter . . . and of course he promised to do just that. But we were still relieved when they broke up. Then, months later, I found out by accident that the two of them had been more involved than we knew—and more than Mackenzie had been comfortable with. What really distressed me was that I hadn't even known about it.

I knew we had to talk about the situation, so I asked Mackenzie to meet me for coffee. My heart nearly broke as I watched her walk into the coffee shop. I could just imagine her hurt, her shame, her embarrassment, and her regret.

She sat down, and I started in, "Mackenzie, this has come to my attention . . ."

Then my heart took over. I leaned over and took her face in my hands and said, "Oh, baby, why didn't you tell me? Why did you carry this with you these months and not talk to me? I could have helped you! I would have walked you through this!"

I'll never forget her response, just as I'll never forget the tears that ran down her face as she said it: "I was so afraid that every time you looked at me, all you would see is what I had done."

My jaw dropped. That was absolutely the farthest thing from my mind. "Honey," I told her, "when I look at you, all I see is how much I love you . . . and how beautiful you are to me."

And it was absolutely true. At that moment, my only response to her was overwhelming love. I knew about her sin, her failure, her inadequacy. I knew how big those things loomed in her mind. But they didn't faze me; I just wanted to help her. Because from my perspective, all I could see when I looked at her was someone I loved dearly.

That was—and still is—enough for me.

Just as I am enough for my loving heavenly Father.

A PERSPECTIVE OF PEACE

Do you hear this good news? Is it enough to change your perspective?

Our inadequacies, our failures, our "not enough" issues are simply beside the point when it comes to the Father's love.

Yes, He has His standards.

Yes, He wants to help us be more like Him.

Yes, He has work for us all to do, and I believe He delights in our hard work and creativity when it's combined with obedience and honest truth.

But even if we never did a thing, our Father would still love us. He continues to love us when we fail, when we run from Him, when our thinking is skewed and our intentions are all wrong. Even when we persist in thinking we can never be enough through our own efforts.

We must sound so silly as we huff and puff and whine and wheeze and try harder and harder and wallow in our worries. But if we let Him, He can love us back to sanity.

He'll give us rest. Even better, He'll give us *peace*.

Remember what Jesus told the woman with the issue of blood? He told her to go in peace. He said the same thing to the Luke 7 woman, the notorious sinner who anointed His feet with perfume. And I believe that's His crowning word for us good Christian girls who try and try and still don't feel like we're enough.

It means "nothing missing, nothing broken."

It means being whole, enough, sufficient. It means being able to relax, not strive, because we're so confident that we're loved. It means doing all our work with a changed perception. An attitude of grateful, peaceful confidence.

Because we're His children.

And because, to Him, we are never anything less than beloved.

WORD OF GRACE FOR DRIVEN CHRISTIAN GIRLS

You don't need to be enough.
And you don't have to do anything.
Quite simply . . . Jesus is all you need.
And His is all you need to be.

9

"How Much Longer, Lord?"

"For I know the plans I have for you," declares the LORD,
"plans to prosper you and not to harm you,
plans to give you hope and a future."
—Jeremiah 29:11

The first time her husband went into rehab, Suzanne was full of hope.

Finally, God had heard her prayers.

Finally, Todd would get the help he needed to kick his alcohol addiction.

Finally, they could have a normal life. A real future. Real hope.

And life hadn't felt that way for Suzanne in a long time. Normal had become anything but normal.

Every year, Todd's drinking problem got worse. Suzanne couldn't believe she had tolerated it for so long, but she kept hoping things would be better. Besides, she loved her husband, and she knew he loved her. He was a fine man, a good provider. He really did love the Lord. But when he drank, Todd became someone Suzanne didn't even recognize—angry, paranoid, unreasonable. His verbal tirades made her cringe, and a few times over the years he had threatened her physically.

Again and again Suzanne cried out to God to heal her husband, to heal her marriage, to get them out of this mess. And now, at last, her prayers were being answered.

After one particularly nasty episode, she'd had to call the police. Todd had spent a miserable night in jail. The next day, a remorseful Todd had finally agreed to check into a residential rehabilitation facility. He was determined to fight this addiction, which threatened the life of his family.

He spent a month going through detox, being monitored and attending group meetings. Suzanne and the boys attended meetings, too, learning more about addiction and how to cope. She spent a lot of time in prayer, asking God to help her forgive her husband, to do her part in moving to a new life together. When Todd came home from rehab, she welcomed him with her whole heart. She was ready to do whatever it took to make a new life possible for them.

Within a year, Todd was in rehab again.

And Suzanne, though still somewhat hopeful, was also discouraged and confused.

She'd known Todd was drinking again—it was hard to hide. She'd known he'd stopped attending meetings. He was under a lot of pressure at work, and his job required a lot of traveling, which made things worse. But this time Todd admitted what was happening and chose rehab for himself. That was a good sign, wasn't it?

Once again, Todd came home clean—chastened, determined to start again. Once again, the whole family supported his efforts, though Suzanne secretly wondered, *How many times can we go through this?*

This time he stayed sober for two weeks. Then the situation deteriorated fast. Suzanne desperately struggled to hold her life and family together as Todd's secrets began to unravel and her life spun out of control.

She learned there were other women—dozens of them, in every town where Todd traveled. Some were women he'd met while traveling. Some were call girls and "escorts." Some were images on the Internet and voices on the other end of a phone sex line. To support his expensive habits, Todd had cashed out several investments earmarked for the boys' college funds. On top of all this, Todd's rages were getting worse. He started sending Suzanne e-mails full of venomous accusations. The late-night tirades frightened her more and more. And sometimes Todd would disappear from home for days on end.

When Todd lost his job, the company called it "restructuring," but Suzanne suspected the alcohol was a factor. He'd called in sick one time too many.

Then, a week or so later, Todd came home drunk yet again. He frightened the children and once again threatened Suzanne. He said he would destroy her reputation . . . take her down . . . tell everyone that the whole situation was her fault. He twisted the knife by insisting that if she would have been the faithful wife he needed, none of this would be happening.

The next morning, with great reluctance, Suzanne asked Todd to move out. She filed a restraining order against him and took the first steps toward a legal separation. When she came home from the lawyer's office that day, all she could do was sit and tremble.

She had been so hopeful. She had tried so hard. For so long, she had trusted God for deliverance from her pain. And yet her situation just kept on getting worse. Instead of deliverance, all she got was disappointment, discouragement, and despair.

Some days, it was all she could do to keep on breathing.

> *Fear breeds a deadening caution, a holding back, a stagnant waiting until people no longer can recall what they are waiting for or saving themselves for. When we fear failure more than we love life, when we are dominated by thoughts of what we might have been rather than by thoughts of what we might become, when we are haunted by the disparity between our ideal self and our real self, when we are tormented by guilt, shame, remorse, and self-condemnation, we deny our faith in the God of love.*
>
> —BRENNAN MANNING[1]

IMPRISONED IN EGYPT, LOST IN THE WILDERNESS

I know so many good Christian girls like my friend Suzanne, women who have struggled for years with the consequences of sin—their own and others. Their pain is chronic, their disappointment deep. Every season of hope seems to be followed by another season of trouble that's worse than before, until their basic reality seems to be "How long, O Lord?"

"When will I find victory over this craving?"

"When will I be delivered from this pain?"

"When will I find freedom from this compulsion?"

"When will this struggle be over?"

"Will anyone ever love me?"

"Will I ever feel good again?"

I so clearly remember feeling this way. One day during a particularly painful period of my life, my journal entry read:

I am a terrified woman . . . again. Tonight I find myself bound by a straitjacket of choices. Mine and those done against me. I can't eat. I can't move. My weakness is sickening even to me. I cry. Cry for what was. What is . . . and what might become of me and this life of mine.

I cry out for release from the ensnarement, this binding harness. Beg for the freedom I once knew. Take me back . . . way back. Oh God, tonight I want my life back. Liberate me from the strength of these shameful ropes. Cut me free.

God, do You hear me? *I want my life back!*

This kind of pain can feel like living in slavery. Eternally trapped in our circumstances. Yearning for release but unable to break free. Sometimes we can't even imagine what freedom would be like.

Or sometimes the real trouble kicks in after we've been released. The affair is over. We've lost the weight or torn up the credit cards or begun the recovery. We've asked for forgiveness and received it. And we know that God is at work in our lives—we've seen the evidence. But still we find ourselves lost and wandering, somehow unable to find our way into the next chapter of our lives.

If any of what I've just described sounds painfully familiar, this chapter is for you. It's different from the others because it doesn't focus on a particular area of brokenness. Instead, it's about long-term brokenness, the kind that threatens to carry us beyond our endurance and our understanding. It's about problems that don't get solved, suffering that doesn't go away, difficulties we can't untangle, habits we can't seem to break, loved ones who keep on hurting us. It's about those times when we've prayed and fasted and tried harder and waited on the Lord and done everything we know to do . . . and circumstances just seem to get worse.

And oh my goodness, it does happen. Let's be honest about that. Some good Christian girls I know seem to spend their whole lives waiting for things to get better . . . and ducking to avoid the next round of discouragement.

I think of my friend Lisa and all those years of being abused.

Or Sara, groping her way toward sobriety.

Or Bobbie, whose heart and finances still haven't recovered from her marriage to a man with bipolar disorder.

Or Annabeth, who lost custody of her two children a decade ago and doesn't know where they are today.

Then there's my new friend Angela, a divorced mom who is raising four little kids alone. I asked her one night about whether she was dating. "Oh, no," she answered wryly. "It's another Saturday night, and I'm here with my integrity." I loved her good-humored honesty, but I also heard the chronic pain and loneliness behind it. This friend is an amazing woman, a strong person who is doing her best to live right. But I can tell that her time in the wilderness is wearing on her.

So where is God in times like those? If we want to talk about real grace, about the love of the Father, about God's offerings to us in our brokenness, I think we have to ask that question. We need to ask how good Christian girls can survive times of extended suffering. How they reach out to their sisters who are trapped in their circumstances or stumbling through a wilderness of pain that just doesn't seem to end.

And what better person to look to than a person who spent half her life in slavery and another half in the wilderness? A strong, resilient woman, a woman of strength and integrity, who passed every test and then finally faltered when she had to wait too long.

Her name is Miriam.

And she is our woman in the wilderness.

Morning Again . . .

Another day in the desert.

Miriam stepped out of her tent, took a deep breath of the arid air, and gazed out over a nearby outcropping of sandstone to the place where the sun would soon come up. She stretched her arthritic back the best she could. Wiggled her toes in the ever-present dust. And sighed.

Two years in the desert. Two years. And Miriam was an old woman, without many years to waste. She'd been well past eighty when her people finally left Egypt, rejoicing in their deliverance. Full of hope for their future in the land that God had promised them.

Now, two years later, they were still out here dithering in the desert.

Miriam snorted her frustration. She didn't blame the people for get-ting restless. She was getting restless herself.

For so many years she had reminded people that God was faithful. That He had a plan for His people. That Moses knew what he was talking about. That they really were going to be free. That the Promised Land was real . . . and just around the corner.

Now she wondered, did she even believe it herself?

All around her, the camp was beginning to stir. Mothers called to children, preparing to go out and gather manna. Neighbors gossiped with one another. As usual, there were complaints—though after that last little incident with the quail, they rarely griped about the food. And though she usually chided the complainers, today Miriam just didn't have the heart.

A movement on the horizon caught her eye, and she squinted to make out the figure—though she knew who it was. Her white-bearded baby brother coming back from the tent of meeting, the place where he went to speak to the Lord. Moses' spine was beginning to stiffen like hers, his legs often unsteady, but he always returned from the tent with a spring in his step. Miriam's sore back ached just looking at him.

Another figure appeared, and Miriam sighed again as the familiar resentment rose in her chest. It was that woman—Moses' foreign wife—walking out to meet him. The two fell in step, walking comfortably together, and Miriam snorted in frustration. It wasn't just that Moses had married an outsider, though that was bad enough. What really bothered Miriam was the sneaking suspicion that Moses trusted his wife and her family more than his own brother and sister. That just wasn't right.

Last night she'd even mentioned it to Aaron . . . put the thoughts into words for the first time. Hinted that Moses was being unduly influenced by a woman who could never understand their heritage. Maybe that was what was keeping them out of the Promised Land. After all, the woman had never known slavery. She'd lived in the desert all her life. How could she understand the importance of pushing on to Canaan? Maybe she was influencing Moses to delay. Or maybe Moses was just starting to like it out here. He talked about the Promised Land, but did he really have the heart to lead them there?

Did he really have what it took to lead a nation?

Miriam shook her head as she bent to fasten her worn sandals. Something had to be done. She hadn't spent all those years as a slave in Egypt just to wander around out here in the wilderness.

God had done His part—Miriam had seen the miracles. And God had clearly promised that Canaan would be theirs. So why were they still here?

Maybe things would be different if Moses wasn't gone so much. If he controlled the people better. If he'd assert himself more directly, speak more eloquently.

And yes, if he'd use Miriam's talents a little more. She could help him if he'd let her. After all, the people loved her. And although God didn't speak to her directly the way He did to Moses, she'd been having visions and dreams long before her little brother had. In fact, she'd been rallying the people back in Egypt while Moses was still an exile, out herding sheep in the Midian desert. If it hadn't been for her, in fact, Moses might not even be alive today . . .

Her mind floated back to that day at the Nile. The little basket-boat with its precious cargo bobbing in the current. And big sister Miriam herself hiding in the rushes, terrified of crocodiles but determined to keep watch, observing the commotion as the princess and her attendants approached the river.

The mixed feelings: What if they found him? What if they didn't? The plan gradually forming in her mind—from God, surely, but could she carry it off? The princess in her delicate floating garments bending down, reaching for the basket. And Miriam herself taking a deep breath and stepping forward.

It had taken a lot for a little Hebrew slave girl to approach a princess . . . especially with such a bold plan. But the plan had worked! Miriam still felt proud that God used her to save her brother so he could lead the people to freedom. Much later, after Moses came back, after the wrangling with Pharaoh, after the plagues and the amazing events at the Red Sea, she had led the people in rejoicing, her heart all but overwhelmed by gratitude to Yahweh for setting them free.

But free for what? To wait around out here in the wasteland because her brother couldn't get his act together?

The light stabbed her eyes as the sun finally chose to lift itself over the horizon. Miriam felt something turn over inside her heart as well, a decision made. She'd talk to Aaron tonight about challenging Moses and getting on with the Promised Land business.

They'd all waited long enough.

Something had to be done. And who would do it if not for her?

Perils of the Long Haul . . . and Grace for the Journey

Do you remember this episode of Miriam's story? To be honest, I'd almost forgotten it.

When I think of Moses' sister, I almost always remember that little girl crouching in the rushes near the Nile, watching her baby brother float down the river in a basket. Or I think of Miriam the prophetess on the desert side of the Red Sea, rallying the Israelites for their journey toward the Promised Land, dancing and singing and playing the tambourine—the ultimate cheerleader for her people.

I think of a courageous, hopeful woman, respected and influential and devoted to her people. And Miriam certainly was all those things. Her story, in a way, was the story of the Israelites. Like them, she suffered in slavery for many long years—she was almost ninety the day she led the singing by the Red Sea. Like them, she experienced the terror of the plagues, the uncertainty of waiting on Pharaoh's whims, the delirious joy of deliverance . . . and the tedium of endless days in the desert.

> *Our questions and questing are crucial, because they can help us live into the answer of the future. I am certain of one thing: the love that is God is at the heart of the answer, just as it is at the heart of each moment—past, present, and future. Faith today, tomorrow, and always seeks to live, to love, and to be loved fully. It seeks the Holy and waits (though not always patiently) to be found; it nurtures and activates wisdom and compassion. It chooses to embrace hope and to be embraced by hope, even when overwhelmed by despair; it seeks life even in the face of death.*
>
> —Jean M. Blomquist[2]

We don't know if she helped build a golden calf when Moses was gone or complained about the food the way many Hebrews did. But we do know that even Miriam eventually grew weary of waiting and trusting the Lord. For that's exactly what she is when we encounter her again in Numbers 12—weary. And impatient.

She had waited so long for deliverance from evil. She'd been so hopeful that soon she'd see the Promised Land. But after two years in the wilderness, discouragement got the better of her. She started complaining bitterly about Moses' wife and then conspired with Aaron to openly question Moses' leadership. She became a source of discord, division, and discontent among the Israelites.

And God didn't put up with it. We read in Numbers 12:10 that He punished Miriam for her rebellion by striking her with leprosy and having her banished from the camp.

I don't know about you, but to me that seems like a harsh punishment for someone who had been faithful for so long. God must have thought so, too, for He responded to Moses' pleas and relented after only seven days, curing Miriam of disease and restoring her to her people.

But Miriam still paid an ongoing price for her lack of faith. Like Moses and a whole generation of Israelites, she would die before the people entered the Promised Land. Though she no doubt continued to receive honor and—I'm guessing—to do good for her people, Miriam never saw the fulfillment of her dearest hope in her own lifetime.

And this is true for other women I know who experience long-term difficulty. Some of them never really completely escape their painful situations. Some never know the complete fulfillment of their dreams or arrive where they hoped they were going.

Some fight temptation all their lives and still fall back into sin from time to time.

Some juggle medications until the day they die.

Some struggle a lifetime with the fallout of their abuse.

Some end their lives still praying for a husband or for a wayward child to come home.

There is certainly no guarantee that my friend Suzanne's husband will finally find true recovery for his addiction. That her shaky marriage will survive. That she'll find someone else to love or find her financial footing. Or that no more trouble will find her.

Yet God's grace is available in abundance for Suzanne and for all of us. In our better moments, we know that. He tells us so in His Word. He's given His Son to make it so.

God's promises hold. His presence is never far. Although life on earth may not offer the specific happily-ever-after we expect, God still has something good in store for each of us—a true future and a real hope. He never abandons us. He never stops working to bring about His plans.

The challenge, for many of us, is remembering.

The even greater challenge is holding on to trust during those drawn-out periods when all we can see are prison walls or desert sand.

Pray for Change . . . but Trust God's Purposes

How do we do that? How do we live past the discouragement and hold on to the promises? How do we keep on walking when we've grown too weary and the constant cry of our hearts is, "How much longer, Lord"?

One thing to keep in mind whether we're languishing in slavery or wandering in the wilderness is that while God wants the very best for us, His best isn't always what we have in mind at the moment. Scripture reminds us that His thoughts are not our thoughts.

So often, we just want to survive. He wants us to thrive.

We want to be free of suffering. God wants us free to love and serve Him.

We want what we want when we want it. God wants us to live close to Him.

We want our lives to just roll along. God wants us to grow.

We want our current problems to be solved. God wants to give us a real future and a hope—something beautifully different from what we've known.

I think this disconnect between God's desires for us and our desires for ourselves, His big picture and our limited view, is one of the biggest reasons we grow discouraged. And remembering God's purposes can be the boost we need when disappointment and discouragement get us down.

We've got to remind ourselves again and again that God wants more for us than we want for ourselves. He will do what is necessary to accomplish His purposes in our lives. And because our vision is limited, we won't always understand what God is doing—or even see that He's doing anything at all. Sometimes, in fact, when things seem to be getting worse and worse and nothing seems to be better, that's actually a sign that God is actively at work.

My friend Suzanne had just such a realization recently, and it made all the difference to her. It came on a day when she had received another volley of e-mail abuse from her estranged—and obviously intoxicated—husband. She was sitting out on her deck trying to have daily devotions, but she just ended up pouring out her pain to God, just as she had a hundred times before. Begging God to soften Todd's heart and change the direction of their lives. Knowing deep inside that Todd's heart wasn't changing at all. Unable to imagine a future for her family that involved anything besides more pain.

Her devotions that day took her to Romans 9, which referred her back to the Exodus story: "For the Scripture says to Pharaoh: 'I raised you up for this very purpose, that I might display my power in you and that my name might be proclaimed in all the earth.' Therefore God has mercy on whom he wants to have mercy, and he hardens whom he wants to harden" (vv. 17–18).

As she sat there, she felt prompted to reread those early chapters of Exodus. And she noticed for the first time the many references to Pharaoh's heart and how it was "hardened" against the Israelites. When Moses first went to Pharaoh to ask for his people's freedom, the Egyptian ruler hardened his own heart. Out of stubbornness and pride, he made a choice of his will to refuse Moses' pleas.

But after this happened a number of times, the Lord Himself stepped in. Following the sixth plague, and several times afterward, it was God who hardened Pharaoh's heart against the Israelites.[3] So God Himself actually made the Hebrews' situation in Egypt worse and worse and their lives increasingly miserable . . . until they finally made up their minds to leave.

Why didn't I notice that before? Suzanne wondered. In that moment, sitting there on her deck with her Bible open, she felt the Holy Spirit whisper to her heart, *Suzanne, I want to take you out of your Egypt. But I have to make things worse so you'll want to go. I have hardened Todd's heart for your sake—so you'll want to be free.*

Are you talking about divorce? she whispered in her heart, dreading the answer.

I'm talking about your heart, the Lord answered. *I'm talking about the part of you that is so accustomed to abuse, disappointment, and rejection that you don't even know what freedom is. But I'm going to move you past that. Regardless of what happens in your life and your marriage, I want your heart to be free.*

I'm going to take you to a place of safety and freedom. But you're going to have to trust Me every step of the way.

Then Suzanne remembered what she'd just read in Exodus 6:9, when Moses went to the Hebrews to tell them about the Promised Land. They were so discouraged, so accustomed to bondage, they couldn't even hear the good news that a better day was coming.

> *The secret of waiting is the faith that the seed has been planted, that something has begun. Active waiting means to be present fully to the moment, in the conviction that something is happening where you are and that you want to be present to it. . . . Hope is trusting that something will be fulfilled, but fulfilled according to the promises and not just according to our wishes. Therefore, hope is always open-ended. I have found it very important in my own life to let go of my wishes and start hoping. It was only when I was willing to let go of wishes that something really new, something beyond my own expectations, could happen to me.*
>
> —HENRI NOUWEN[4]

And doesn't that happen to us too? We can be so tangled up in our pain that we don't have it in us even to care about our future. We get stuck, attached to our familiar trauma. And we resist change—even the change that's necessary to set us free.

That's something to keep in mind in those dark times when we see no way out of our pain. Sometimes God allows the situation we are in to get worse and worse so we will be willing to let go. So we'll finally be motivated to leave what we know and trust Him to take us into something better.

PREDICTABLE PITFALLS

As Miriam and the people of Israel discovered, of course, freedom isn't the same as instant gratification. Deliverance usually takes time. The miracles we receive aren't always the ones we would have chosen. And as we've pointed out, often those who escape the bondage of a particular form of brokenness still spend some time in the wilderness, waiting for things to get better and a new life to materialize.

Very few of us are good at holding on to trust in those situations. (I know I'm not.) The longer we have to wait to see God's promises fulfilled, the more likely we are to fall into some dangerous traps.

Faulty memory is one of the most treacherous of these. It's what happened to the Israelites in the wilderness when they started to long for Egypt. The memory of Pharaoh's oppression grew dim. Their deliverance lost its wonder. And all they could think of is what they used to eat in Egypt: "If only we had meat to eat! We remember the fish we ate in Egypt at no cost—also the cucumbers, melons, leeks, onions and garlic. But now we have lost our appetite; we never see anything but this manna!" (Num. 11:4–6).

It would be funny if it weren't so sad. But it's so human, so typical. When waiting wears us down, it's so easy to forget what God has done for us, to minimize our past pain and long for what we know—even if what we know is dangerous or destructive. We remember the sexual "freedom" but not the shame, the financial security but not the abuse, the ability to eat anything we wanted but not the terrifying sense of being out of control. If we're not careful, we may fall back into the behavior or the circumstance that brought us so much suffering.

Like the Israelites, we may slip into chronic negativity and become complainers, constantly finding fault with our circumstances, constantly second-guessing God's handling of our situation, unable to experience any present joy because we're convinced anything would be better than where we are now.

Or we may fall into Miriam's temptation instead—impatience. Instead of trusting God's timing and provision, we take matters into our hands and do whatever we can think of to control our own destiny. We stop listening to the Lord and start doing things our way.

Oh, I relate to Miriam! You probably do too.

Maybe you've grown tired of praying for your husband to come to the Lord . . . so you've started to nag a little.

Or you've about given up waiting for a mate or trying to live pure as a single and decided you deserve a little sexual gratification.

Or you've about decided your attempt to live credit free just isn't practical and gone back to depending on credit cards.

You've given in to the urge to go on the offensive and defend your honor instead of waiting for God to vindicate you.

Or you've just given up on God without even realizing it. You've stopped believing your life has a higher purpose. You've stopped listening for His voice and fallen back into doing things your own way.

It's so easy to do that when you've waited so long. It can happen to anyone. We may not even know we're doing it at first.

After all, following God is not a completely passive activity. In the words of the Serenity Prayer, there are times when we are called to make brave changes in our lives. But there's a big difference between bold decision making and the panicky manipulation that comes when we're just tired of waiting for things to work out. It's that kind of desperate striving that gets us in deep trouble.

> *I love that . . . abiding . . . is for the weak. A tired woman like you or me. We can do that. We can lean in and ask God to take hold of us. To abide is to consent in your mind and in your spirit to give yourself to God for His keeping. Here is where you can be assured, the wallflower can fall into the strong arms of God and agree to stay there. He is the One who will lift you up to dance at exactly the right time.*
>
> —Angela Thomas[5]

The story of Miriam and the Israelites reminds us that while grace is always available when we fall into wilderness pitfalls, the consequences are real and painful. We might not be struck with fire or leprosy. But each time we try to take over from God and stop trusting His purposes, we delay our entry into the better future God has in mind for us. The more we fight Him, the more we question, the longer it will take us to get to our Promised Land.

PRACTICAL STRATEGIES FOR THE CHRONICALLY BROKEN

So how can we steer clear of the wilderness pitfalls? How do we resist the temptations to turn back or move forward too fast . . . or just to give up? How do we even manage to survive—to take another step in faith when we have no idea where we're going?

I'm no final authority because I'm still traveling too. But I've been traveling a while now, and I can recommend some strategies that have helped me:

Strategy #1: Look for God's Provision

One of the most amazing things to me about the Israelites' experience in the wilderness is that God's presence and provision for them was so constant and obvious . . . and they still grew discouraged. From the moment they left Egypt, a pillar of cloud or fire went before them. When Pharaoh's army pursued them, God parted the Red Sea. When the people were hungry, He provided manna or quail. When they were thirsty, God showed them how to find water. He spoke directly with their leader, Moses, providing explicit instructions on how they could live together peacefully.

And in spite of these amazing acts of provision, the people of Israel complained and rebelled. They actually convinced themselves that

God wasn't looking out for them. And when they did, they robbed themselves of their own confidence in God's love and care.

Well, as I said, it would be funny if it weren't so sad. But I do the same thing. Don't you? We focus on our own need and our pain instead of on God's sustaining gifts in the midst of our pain . . . and that's when our trust begins to waver.

So one of the most helpful things we can do in times of extended brokenness—I'm saying this to myself as well as you—is to consciously look for our provision, then receive it thankfully. Sometimes I actively pray for reminders of the way God is sustaining me—and write down my answers in case I forget.

But what exactly do I mean by provision? It can be large (an unexpected check that covers the mortgage) or tiny (a note from a friend). It can be intensely spiritual (a meaningful daily devotion) or completely practical (a friend drops by a casserole so you don't have to cook).

Often, I've seen, God's provision for our difficult times comes in completely unexpected but absolutely appropriate ways.

One woman I know has struggled for years with both her weight and her marriage. A recent cholesterol scare prompted her to lose thirty pounds, and it happened far more easily than it ever had. Then she discovered her husband had been unfaithful. And as she fumbled around for guidance and encouragement in the midst of her pain, she received a distinct word from the Holy Spirit about her weight loss: *This is My provision for you.* She realized that she was able to cope with this particular situation with more strength and confidence knowing that she looked better than she had in years.

That may sound like a strange form of provision, but I'm astounded by both its timeliness and its very personal nature. God provides exactly what we need when we need it. And He provides exactly what is needed for His purposes to be accomplished.

That's why I think praying for awareness of provision is as important as praying for provision itself. The awareness of God's provision helps us trust His power. Our chosen attitude of thankfulness helps us trust His goodness. Our reliance on Him helps us follow step by step through the wilderness and on toward the future God has in mind for us.

Strategy #2: Don't Travel Alone

One of the most crucial things you can do if you find yourself in an extended period of brokenness is to surround yourself with people who can speak hope to you and encourage your trust. People who can jog your memory when you forget what God has done for you. People who can help you see the big picture of what God is doing in your life. People who are willing to be your companions in your journey out of bondage and on toward a hopeful future. In times of extended waiting, the companionship and support of other people can be the Lord's most important provision.

And yes, I know it's not always easy to come by. Old friendships won't necessarily stand up to new pressures. Church friends, sadly, may be sources of condemnation instead of encouragement. It's hard to reach out to new friends when you're feeling needy. And sometimes it's just hard to meet people, especially if your circumstances have changed.

You might need to pray specifically for God to send you the friend you need. I believe He will honor that prayer—although you might need to keep your eyes and heart open, because the person the Lord sends to help you may not be the kind of person you had in mind.

One helpful place to look for support and companionship is someone who has gone through the same kind of brokenness you're experiencing. Your pastor may be able to recommend support groups in your church or your community. Libraries, hospitals, and community organizations may offer referral services. Your computer can help you find local resources or online communities. Or perhaps you can remember meeting someone whose circumstances now seem familiar—because it's happened to you too. You may be able to help each other.

Through it all, never forget that you have a constant Friend in the person of the Holy Spirit. He is always present with you, a dependable Helper and Comforter. The more time you spend in quietness, waiting on the Lord, the more you will experience His closeness and know His practical grace. He is the Companion you need most for your journey . . . and He is always there for you.

Strategy #3: Lament Before the Lord

I love Michael Card's book *A Sacred Sorrow,* which encourages us to "learn the lost language of lament" and pour out our pain before God. He actually says that complaining can be a form of worship, a way of drawing close to God. It's what Job did. So did King David (in psalms of grief and complaint) and the prophet Jeremiah and even Jesus on the cross. The Bible never tells us to just suck it up and bear our pain stoically. Instead, we are told to cast our burdens on the Lord, including our doubt and pain. Until we trust Him with our honest pain and true doubt, we can't receive the gift of His comfort.

This is a tricky issue, especially when we're thinking about the Exodus. Didn't the Israelites and Miriam get in trouble for constantly complaining? Does God really want us to go around griping about everything that's wrong in our lives?

But lament is really something quite different from griping, complaining, and whining. The difference is trust. The Israelites grew restless when their trust in Yahweh's goodness and ability waned. Their complaints were really accusations, expressions of mistrust. And these complaints were made about the Lord, not to the Lord.

If, as you are reading this, you find yourself in the wilderness, realize that though you may not feel like it at the moment, you are in the very place where the Bible reveals that true worship can begin. If you're like me, you might sometimes find that you have nothing to say from where you are, no words to articulate the depth of the dimensions of your hunger, thirst, disappointments, frustrations, guilt, or anger. If this is where you find yourself, then the biblical laments are there just for you. Reading out loud from passages such as Psalm 13, 22, 55, or 86 can help you express your sorrow and also find comfort that others have lived through similar pain and even come out on the other side. [6]

Healthy lament means taking our suffering to the Lord and weeping in His presence, trusting Him with our pain, pouring out our distress to Him, and letting Him gradually lead us into an attitude of true worship. That's exactly what we see in most of the psalms of lament—a gradual shift from complaint to praise and thanksgiving. And that's what I almost always experience when I dare let down my guard, stop ignoring my pain or spouting off to others, and bring my distress directly to God. No matter how painful my distress, my heart eventually turns a corner and moves toward hope.

> *My Lord is with me in my pain, but he also is greater than pain, greater than fear, greater even than death. He is with me in the midst of my suffering, but he will also carry me beyond it. If I continue holding up my cup to him, he will do more than fill it, he will also transform it. . . . This is not a consolation prize. This is not a paltry offering I get in return for giving up on earthly happiness. What God promises me in the midst of my pain is real life, real joy, incredible growth, unbelievable beauty. This is what God has had in mind for me all along.*
>
> —EMILIE BARNES[7]

This happened, in fact, with the journal entry I quoted earlier. I wasn't consciously trying to write a psalm, but I did. As I poured out my heart in lament to God, my complaints and demands gradually calmed into a kind of trusting prayer:

Today, O Father, kiss my heart again. Remind me that You are the freedom and deliverance I so long for. It is You. . . . You are my strength and courage. Remind me again . . . it is in Your embrace I find life and liberty, the only love that lasts and never disappoints.

Teach me again. Give me courage to believe that I must be willing to release the life I have planned to embrace the life that is waiting for me.

I love rereading that journal entry. To me, it's a tangible proof of God's work in my heart—a written record of what God can do when I trust Him with my laments. It's nice to get my worries off my chest. But it's even better to take my pain to the one who can handle it . . . and, eventually, turn my complaints into worship, my tears to joy.

Strategy #4: Make a Life in the Wilderness

Miriam never made it to the Promised Land in her lifetime. Neither did Moses or Aaron.

And neither, to be truthful, will many of us.

We will experience times of deliverance and times when our hopes are fulfilled—true gifts from a loving God. But life here on this fallen planet is by definition a trip through the wilderness. We see God as a poor reflection in a dark mirror instead of face to face (see 1 Cor. 13:12). We rejoice in Jesus's coming but still wait His coming again.

And here on earth, as our Lord promised, we will have trouble (John 16:33). We are sustained by the Lord, but we're still, as the old hymns put it, "just a-travelin' through." So we can't just duck our heads when life gets hard and wait until it's over—because it might not be over for a while.

So whether we're waiting for deliverance or on the road to freedom, we need to learn the art of living richly "in the meantime." There's so much we can do while we're waiting for God's plans to unfold—so much life we can share with others. Gathering quail and manna and enjoying the Lord's provision. Cultivating meaningful relationships. Taking care of ourselves the best we can. Study the Bible to learn more about the God who is in charge of the journey. Trying to lighten the load by setting aside old habits that are dragging us down.

Most important of all, I think, is to make a point of reaching out to others. Even while you're marking time in Egypt or trudging toward your Promised Land, there are others you can help—perhaps other good Christian girls who need to make a confession, to be loved and encouraged. (That's what the next chapter is all about.)

What I have learned as I've slogged through my own times of extended brokenness is that joy and celebration are possible even in the midst of chronic pain and difficulty. I would even say that joy and celebration are essential. Karen Burton Mains expresses this so beautifully in *Lonely No More*:

> If you don't want the birthing of agony to tear you apart, give it a hard look only when you are in the middle of celebrating life. Let the pain come, because it must come. Let it rend your soul asunder, but only when you are surrounded by newborns and the conversations of friends. Cry in the night because . . . you have no choice, but also rejoice. Celebrate life passages no matter the distress, no matter death or terror or loss. How do I rejoice today? By picking out the bugs that crawled from the irises into the water glasses and laughing. By being grateful for all the hands that helped. By finding a corner out of the commotion to let down my hair with my longtime buddy Marlene . . . and to howl with healing laughter.[8]

That's such a word of hope for all us good Christian girls. There is grace to be found in ordinary life even when nothing seems ordinary. A dinner with friends, a hot bath, a half-hour playing with a baby, a whiff of a newly opened rose, a quiet cup of coffee before the day begins—any of these can be just what you need to adjust your perspective and travel with more trust.

And remember: always, in the midst of it all, as we wait for deliverance or wander in the desert, God's kingdom is still unfolding.

All is being made new.

Our best and brightest future is coming about, and we will see it all, in God's time—a foretaste in this world and its full joy in the next.

In the meantime, we have a future and a hope and a Traveling

Companion who will never let us down. Isn't that reason enough for Suzanne and Miriam—and all us good Christian girls who are sick and tired of waiting—to rejoice?

Hang on, sister. It's going to be all right. I'll meet you in the Promised Land!

WORD OF GRACE FOR DISCOURAGED CHRISTIAN GIRLS

God keeps His promises.
You can trust Him—even for the long haul.

10

"Lord, That Was So Cool!"

May God our Father himself and our Master Jesus clear the road to you!
And may the Master pour on the love so it fills your lives
and splashes over on everyone around you.
—1 Thessalonians 3:11–12 MSG

Only twice in my life have I directly heard the voice of God.

Oh, I've heard Him all my life through the words of Scripture and the wisdom of other Christians. I've seen His work in the unfolding of events in my life and felt His abiding presence. But only those two times did actual words echo in my spirit.

The first I've already told you about. That was when I sat in my car in the garage with the ignition on, waiting to die . . . and the Spirit told me I needed to drink water. Just a few simple, mundane words—though absolutely clear to me. And they saved my life.

The second time I heard the Spirit, I was in my car again. And these words were lifesaving, too, though in a far different context. They have sounded constantly in my heart as this book became a reality.

It happened one day when I was driving down Roller Coaster Road.

And yes, that's the real name for a road near my house in central Colorado. If you drove down it, you'd immediately understand why they call it that—it's one long series of humps and dips, hills and valleys, one after another—up, down, up, down. If you're driving that road in a good mood, it feels like an adventure—you almost want to yell out, "Whee!"

I was not in a good mood on that particular day.

My life had been on a roller coaster for way too long, with way too many dips and a few recent heart-stopping plunges. I'd had my fill of disappointments and shame and worry and pain—especially about my teetering marriage, which had just suffered another blow that very afternoon. I felt like such a failure—not even close to a good Christian girl. So I was pouring out my heart to God that day as I drove my big Suburban up and down Roller Coaster Road.

"Lord, when is this enough?" I cried. "I've served You. I've loved You. I've tried to do what's right—and everything's falling apart. I mean, You're telling me to write a book about shame, and I feel like I have a big S right on the top of my forehead!"

The tears were coming fast now. I had to blink them away just so I could drive. I crested another hill and headed down into the next valley. And that's when I heard the words, clear and unmistakable, echoing in my spirit:

I have called you into the ministry of deeper still.

"Deeper still?" But I knew immediately what the words meant. God was calling me to serve Him right in the middle of my pain. He was calling me to serve Him through my pain.

The brokenness, all the shame, all the failure and humiliation—none of it was going to be wasted. Because everything I was going

228

through was preparing me to "go deep" in my own life and in the lives of other good Christian girls. Down below the pat answers and the knee-jerk assumptions. Down beneath the shallowness of Sunday morning small talk. Down to the secret places where we go to lick our wounds and protect our hearts.

God wanted me to dive deeply and honestly into my own pain so I could experience His comfort and healing and freedom. And so I could speak peace to other women who were just like me. Women who were desperate enough to give up on their lives. Women who had been broken by sexual sin or left desolate by abuse. Heartbroken women mourning failed relationships . . . or trap-ped in addictions . . . or tormented

> *Some people are uncomfortable with messy life stuff. They don't want to be around it. They want you to get over it. They don't want to talk about it, unless it's the final purge on your way to a healing.*
>
> —NAN E. COOK[1]

by mental illness . . . or driven to exhaustion by a nagging sense of inadequacy. Or struggling through some other crisis that left them feeling lost and ashamed and forgotten.

By taking me deeper still, God wanted to move me from being the good Christian girl I've always been—someone who knew all the right answers and had the best intentions and ran with the right crowd and tried to be nice and decent—to something far more real.

Not just a good Christian girl.

But God's Christian girl.

No more zipped-up, safe religion. No more religious happy talk. No more spiritualizing tricky real-life issues or covering up problems I didn't have easy answers for. No more pretending to have it all together for the sake of my "witness."

Instead, I was being called to plunge deeper still into the dark valleys of life.

The place where His light can shine the brightest.

THE GOD WHO GOES THERE TOO

I got the message, loud and clear. But as I've said, I was not in a good mood that day. At that moment, to be honest, I didn't feel much like being God's Christian anything.

So I answered back, "All right, Lord. So who's going to be there at the very bottom of this pit You've allowed me to go to? Who's going to be there for me?"

That's when I heard the Holy Spirit say, with infinite tenderness, *I am deeper still.*

And deep in my spirit, I knew it was true.

For I realized He had already kept me going through the previous traumatic months and years. And He has continued close through the writing of this book, which opened my eyes to pain I didn't even know was out there. Through surprises and revelations that shook me to the core—the sobering realization of the depth of my own sin and truly shocking revelations of sin by those I trusted most.

Just this past month, as I was finishing the final chapters, I and my church and the rest of the nation learned that my very prominent (and beloved) pastor had been involved in sexual sin and drug abuse. And while I've never believed that any of us is immune to sin, that was yet another trauma. Yet another blow. Some days I still couldn't breathe.

And still, the deeper I went into all of this messiness, the more I had to echo the psalmist's prayer (talk about a roller coaster!):

> If I go up to heaven, you are there;
>
> > if I go down to the place of the dead, you are there.
>
> If I ride the wings of the morning,
>
> > if I dwell by the farthest oceans,
>
> even there your hand will guide me,
>
> > and your strength will support me. (Ps. 139:8–10 NLT)

In everything I've gone through—even in the most agonizing ugliness—the Lord has been right there with me. Listening to my whining and complaining. Holding me close and comforting me. Teaching me and correcting me. Forgiving my many, many mistakes. Moving me (sometimes imperceptibly) toward strength and insight and purpose. Pouring grace and reconciliation and even joy into me through His Word. Through His felt presence. Through the miraculous timing of events and the miracle of changed perspective.

And also, profoundly, through the love and support of—you guessed it—other good Christian girls.

For I literally couldn't have made it through the past few years without my tough and tender and totally valiant sisters in Christ. These were the women who listened to the Lord's voice, obeyed His promptings, and dared to go deeper still into my world of pain. Women who have listened to me, cried with me, run errands for me, brought me soup and cookies, helped out at parties, hired my children, prayed for me faithfully, and dared tell the truth to me even when it hurt. Women who have inspired me to reach out to my sisters and weep with them, too, to comfort within the comfort I have been given (see Rom. 12:15; 2 Cor. 1:4).

And yes, of course there were men too. Wonderful godly men who helped me immensely. I thank God for them. But this is a book for women, so it's women I'm speaking to now. It's to you, my fellow good Christian girls, that I want to address this final chapter.

True Confessions

This book is called *Confessions of a Good Christian Girl*. And yes, the title is meant to be a little provocative. I wanted to pique your interest, to draw you in with something that sounded "juicy."

But now I want to leave you with something even juicier—in the best sense of the word. Something nourishing and lovely and full of life, just like the beautiful women who have ministered to me in the past few years. Just like I, in my deepest heart, aspire to be.

You see, a confession is more than just admitting what is wrong.

A confession is also a proclamation of what is right.

It's a statement of strong belief, a declaration of faith. And as such, this chapter is my confession about what it really means to be God's Christian girl.

For if I have been called to a ministry of deeper still, I believe you've been called as well. God wants us to be what He created us to be . . . and redeemed us to be . . . and taught us and loved us to be. His beloved daughters—treasured and cherished by a loving Father. But also His flesh-and-blood representatives in the world.

Stop for just a minute and think about what that means. It means that God not only loves us but trusts us. He values our input and our cooperation; He has confidence in our potential. He actually chooses to work through us. And if He sometimes has to do some quick stepping to bring good out of our mistakes (He's done some amazing dances to redeem some of my goofs!), well, He thinks we're worth it.

We have the honor of being the Lord's hands and feet and voice

> *The longer I work with wounded women, the more I am convinced*
> *that if a heart is open and truthful, there is no pain so deep or pervasive*
> *that God cannot heal it. Those who have been wounded and healed are*
> *then gifted in helping others heal. Wounds change us. They call forth*
> *our courage. They demand that we grow mentally, emotionally, and*
> *spiritually. When we face and embrace our pain, we are never again the*
> *same. We are better. And . . . the broken places of our life—the fractures,*
> *fissures, and jagged edges—can become the very locales where God's glory*
> *spills through in a torrent of light, hope, and healing. Out of our own*
> *personal darkness, God's penetrating light can touch*
> *those who still grope in the shadows.*
>
> —PAM VREDEVELT[2]

on earth. Telling the world who He is and what He's done. More important, showing the world what He's like. And going deeper still to serve as active agents of His grace to the broken people all around us—including good Christian girls who have lost their way or come to the end of their rope.

What does this mean in a practical sense? Let's take just a minute to explore what a call to deeper still looks like in the life of God's Christian girls.

CALLED TO BE REAL

In the first place, it means we're called to authenticity. Authentic means genuine. It means real. It means not hiding ourselves behind a facade— even a good Christian facade—but being honest with ourselves and others about our struggles, our failures, and our weaknesses. And not just the interesting ones. Not just the ones we're pretty sure will be excused or accepted. But also the messy, embarrassing ones. The ones that make us cringe and squirm just to admit they apply to us.

Authenticity, in fact, is the whole point of confession. It's a matter of opening our lives to God so we'll find healing . . . and opening our lives to others so we can learn from each other, help each other, speak truth to each other, and share God's healing grace. The book of 1 John calls this "living in the light":

> If we are living in the light of God's presence, just as Jesus is, then we have fellowship with each other, and the blood of Jesus, his Son, cleanses us from every sin. If we say we have no sin, we are only fooling ourselves and refusing to accept the truth. But if we confess our sins to him, he is faithful and just to forgive us and to cleanse us from every wrong. (1:7–9 NLT)

Living in the light isn't the same as emotional exhibitionism. It doesn't mean we dump all our issues on any poor soul who happens to be nearby. That kind of over-the-top confession can easily teeter over into reverse pride. ("Look how much I've sinned, how awful my life is!") With just a little bit of spin, it can become every bit as false as pious hypocrisy, a cover-up for real issues. It can also be abusive, a way of manipulating others. (It always amazes me how we humans tend to twist God's good gifts and use them for our own sinful purposes.)

But how different it looks when a good Christian girl dares to live transparently. Not hiding in shame or vying for attention. Not using one sin to distract from other, less embarrassing ones. Not trying to one-up anyone else's confession. But simply trusting God with the whole of her reality . . . letting His light into the dark places of her heart and soul and spirit and then shine through her as well. Seeking true healing and forgiveness instead of cover-ups and secrecy. And daring to let other people in on the process.

> *It was no small impact when I finally realized my religious pretense looked little like the life of Jesus and much more like a Pharisee. Discipleship for me had been defined by memorizing Bible verses, church attendance, praying before meals, some Bible reading, watching my language, and not getting drunk with my friends. Though I had read the Bible for years, it never really hit me that Jesus, God in the flesh, hung out among prostitutes, lepers, tax collectors, and betters. . . . God's invasion into time and space was vulgar to religious people, who dressed right, acted right, and played by society's rules. But Jesus did not. As a friend of sinners, he identified with, ate with, and touched the culture's rejected ones. What must happen in our churches to accept such behavior as normal, not exceptional? . . . When will we have the courage to condemn like Jesus did our own Pharisee-like behavior?*
>
> —JIMMY DORRELL[3]

And oh, this kind of authenticity can be hard. Sometimes it feels like humiliation rather than humility. We feel exposed and vulnerable. Shallow, surface Christianity starts to look good. Hypocrisy starts to sound like a plan.

But it's only when we dare unveil our deepest pain and shame to ourselves, to Christ, and to others that we find a way to connect to their deep pain. Only in this way do we earn "street cred"—the right to be heard and to be trusted.

Not that we'll ever do it perfectly. Not that we'll ever get the balance right. Not that we'll ever break entirely free of sin and self-deceit as long as we're on the earth. But just making the choice to seek the light with our lives makes such a difference. When we strive for authenticity, doing our best to let God's light into the dark places of our souls, we open up our lives—and the lives of others—to the healing flow of God's grace.

CALLED TO COMPASSION

In addition to being authentic, I absolutely believe we're called to be compassionate. And compassion means something far different than sympathy. It's more than feeling sorry for someone or having kindly thoughts.

The word *compassion* literally means "suffer with." We extend compassion to another person when we make an effort to enter her world and try to understand her—when we really see her potential and her pain, really listen to her needs, genuinely care about her feelings, and respond kindly and lovingly to her.

Compassion comes easiest when we've been there ourselves. One way God uses our pain is to help us understand the pain of others and to teach us what forms of ministry are most helpful. But compassion doesn't arrive automatically with difficulty. Pain can make us selfish. It can drive us to isolate ourselves, to avoid other people's problems, or to compare our pain with others and complain because we're worse off than they are.

Compassion is a choice, even for those who have known suffering. We must choose to see. We must choose to reach out to the other person and weep when they weep. We must choose to use our tears and pain (and some holy imagination) to relate, to build a bridge into another person's life instead of putting up a wall.

We may or may not be called to fix her problems. That may not be possible or appropriate. Her pain may require professional intervention or may be a matter between her and God. But taking the time to notice and care—to listen with our hearts as well as our ears, to weep when she weeps (Rom. 12:15)—is in itself a form of ministry.

This is how Jesus responded again and again to the sick and needy people who came to Him. He saw their hurt—that they were sick (Matt. 14:14; Mark 1:41) or hungry (Matt. 15:32) or "harassed and helpless, like sheep without a shepherd" (Matt. 9:36). (I don't know about you—but I know how those poor people felt!) And because He saw them, He was moved to heal them, feed them, and teach them.

> *When we honestly ask ourselves which people in our lives mean the most to us, we often find that it is those who, instead of giving advice, solutions, or cures, have chosen rather to share our pain and touch our wounds with a warm and tender hand. The friend who can be silent with us in a moment of despair or confusion, who can stay with us in an hour of grief and bereavement, who can tolerate not knowing, not curing, not healing and face with us the reality of our powerlessness, that is a friend who cares.*
>
> —HENRI NOUWEN[4]

CALLED TO PRACTICAL MINISTRY

And that, too, is part of God's deeper-still call to good Christian girls. He wants us to move from understanding and caring to practical, hands-on support. Not just giving a cup of cold water (or a casserole or a pot of soup) in the Lord's name—though that's a start—but doing whatever we can to ease another person's burdens.

Practical ministry, like compassion. begins with really seeing another's need. But it then applies energy, imagination, and elbow grease to help meet that need.

Jesus's words on this subject are pointed and clear. He stated that when we feed the hungry and clothe the naked and visit prisoners and take care of the sick we are actually ministering to Him (Matt. 25:31–46). And surely that applies to those who are hungry for friendship, naked of confidence or self-esteem, imprisoned by addiction or debt, or sick with worry. Whatever the need, a little thought and prayer is something practical we can do to help.

It could be an invitation to lunch . . . or an invitation to get involved preparing lunch for someone else. It could be as simple as taking dinner to a neighbor or as complicated as asking a single mom and her kids to live with you. Researching respite-care facilities, doing someone's taxes, mowing a busy neighbor's lawn as well as your own, helping a friend sort through her mother's effects—the possibilities are endless. And I consider prayer to be an intensely practical and effective offering. In fact, I've come to believe that prayers offered along with practical help double the effectiveness of the offering.

The point is, practical care isn't limited to food baskets and clothing drives, and it's certainly not just for certain categories of people. Anytime you notice a need and take steps to help meet that need—and you do it out of love—you're fulfilling God's call to practical ministry.

CALLED TO BE ENCOURAGERS

The wonderful thing about a commitment to authenticity and to practical acts of love and support is that they fulfill another kind of call, the call to provide encouragement. To encourage someone essentially means to give her courage or confidence or strength—to change her life, to keep trying, to do what's right, to draw closer to God.

I think of it as a ministry of motivation. It's what happens when you notice that someone's steps are faltering then come alongside to help her keep moving forward. To me, it's almost like locking arms with another person to give her strength. And the best thing about this kind of encouragement is that it's a two-way street. One day I'm the encourager; the next day I'm the one in need of a boost. So we move forward arm in arm, ministering grace to one another. In the words of Hebrews 10:24, we "spur one another on toward love and good deeds."[5]

There are so many ways to share encouragement—a word of confidence, a hug that reminds her she's loved, a helping gesture that saves time or energy, a note that says you're praying for her, even an honest comment that helps shift her perspective and focus her goals. Sometimes it's just a simple reminder that things will get better.

I'll never forget a woman who did that for me years ago, when my youngest child was about three. Mikia has always been a free spirit with a mind of her own—both a delight and a challenge. On this particular day she had insisted on wearing her favorite princess costume—complete with long white gown, gloves, and tiara—on a trip to the grocery store. I decided not to fight her on that—I had enough on my hands with four kids under seven and a mile-long grocery list. We got to the store, and I was hurrying to get my shopping done, when Mikia somehow got away from me. She shot around the corner with seven-year-old Mackenzie in hot pursuit. Mackenzie returned within seconds, a horrified look on her face.

"Mother," she gasped, "you have to come right now. It's an emergency." With my heart in my throat, I grabbed the other kids and followed Mackenzie.

I'll never forget the scene. Five or six other mothers had parked their carts—with their kids primly buckled into the seats—along the edges of the bean aisle. They were watching Mikia, in full royal regalia, turning cartwheels down the center of the aisle—with no underwear on.

> *Biblical encouragement is soul work. God unleashes its mysterious power every time a child of God follows the Holy Spirit's direction and steps into the suffering of another person. . . . As children of God, we have every tool we need to mend broken hearts and lives. So instead of isolating ourselves in a self-made cocoon of protection, we need to find out what those tools are, learn how to use them, and get to work.*
>
> —SHARON W. BETTERS[6]

I thought I would die. And then I was afraid I wouldn't! I thought, *Oh my goodness, I am actually going to live through this!* I knew the women where thinking, *What kind of a mother are you to bring your daughter into a grocery store with no underwear?* I just stood there mortified—until an older woman walked over to me, put her arm around me, and said, "That's okay, honey. That's okay. She'll wear underwear again someday."

That one little act of encouragement changed everything. I went from mortified embarrassment to relieved laughter, and the other women laughed with me—all because somebody cared enough to come alongside me and do something to lighten my load with a little perspective. In the process, she assured me that I wasn't alone, that someone cared, that there was grace for my mistakes and my failures.

And here's the great thing. Almost a decade later, I was able to pass along some of that encouragement to another young mother in another grocery store. I was there with my kids again, but this time they were teenagers. And as I stood in line to check out, my attention gradually focused on the woman in front of me. A woman with whom I obviously had nothing in common.

She was about nineteen. Every inch of her that I could see—and I could see a lot!—sported a tattoo of some sort or a piercing. Some places had multiple piercings. Her hair was dyed several different colors. And she was obviously having a bad day. She was skinny and pale and looked exhausted. Her little baby in the infant carrier was screaming. Her toddler grabbed for a package of candy and opened it, and she yelled at him while digging through her purse for food stamps and money—it was clear she was going to come up short. Everyone around was watching and frowning. You could feel that young woman's shame and desperation.

Then for some reason—it had to be the Holy Spirit—I looked at that young girl with her tattoos and piercing and multicolored hair and saw . . . me.

I saw that life was not working for her at that moment. And I had absolutely been there, especially as a mother. Though our worlds were far apart, we were more alike than different.

So I spoke to her, a little nervously. I asked about her baby and asked if I could hold her. I jiggled that sweet baby and told her I remembered what it was like to be a young mom. (It was about this point that my own kids disappeared, obviously thinking, *Oh brother. There goes Mom again, talking to a complete stranger.*)

Nothing much happened after that. We chatted as she went through the line and paid. We chatted a little more as my groceries started down the conveyor belt. I told her that being a parent is one of the hardest jobs around no matter what the situation and that it can seem overwhelming when life is pressing. I said what really matters is to be a mom who shows up, who works to love and care for her kids. And, of course, I said her kids were adorable.

She gathered up her toddler and baby and pushed her cart out of the store. My kids reappeared from somewhere. We started to load our bags of groceries back into a cart for our own trip to the parking lot. And then, out of nowhere, the young mother appeared. She slowly walked up to me with tears in her eyes and said, "I just have to thank you. That's the most encouragement I think I've ever had in my whole life."

Her whole life? My heart nearly broke to realize how difficult her life must be—that a random conversation with a stranger meant so much. But I also had to smile at the joy of being God's point person in encouraging that young woman. I knew she would be in my prayers for a long time.

We hugged. I whispered a few more words of encouragement. She left again. And I heard my daughter Mackenzie whisper at my elbow, "Mom," she said, "that was so cool."

That was when I realized that my simple decision to come alongside someone who was hurting . . . to look past our differences and really see her, to speak to her, to give a little bit of practical help and some encouraging words . . . had done so much more than I had intended. It had also shown my children how a deeper-still ministry could work. It ended up encouraging them and me too.

CALLED TO RECONCILIATION

Since that day in the grocery store, I have prayed that God would use our encounter not only to encourage that young woman in her current life but to bring her to a new kind of life altogether in Christ, to help repair the connection between her and her heavenly father. For one of the most powerful parts of a deeper-still ministry is the call to what the apostle Paul called a "ministry of reconciliation."

Reconcile is a word used for settling arguments, bringing harmony out of discord, restoring strained relationships, and bringing peace. Its root meaning is to repair or to make good again (remember "nothing missing, nothing broken"?), and it usually refers to healing or restoring relationships. As ministers of reconciliation, we're called to bring new life to people by helping restore their relationship with God and each other. Or more accurately, to relate to people in such a way that they're more open to God's reconciling and renewing work in their lives. Paul explains it this way:

> Therefore, if anyone is in Christ, he is a new creation; the old has gone, the new has come! All this is from God, who reconciled us to himself through Christ and gave us the ministry of reconciliation: that God was reconciling the world to himself in Christ, not counting men's sins against them. And he has committed to us the message of reconciliation. We are therefore Christ's ambassadors, as though God were making his appeal through us. (2 Cor. 5:17–19)

God's the one who does the real healing, restorative work in people's lives. But we're the messengers, the ambassadors, the go-betweens. Our job is to build relationships, make connections, establish a presence in people's lives that God can then use to restore their relationship with Him and with others. We are to present God's offer of healing so accurately that people can see how irresistible His offer is.

And note that this ministry isn't just to unbelievers. We're certainly charged with bringing the message of Christ to those who don't know Him, to showcase His irresistible love and show the power of His grace and forgiveness. But I believe we're also called to reach out to our fellow Christian girls who have lost their way and become estranged from their heavenly Father.

> *There is much more involved in reconciliation than in forgiveness. The two are not the same. Reconciliation requires two people who are willing to take ownership, in some way, for the problem. It means addressing the actual issues that led to the need to forgive in the first place. In being willing to forgive, we open our hearts to the possibility of a new relationship. . . . But the only part that is under our control is the ability to forgive. As the Bible says, "So far as it depends on you, be at peace with all men."*
>
> —PAULA RINEHART[7]

How do we carry out this healing work? Partly through our words—our honest and loving attempts to explain why we're Christians. But more powerfully by the way we live—through our honesty, our compassion, our practical help and encouragement. First Peter 3:15–16 brilliantly describes an effective ministry of reconciliation: "Worship Christ as Lord of your life. And if someone asks about your Christian hope, always be ready to explain it. But do this in a gentle and respectful way. Keep your conscience clear."

And of course, one of the most powerful ways to reconcile others with God is to make reconciliation a priority in our own lives—being willing to extend mercy and forgiveness to those who have hurt us, seeking forgiveness from those we have hurt and from God, seeking to reconcile our own painful and broken relationships. We won't always succeed right away, because true forgiveness often takes time and healing. We may not succeed at all in certain cases, because reconciliation requires the willingness of both parties. But the more we make the ministry of reconciliation a priority in our lives, the stronger our relationship with our heavenly Father will grow.

What God Can Do with a Yes

As good Christian girls, we're all called to a deeper-still ministry. We're all called to live real and authentic lives . . . to extend compassion to those who are hurting . . . to offer practical help . . . to encourage those who are lagging behind. We're all called to be Christ's ambassadors, living in such a way that we help restore people's relationships to God and each other.

But it goes without saying we won't always get it right.

If you're anything like me, in fact, you'll get it wrong a lot of the time!

You won't always have the courage to live authentically. Sometimes you'll be so caught up in denial that you won't even know you're being dishonest. Or you'll be so paralyzed by fear that you just can't face admitting your failures to another person. You'll fail to speak the truth as you understand it, or you'll speak the truth harshly and alienate people instead of drawing them to God.

Sometimes you won't have the insight or the energy—or even the interest—to be compassionate. Or your pain will loom so large you'll have a hard time caring about somebody else's suffering. Or you'll hide from your own sins by obsessing over others' failures, offering them judgment and condemnation instead of grace and compassion.

Sometimes you'll be too busy or preoccupied or just plain selfish to reach out in practical ways, too mired in your own sense of inadequacy to encourage someone else, too angry at God or someone else to even consider being a reconciler. Sometimes you won't even want to try.

And yes, I've been there. Multiple times. So, I'm willing to guess, have you.

The truth is, as long as we're sinners living in a fallen world, we're going to have trouble living as God's Christian girls. But the good news is that we don't have to be successful in order for God to use us. All we have to be is willing. All we really have to say is yes . . . and He'll take us from there.

God can do so much with a yes! He doesn't ever require us to be perfect—perfecting us is His job. But because He's given us free will, He won't do a thing with us until we say yes to Him.

Yes to what He wants to do in our lives.

Yes to letting Him change us and shape our destiny.

Yes to learning and adopting His point of view and sharing His concerns.

Yes to trying to be authentic and compassionate and practically helpful and encouraging and reconciling.

Yes to letting Him heal and comfort us "in all our troubles so that we can comfort others" (2 Cor. 1:4 NLT).

Yes to letting Him forgive our failures to get it right!

And yes to His view of what our part is in all of it—because that's one of the hardest things for any of us to get right. We just can't seem to keep straight what we're called to do and what God wants to do. That's why His call seems to be overwhelming at times. That's why we get so weary in well doing, why we burn out. That's why we turn into control freaks or fail to live up to our promises—or both! We keep trying to do God's job instead of ours.

You see, it's not our place to fix people or to save their souls. It's not our place to convict them of sin or grant them forgiveness (though we may be called to speak truthfully about sin and grace). All that is God's job—and He does it beautifully. He's the one in charge of the whole process. He's the one who works through us to love and guide others. And of course He's the one who keeps caring for us in all our roller-coaster ups and downs.

So what is our job? It's really a lot simpler than we think it is.

Our job is to listen to Him.

Our job is to obey Him.

Our job is to step out in faith, moving forward even when we don't think we can.

Our job is to keep coming to Him for help and comfort and forgiveness.

And our job, most of all, is to remember who we are . . . and who God is.

And then to get ourselves out of the way so God can do His work.

Letting God Show Off

I learned this anew recently when I traveled to speak at a women's conference. I had been booked as the keynote speaker many months in advance. But so much had happened between the time I signed the contract and the time I was called to speak. By the time I boarded the plane that autumn afternoon, I couldn't remember being so discouraged. I was simply overwhelmed by events in my life, all the upheaval in my family. And here I was scheduled to bring inspiration and comfort to several thousand women. I just didn't think I had it in me.

I didn't sleep that night. In fact, I cried most of the night. And I woke up that next morning to find my eyes were literally swollen shut. I mean, I looked like someone had beaten me with a stick. No kidding!

How can I do this? I thought. There I was squinting at the mirror trying to curl my eyelashes, applying cold packs to eyes that wouldn't even open . . . and I was supposed to speak on "The God Who Sees You." And I'm thinking, *God, I hope Your eyes are not as swollen as mine, because I can't see a thing!*

The phone rang as I was trying to apply my lipstick. My dear friend Emily was calling to see how I was and to pray with me. "I had the worst night last night," I told her. "I don't think I have anything to give."

"Well that's good, Tammy," she said. (She's a wise woman.) "Because when you are weak, God is strong."

"Well," I said with a sigh, "God gets to be a big show-off today."

And He was. I stumbled onto the stage that morning in all of my bleary-eyed glory. I opened my mouth to speak though I felt I had nothing to say. And that's when God showed up—and He showed up big. I have never felt such anointing in my life. I shared honestly about what I was walking through, what I was learning about God's love. And the women responded with floods of tears. Hundreds came down for prayer at the end of my talk. Hundreds more stood in line to talk to me afterward. They thanked me. They also reached out to minister to me. Some of them held my hand and prayed.

When I boarded the plane for home that night, I found my seat, sank down, and burst into sobs of exhaustion and wonder. "Only You could do that, God. You really were a show-off today, weren't You?

I could almost hear Him saying, *Good. Finally, this is not about you. Finally it's about Me!*

And thank God it is. That's the way it should have been all along.

It's not about me! It's about what God's doing in my life . . . and the lives of all His girls. And through it all, we can trust Him to keep loving us. To keep us growing. To strengthen us and move us forward. To find us when, once again, we lose our way.

And we will. That's another given for good Christian girls living in a fallen world.

No matter how many times we've been lost and found, we may still be lost again.

We may feel forgotten, alone, bereft. We may feel we have nothing to give.

But the problem is with our own vision, not God's provision.

It's with our faith, not His faithfulness.

Because even when we are weak, He is strong.

And even when we think He's not doing anything, He's moving heaven and earth to bring us home to Him—as I realized a few years ago when my son Samuel got stuck at the airport.

> *I'm just one small part in what God is doing in my corner of the world. But I love to see how I fit in—how blessings given to me have multipled manyfold in the lives of so many others. This, in fact, is the greatest blessing of all.*
>
> —Emilie Barnes[8]

He Knows

When my son Samuel was about twelve or thirteen, he went away to camp. Far away—all the way from our Colorado home to upstate New York. It was a big rite of passage for him, and it went great. Phone calls and a few letters let us know he was thriving . . . and that he'd be home soon.

I couldn't wait. I'm crazy about my son. I've been crazy about him from the moment he was put in my arms from Korea. He's just a treasure of my heart. And I'd missed him terribly—he'd never been away from home so long before. So I spent days getting everything ready for him. I'd changed his sheets and cleaned his room and stocked up on his favorite snacks. I'd cooked a huge roast—we always joked about Sam's fondness for "dead animal." I was thinking about him every moment. I had his airline schedule posted promptly on my calendar. I was literally counting the hours.

Around breakfast time, when Sam's plane was scheduled to take off from New York City, the phone rang. It was the camp. Sam had missed his flight that morning and would have to be put on another flight. I'd have to pick him up a little later than I planned.

"Oh, all right," I said. I wasn't thrilled with the delay, but I wasn't that worried either. I just said a little prayer and continued puttering around the house . . . until the phone rang again. This time it was the airline.

"Mrs. Maltby, we're sorry to tell you, but your son's flight has been canceled. We're going to have to put him on another one."

Again? I was beginning to get a little anxious. I knew these things happened. But I didn't like the idea of my son spending all that time by himself at the airport. Still, I was glad they caught me before I started the drive to the Denver airport to pick him up. I puttered around a little more, keeping one eye on the clock.

I was just heading for the garage with my keys in hand when the phone rang again. And again it was "Mrs. Maltby, I'm sorry . . ." This time the crew of Sam's flight had gone into overtime and couldn't fly. You guessed it. Sam would have to be put on yet another flight.

Well, by this point I was getting a little hysterical. I was upstairs on the World Wide Web, searching frantically for alternate ways to get Sam home.

I thought about cashing in airline miles. I made a list of everybody I knew in New York City who could go pick him up. I was ready to get in my red Suburban and drive all the way to New York and get him. I mean, I was getting anxious. I was screaming downstairs at my husband, telling him he needed to be upstairs as upset about this as I was. The whole house was in chaos because I was so concerned about my son being stuck at the airport. He was all I could think of.

Finally, about five-thirty that afternoon, the phone rang again. And this time it was my son.

"Hi Mom," he said. "This is Sam."

I laughed. "I know!"

Then he said, "Mom, do you know I've been at the airport all day long?"

He thought I had forgotten about him!

And I was absolutely horrified that he would think that.

I said "Samuel, I have been thinking about you all day long. You are the only thing I have been thinking about all day long. I've been on the phone. I've been on the World Wide Web. I've been doing everything I possibly can to get you home to me!"

It was only after I hung up the phone that the Holy Spirit spoke to me. Not in clear words this time, but the picture was clear:

Tammy, I do that for you all the time. You are lost and stuck in your guilt and your shame and your mistakes and your failures . . . and you don't think I know. You think I've forgotten you, that I don't understand what you're going through. Even that I don't care.

But I see you. I care passionately about what you're going through.

251

And not only that—I'm hard at work on your behalf. I'm on the real World Wide Web, arranging events for your benefit. And I am calling Sue and Jennifer and Lisa, stirring up My good Christian girls to help you and encourage you.

You don't think I see. You don't think I'm at work.

But just because you don't see it doesn't mean that I'm not doing it.

And it's all because I love you. Because I see you.

Because I want you and all My girls home with Me.

Don't you love that picture?

A loving God in charge, and all of us good Christian girls (and boys!) listening to His heart, following His lead—reaching out, going deep, living out His grace in absolutely irresistible, life-changing ways.

I've seen it happen in some of life's deepest, darkest muck.

And you've seen it too. I know you have.

You've caught the vision and said yes to God's call.

You're living in the light, reaching out in compassion, putting hands and feet to the gospel, linking arms with other Christians. Going deep—and deeper still. Reaching out wide to one another and to God. Going with the flow of endless mercy and grace, and taking the roller-coaster hills and valleys as they come.

Safe in the Father's arms.

Side by side with your sisters and brothers in Christ.

On a good day—and there'll be plenty—maybe you'll even want to yell, "Whee!"

And this good Christian girl is going to be yelling it right beside you!

❧ WORD OF GRACE FOR GOD'S CHRISTIAN GIRLS ❧

Not "There but for the grace of God go I."
But "There in the grace of God . . . we're traveling together."

Appendix A

- Listen first! The very act of listening with care and attention eases pain and brings healing.

- Even if the confession shocks you, try not to judge or condemn. (Jesus wouldn't.) Try to focus on the person, not the sin. Remind yourself that she is a child of God, that God loves her despite her sin, and that the very act of confession is positive.

- Pray! Ask God to love the other person through you. Put her in God's hands.

- Don't sit on an emergency. If there is a threat of suicide or you suspect physical abuse, urge the person to contact a helpline or a professional immediately—or do it for her. Check back to see if she has followed through and gotten help.

- Don't hold back your tears. Weeping with those who weep is an incredibly powerful and biblical strategy. We aren't called to heal people or make them change. We're called to come alongside, love them, and let God do the rest.

- Don't rush in to fix things or explain the unexplainable. Concentrate on coming alongside with practical support and emotional companionship.

- Be clear about what you're called to be. You're a friend and a Christian sister. You're not a therapist (unless you happen to be one!), a police officer, etc. And you're not God. So offer your listening, your support, your prayers, your presence, and if necessary your help in locating further guidance. Keep on checking your balance: what is your role, what is Jesus's role, what is the role of trained professionals?

- Remind yourself and the other person that God's not finished yet. Despair is always shortsighted and presumptuous. God always has a plan B.

- Share your own brokenness—if appropriate, your own confession. (But beware of being caught up in a round of "dueling traumas.")

- Honestly share the "comfort [you yourself] have received from God" (2 Cor. 1:4). But don't mouth platitudes just to have something to say.

- Be careful about volunteering advice. Love silently until the other person asks or the Holy Spirit prompts strongly. Then be willing to speak the truth in love.

- If you're having difficulty being there for the other person, consider what factors may be holding you back. Are you afraid of doing the wrong thing? Is denial about your own sin making you judgmental? Are you afraid of being "sucked in" to the problem? Are you doubtful that even God can help? Make these issues a focus of prayer.

- Ask God for ideas of how you can be of practical assistance— and obey any "nudge" from the Holy Spirit as quickly as you can.

- Do your best to keep promises. Don't offer help that you're not prepared to follow up on. A Christian sister who's hurting doesn't need to be let down again by you. Be honest with yourself and the other person about what you can take on. At the same time, if you honestly feel you're called to come alongside . . . do it.

- Do something to help, even if it's small. You're not called to be all things to all people, just to be an obedient part of what God is doing for this person. If offered sincerely and prayerfully, your brief note or little box of cookies can be just what someone needs.

- Remember to extend grace and forgiveness to yourself, to accept God's grace for your efforts. You won't always get things right, but God can do a lot with your loving intentions.

Appendix B

God's provision for the hurting times in my life often comes through face-to-face contact with loving people, but it also arrives through books and other resources that both teach me and minister to my soul. Here are some resources that have been meaningful to me—I hope they help you too.

GRACE-FILLED RESOURCES
FOR ANY HURTING CHRISTIAN GIRL

American Association of Christian Counselors Web site. This site offers helpful articles on a number of topics plus help in finding a reputable Christian counselor. Access at http://www.aacc.net.

Gire, Ken. *Windows of the Soul.* Grand Rapids: Zondervan, 1996.

Graham, Ruth with Stacy Mattingly. *In Every Pew Sits a Broken Heart: Hope for the Hurting.* Grand Rapids: Zondervan, 2004.

Manning, Brennan. *Abba's Child: The Cry of the Heart for Intimate Belonging.* Colorado Springs: NavPress, 2002.

Manning, Brennan. *The Ragamuffin Gospel: Good News for the Bedraggled, Beat-Up, and Burned Out.* Sisters, OR: Multnomah, 2005.

Stephens, Steve and Pam Vredevelt. *The Wounded Woman: Hope and Healing for Those Who Hurt.* Sisters, OR: Multnomah, 2006.

Today's Christian Woman Web site. Contains great articles for good Christian girls who are hurting *and* good Christian girls who want to help. Access at http://www.christianitytoday.com/women.

Troubledwith Web site. This excellent site, sponsored by Focus on the Family, provides articles, resources, and referrals on a number of family-related topics including abuse and addiction, life pressures, love and sex, parenting, relationships, and transitions. Access online at http://troubledwith.com.

Yancey, Philip. *What's So Amazing about Grace?* Grand Rapids: Zondervan, 1997.

RESOURCES FOR DESPERATE CHRISTIAN GIRLS (SUICIDE)

National Suicide Prevention Lifeline. This confidential, twenty-four-hour service routes callers to local crisis centers across the country. For more information access http://www.suicidepreventionlifeline.org or call the hotline at 1-800-273-TALK (8255).

Blauner, Susan Rose. *How I Stayed Alive When My Brain Was Trying to Kill Me: One Person's Guide to Suicide Prevention.* New York: HarperCollins, 2003.

Center for Disease Control and National Center for Injury Prevention and Control. "Suicide: Fact Sheet." Access at http://www.suicidepreventionlifeline.org or call the hotline at 1-800-273-TALK (8255).

Cox, David and Candy Arrington. *Aftershock: Help, Hope, and Healing in the Wake of Suicide.* Nashville: Broadman & Holman, 2003.

Hsu, Albert Y. Hsu. *Grieving a Suicide: A Loved One's Search for Comfort, Answers and Hope.* Downers Grove, IL: InterVarsity, 2002.

Suicide Prevention Action Network USA (SPAN USA) Web site. Access at http://www.spanusa.org.

Suicide Prevention Resource Center. Access at http://www.sprc.org/index.asp.

RESOURCES FOR SEXUALLY BROKEN CHRISTIAN GIRLS (SEXUAL ISSUES)

Dillow, Linda and Lorraine Pintus. *Intimate Issues: 21 Questions Christian Women Ask about Sex.* Colorado Springs: Waterbrook, 1999.

Ethridge, Shannon. *Every Woman's Battle: Discovering God's Plan for Sexual and Emotional Fulfillment.* Colorado Springs: Waterbrook, 2003.

Laaser, Mark R. *Healing Wounds of Sexual Addiction.* Grand Rapids: Zondervan, 2004.

Schaumburg, Harry W. *False Intimacy: Understanding the Struggle of Sexual Addiction.* Colorado Springs: NavPress, 1992.

Willingham, Russell. *Breaking Free: Understanding Sexual Addiction and the Healing Power of Jesus.* Downers Grove, IL: InterVarsity, 1999.

RESOURCES FOR DESOLATE CHRISTIAN GIRLS (ABUSE)

National Domestic Violence Hotline: 800-799-SAFE (7233).

Allender, Dan B. *The Wounded Heart: Hope for Adult Victims of Childhood Sexual Abuse.* Colorado Springs: NavPress, 1990.

Bancroft, Lundy. *Why Does He Do That?: Inside the Minds of Angry and Controlling Men.* New York: Berkley, 2003.

Barnhill, Julie Ann. *She's Gonna Blow: Real Help for Moms Dealing with Anger.* Eugene, OR: Harvest House, 2001.

Branson, Brenda and Paula Silva. "Domestic Violence Among Believers: Confronting the Destructive Secret." *Christian Counseling Today.* Vol. 13 (2005), 3:24–27. Access online at http://www.focusministries1.org/pdf/CCT2005.pdf. The Focus Ministries Web site (http://www.focusministries.org) provides a wealth of excellent help for Christian women.

Fortune, Marie M. *Keeping the Faith: Guidance for Christian Women Facing Abuse.* San Francisco: HarperSanFrancisco, 1987.

Hegstrom, Paul. *Angry Men and the Women Who Love Them: Breaking the Cycle of Physical and Emotional Abuse.* Kansas City, MO: Beacon Hill, 2004.

Hegstrom, Paul. *Broken Children, Grown Up Pain: Understanding the Effects of Your Wounded Past.* Kansas City, MO: Beacon Hill, 2005.

Kroeger, Catherine Clark and Nancy Nason-Clark. *No Place for Abuse: Biblical and Practical Resources to Counteract Domestic Violence.* Downers Grove, IL: InterVarsity, 2001.

Miles, Al. *Violence in Families: What Every Christian Needs to Know.* Minneapolis: Augsburg Fortress, 2002.

Safeplace Ministries Web site. An excellent source of information and help on many different kinds of abuse. Access at http://www.safeplace.com (not www.safeplace.org.)

White, Amy Wildman. "The Silent Killer of Christian Marriages." In Catherine Clark Kroeger and James R. Beck, eds. *Healing the Hurting.* Grand Rapids: Baker, 1998. Access online October 2006 at http://www.safeplaceministries.com/EmotionalAbuseArticle.htm.

World Evangelical Fellowship Task Force to Stop Abuse Against Women, "The Teaching of Scripture," *Biblical Statement of Human Dignity.* Access online at http://www.abuseofwomen.org/thesis_sec3.html.

Appendix B

RESOURCES FOR HEARTBROKEN CHRISTIAN GIRLS
(FAILED RELATIONSHIPS AND DIVORCE)

Barna Group, The. "The Barna Update: Born Again Christians Just As Likely to Divorce As Are Non-Christians." September 8, 2004. Access at http://www.barna.org/FlexPage.aspx?Page=BarnaUpdate&BarnaUpdateID=170.

Clinton, Tim and Gary Sibcy. *Attachments: Why You Love, Feel, and ACT the Way You Do: Unlock the Secret to Loving and Lasting Relationships.* Brentwood, TN: Integrity, 2002.

DivorceCare Web site. Excellent site featuring helpful information on groups and dealing with kids. Access at http://divorcecare.com.

Growthtrac Web site. This site http://www.growthtrac.com offers some excellent articles on living through failed relationships as well as help for strengthening a struggling relationship. Access the divorce articles at http://www.growthtrac.com/artman/topics/10.php.

Lucado, Max. *The Dark Country of Divorce.* San Antonio, TX: UpWords Ministry, 1996. Electronic version available at http://www.maxlucado.com/pdf/divorce.pdf#search=%22Malachi%20%22God%20hates%20divorce%22%22.

Nelson, Carla Sue, Connie Wetzell, Michelle Borquez, and Rosalind Spinks-Seay. *Live, Laugh, Love Again: A Christian Woman's Survival Guide to Divorce.* New York: FaithWords, 2006.

RESOURCES FOR TRAPPED CHRISTIAN GIRLS (ADDICTIONS)

12-Step.org Web site. This Web site is a good place to start for information about the many recovery programs based on the "Twelve Step" recovery model of Alcoholics Anonymous. Includes a list of specifically Christian resources. Access online at http://www.12step.org.

Alcoholics Anonymous World Services. *Alcoholics Anonymous.* 4th Ed. New York: Alcoholics Anonymous World Services, 2001 (original copyright 1939). Access online at http://www.aa.org/bigbookonline.

Baker, John. *Stepping Out of Denial into God's Grace, Participant's Guide #1,* Celebrate Recovery Program. Grand Rapids: Zondervan, 2004.

Baker, John. *Taking an Honest and Spiritual Inventory, Participant's Guide #1,* Celebrate Recovery Program. Grand Rapids: Zondervan, 2004.

Baker, John. *Getting Right with God, Yourself, and Others, Participant's Guide #1,* Celebrate Recovery Program. Grand Rapids: Zondervan, 2004.

Baker, John. *Growing in Christ While Helping Others, Participant's Guide #1,* Celebrate Recovery Program. Grand Rapids: Zondervan, 2004.

Beattie, Melody. *Codependents' Guide to the 12 Steps: How to Find the Right Program for You and Apply Each of the Twelve Steps to Your Own Issues.* New York: Fireside/ Simon & Schuster, 1998.

Celebrate Recovery. This Christ-centered "twelve step" recovery program originated in Lake Forest, California's Saddleback Church's and has been duplicated in more than five hundred churches across the nation. Celebrate Recovery applies biblical principles and small group support to help people grow spiritually and break free from addictive, compulsive, and dysfunctional behaviors. More information on this program can be found in the four books by John Baker listed above and at http://www.celebraterecovery.com.

Dodes, Lance M. *The Heart of Addiction: A New Approach to Understanding and Managing Alcoholism and Other Addictive Behaviors.* New York: HarperCollins, 2002.

May, Gerald. *Addiction and Grace.* San Francisco, HarperSanFrancisco, 1988.

Miller, J. Keith. *A Hunger for Healing: The Twelve Steps As a Classic Model for Christian Spiritual Growth.* San Francisco: HarperSanFrancisco, 1991.

Minirth, Frank et. al. *Love Hunger: Breaking Free from Food Addiction.* Nashville: Thomas Nelson, 2004.

Spickard Jr., Anderson and Barbara R. Thompson. *Dying for a Drink: What You and Your Family Should Know about Alcoholism.* Nashville: W Publishing, 2005.

Stoop, David A. and Stephen Arterburn. *Twelve Step Life Recovery Devotional: Thirty Meditations from Scripture for Each Step in Recovery.* Wheaton, IL: Tyndale House, 1991.

Thompson, Tom. "Myth 2: 'Addiction Is Not a Sickness; It Is Simply Repetitive Sin." Article on American Association of Christian Counselors Web site. Access online at http://aacc.net/2006/04/11/myth-2-â??addiction-is-not-a-sickness-it-is-simply-repetitive-sinâ?.

RESOURCES FOR TORMENTED CHRISTIAN GIRLS
(MENTAL ILLNESS)

Bloem, Steve and Robyn Bloem. *Broken Minds: Hope for Healing When You Feel Like You're "Losing It."* Grand Rapids: Kregel, 2005.

Brunson, Harold. "Mental Illness and Demon Possession." Sermon preached September

18, 2005 at Parker Baptist Church, Parker, Texas. Available online as an audio file at http://www.sermonaudio.com/sermoninfo.asp?SID=10300514137.

Greene-McCreight, Kathryn. *Darkness Is My Only Companion: A Christian Response to Mental Illness.* Grand Rapids: Baker, 2006.

Hope to Healing. A Web site that shares stories of hope from those suffering from mental illness. Access online at http://www.hopetohealing.com.

National Alliance on Mental Illness. An excellent source of information and support. Accessed online at http://www.NAMI.org.

Resources for Driven Christian Girls
("Not Enough")

Anderson, Fil. *Running on Empty: Contemplative Spirituality for Overachievers.* Colorado Springs: Waterbrook, 2004.

Card, Michael. *A Sacred Sorrow: Reaching Out to God in the Lost Language of Lament.* Colorado Springs: NavPress, 2005.

Gire, Ken. *The North Face of God: Hope for the Times When God Seems Indifferent.* Wheaton, IL: Tyndale, 2005.

Rohr, Richard. *Simplicity: The Freedom of Letting Go.* Revised Edition. New York: Crossroad, 2004.

Sorge, Bob. *Secrets of the Secret Place: Keys to Igniting Your Personal Time with God.* Greenwood, MO: Oasis, 2001.

Resources for God's Christian Girls
(How to Help Others)

Betters, Sharon W. *Treasure in the Darkness: A Grieving Mother Shares Her Heart.* Phillipsburg, NJ: P&R, 1996.

Betters, Sharon W. *Treasures of Encouragement: Women Helping Women in the Church.* Phillipsburg, NJ: P&R, 1996.

Dorrell, Jimmy. *Trolls and Truth: 14 Realities about Today's Church That We Don't Want to See.* Birmingham, AL: New Hope, 2006.

Heavilin, Marilyn Willett. *Roses in December: Comfort for the Grieving Heart.* Eugene, OR: Harvest House, 2006.

Nouwen, Henri. *The Wounded Healer.* New York: Doubleday, 1979.

Notes

Chapter 1: "Daddy, Are You There?" Why Even Good Christian Girls Need a Word of Grace

1. Retold from a story in Ken Gire, *Windows of the Soul* (Grand Rapids: Zondervan, 1996), 215.
2. Brennan Manning, *The Ragamuffin Gospel: Good News for the Bedraggled, Beat-Up, and Burned Out* (Sisters, OR: Multnomah, 2005), 85.
3. Angela Thomas, *A Beautiful Offering: Returning God's Love with Your Life* (Nashville: Nelson, 2004), 18–19.
4. Charles H. Spurgeon, from *Morning and Evening* (Grand Rapids: Christian Classics Ethereal Library), Evening, August 22. Accessed 1 October 2006 at http://www.ccel.org/ccel/spurgeon/morneve.d0822pm.html.
5. Some of these modern-day women have given me full permission to tell their story as it happened and to use their real names. Others have asked that I change names and recognizable details, usually to protect the privacy of children and other family members. I have honored their requests. For the same reasons, I have changed a few details about my own circumstances. The essentials of every story, however, are entirely true and were told to me by the women involved.

Chapter 2: "I Can't Take It Anymore" The Desperate Pain of Suicide

1. Thomas Merton, *New Seeds of Contemplation* (New York: New Directions, 1961), 15.
2. From Robert Robinson's wonderful hymn, "Come, Thou Fount of Every Blessing," written in 1758. The entire line is "Prone to wander, Lord, I feel it, prone to leave the God I love. Here's my heart, O take and seal it. Seal it for thy courts above."
3. Susie Davis, *The Time of Your Life: Finding God's Rest in Your Busy Schedule* (Sisters, OR: Multnomah, 2005), 43.

Notes

4. Larry Crabb, *Shattered Dreams: God's Unexpected Pathway to Joy* (Colorado Springs: Waterbrook 2001), 57.

5. Brennan Manning, *The Ragamuffin Gospel: Good News for the Bedraggled, Beat-Up, and Burned Out* (Sisters, OR: Multnomah, 2005), 85.

Chapter 3: "I Just Want to Be Loved" The Shadowy Secrets of Sexual Brokenness

1. Rick Warren, "Saddleback Sayings," *Rick Warren's Ministry Toolbox: Rick Warren's Free Newsletter to Help Those in Ministry Grow Healthier Churches*, No. 1 (March 19, 2001), accessed 1 October 2006 at http://www.pastors.com/RWMT/printerfriendly.asp?issue=1&wholething=1.

2. Claire shared all this with me in a personal e-mail—used by permission.

3. *Aspiring Women* interview, episode #0516, "Hooked on Sex," first aired 23 January 2006. Used by permission.

4. Details taken from an e-mail and a phone interview. Used by permission.

5. Michael Card, *A Sacred Sorrow: Reaching Out to God in the Lost Language of Lament* (Colorado Springs: NavPress, 2005), 65.

6. From transcript of "Hooked on Sex."

7. Mario Bergner, "Go! And Sin No More" *Redeemed Lives News*, Autumn 2003, accessed at http://www.redeemedlives.org/Resources/Nws_atcl/2003/autumn03sin-print.htm.

Chapter 4: "You Can't Treat Me This Way!" The Desolation of Family Violence and Abuse

1. Catherine Clark Kroeger and Nancy Nason-Clark, *No Place for Abuse: Biblical and Practical Resources to Counteract Domestic Violence* (Downers Grove, IL: InterVarsity, 2001), 15–16.

2. Unfortunately, there are no specific studies into the percentage of Christian homes that are touched by all kinds of abuse, but we can get a good picture from studies of smaller samples and of the larger population. For instance, a United States Department of Justice 1998 publication reported that 22.1 percent of American women have been physically assaulted by an intimate partner in their lifetime. A smaller-scale study by the Christian Reformed Church in North America revealed that 28 percent of church members surveyed had experienced at least one form of abuse.

3. Women do abuse men, although statistically speaking, this is far less common—not because women are less sinful, but because in our culture men are usually more powerful. Al Miles discusses this helpfully in *Violence in Families: What Every Christian Needs to Know* (Minneapolis: Augsburg Fortress, 2002), 32–33.

4. Julie Ann Barnhill, *She's Gonna Blow: Real Help for Moms Dealing with Anger* (Eugene, OR: Harvest House, 2001), 131.

5. Ibid.

6. According to Catherine Clark Kroeger and Nancy Nason-Clark, "Between 50 and 75 percent of the men who batter their wives experienced or witnessed abuse in their own childhood home." Quoted in Kroeger and Nason-Clark, *No Place for Abuse*, 33.

7. Quoted in Kroeger and Nason-Clark, *No Place for Abuse*, 67. Reference given is www.weaveinc.org/facts.html.

8. For a concise and extremely helpful discussion of emotional abuse, see Amy Wildman White, "The Silent Killer of Christian Marriages" in Catherine Clark Kroeger and James R. Beck, eds., *Healing the Hurting* (Grand Rapids: Baker, 1998). Accessed online 1 October 2006 at http://www.safeplaceministries.com/Emotional%20Abuse%20Article.html.

9. Kroeger and Nason-Clark, *No Place for Abuse*, 34–35.

10. Ibid., 121.

11. World Evangelical Fellowship Task Force to Stop Abuse Against Women, "The Teaching of Scripture," *Biblical Statement of Human Dignity*. Accessed online at http:www.abuseofwomen.org/thesis_sec3.html.

12. Kate Dunn, "Fears, Foes and Family," Sermon preached at Rutgers Presbyterian Church, NYC, 20 June 1999.

13. World Evangelical Fellowship Task Force to Stop Abuse Against Women, "Hope for the Abused and the Abuser," *Biblical Statement of Human Dignity*. Accessed online at http://www.abuseofwomen.org/thesis_sec11.html.

14. Nicholas Wolterstorff, *Lament for a Son* (Grand Rapids: Eerdmans, 1987), 80–81.

15. Bonnie Nicholas, "Tamar and Amnon," a talk based on 2 Samuel 13, given at a one-day retreat for survivors of abuse. Accessed online at the InterVarsity Ministry Exchange: http://www.intervaristy.org/mx/item/4891/?PHPSESSID=0d53cae781638d4a442f48915cbf9c3327.

Chapter 5: "It Should Have Been Forever" The Heartbreak of Divorce and Failed Relationships

1. The Barna Group, "The Barna Update: Born Again Christians Just As Likely to Divorce As Are Non-Christians," 8 September 2004. Accessed October 2006 at http://www.barna.org/FlexPage.aspx?Page=BarnaUpdate&BarnaUpdateID=170.

2. Nancy Pickering, column in *The Parish Paper*, Church of the Ascension, Knoxville, TN, 15 August 1999.

3. Kari West and Noelle Quinn, *When He Leaves: Help and Hope for Hurting Wives* (Eugene, OR: Harvest House, 1998), 247.

4. Remember, I'm guessing at these details of her life. Based on the biblical evidence, however, I think it's a good possibility . . . or something like it.

Notes

5. Ruth Graham, *In Every Pew Sits a Broken Heart: Hope for the Hurting* (Grand Rapids: Zondervan, 2005), 213.

6. Arthur Schopenhauer, *The Essays by Arthur Schopenhauer, Studies in Pessimism,* tr. T. Bailey Saunders (London, 1892), Project Gutenberg eBook #10732, 17 January 2004, 55. Accessed 30 May 2006 at http://www.gutenberg.org/catalog/world/readfile?fk.files=44977.

7. Wendy M. Wright, *The Vigil: Keeping Watch in the Season of Christ's Coming* (Nashville: Upper Room, 1992), 42.

8. D. Moody Smith, "The Woman of Samaria," BibleTexts.com Glossary of Terms, from James Luther Mays, ed., *Harper's Bible Commentary* (New York: Harper and Row, 1988). Accessed 21 September 2006 at http://www.bibletexts.com/glossary/woman-of-samaria.htm.

9. According to several sources I consulted, the Hebrew word used in this scripture is actually the word for when a man put his wife out of the house without a formal bill of divorcement—effectively abandoning her without a means of support or the freedom to marry again. And yes, I'd say that God hates that! For further explanation see Stephen Gola, "Which 'Divorce' Does God Hate? Does God Really 'Hate Divorce'? on Gola's Divorce Hope Web site, http://www.divorcehope.com/godhatesdivorce.htm.

10. Max Lucado, *The Dark Country of Divorce* (San Antonio, TX: UpWords Ministry, 1996), 6–7. Electronic version accessed 24 September 2006 at http://www.maxlucado.com/pdf/divorce.pdf#search=%22Malachi%20%22 God%20hates%20divorce%22%22.

Chapter 6: "I Never Meant to Go There" The Treacherous Trap of Addiction

1. Eating disorders such as anorexia nervosa and bulimia are tricky to classify. Some sources list them as forms of mental illness, some consider them purely a psychological result of cultural and family pressures, and others—especially in the past few decades—consider as reverse or "avoidant" addiction. Regardless of their classification, these disorders share many traits with "classic" addictions and have responded to similar treatment, including the twelve-step program Overeaters Anonymous. I have chosen to follow the lead of Gerald May in his book *Addiction and Grace* (San Francisco: Harper & Row, 1988) and include them in this chapter.

2. Anderson Spickard Jr. and Barbara R. Thompson describe several such scenarios in their superb book, *Dying for a Drink: What You and Your Family Should Know About Alcoholism* (Nashville: W Publishing, 2005), 3.

3. Spickard and Thompson describe several such scenarios in their superb book, *Dying for a Drink: What You and Your Family Should Know about Alcoholism.* See, for example, chapters 2 through 5.

4. David Eckman, *Sex, Food, and God: Breaking Free from Temptations, Compulsions, and Addictions* (Eugene: Harvest House, 2006), 32.

5. Luci Swindoll, *The Alchemy of the Heart: Life's Refining Process to Free Us from Ourselves* (Sisters, OR: Multnomah, 1984), 182.

6. Stephen Arterburn, *Healing Is a Choice: Ten Decisions That Will Transform Your Life and Ten Lies That Can Prevent You from Making Them* (Nashville: Thomas Nelson, 2005), 215. Reprinted by permission. All rights reserved.

7. Tom Thompson, "Myth 2: 'Addiction Is Not a Sickness; It Is Simply Repetitive Sin,'" American Association of Christian Counselors Web site, accessed August 2006 at http://aacc.net/2006/04/11/myth-2-â??addiction-is-not-a-sickness-it-is-simply-repetitive-sinâ?.

8. Spickard and Anderson, *Dying for a Drink,* 30.

9. Ibid.

10. Pam Vredevelt, in Steve Stephens and Pam Vredevelt, *The Wounded Woman: Hope and Healing for Those Who Hurt* (Sisters, OR: Multnomah, 2006), 150–51.

11. Henri Nouwen, *Turn My Mourning into Dancing: Finding Hope in Hard Times*, comp. and ed. Timothy Jones (Nashville: W Publishing Group, 2001), xv. Reprinted by permission. All rights reserved.

12. Beth Moore, *Jesus the One and Only* (Nashville: Broadman & Holman, 2002), 130.

Chapter 7: "Can God Hear a Crazy Woman?" The Torment and Stigma of Mental Illness

1. Steve and Robyn Bloem, *Broken Minds: Hope for Healing When You Feel Like You're "Losing It"* (Grand Rapids: Kregel, 2005), 11–12.

2. Mental Health Association of New York City, "What Is Mental Illness?" http://www.mhaofnyc.org/6aboutmi.html.

3. Judith Davis, "A Sermon for 5 Epiphany B," sermon given at Christ Church, Washington Parish, Washington, D.C., 5 February 2006, accessed at http://www.washingtonparish.org/sermon%20for%205%20epiphany%20yr%20b.html.

4. According to Mental Health Association of New York, the most common adult mental illnesses are depression, bipolar disorder, and schizophrenia. The most common child and adolescent include depression, attention-deficit/hyperactivity disorder, bipolar disorder, conduct, anxiety and eating disorders, and schizophrenia. See "What Is Mental Illness?" on the Mental Health Association of New York Web site: http://www.mhaofnyc.org/6aboutmi.html.

5. Jackson H. Day, "Mental Illness Awareness Sunday," sermon preached at Grace United Methodist Church, Upperco, Maryland, 12 October 2003,

accessed online at http://www.gbgm-umc.org/grace-hampstead/031012.htm, 1 October 2006. Note: Jackson H. Day has served as program director for healthcare and mental illness issues at the United Methodist General Board of Church and Society. He currently cochairs a convention subcommittee on ministry to persons with mental illness and their families.

6. I'm indebted to Harold Brunson, a Baptist pastor, author, and speaker who also spent several years teaching in a high-security mental institution, for these insights. See "Mental Illness and Demon Possession," sermon preached 18 September 2005 at Parker Baptist Church, Parker, Texas. Accessed online as an audio file at http://www.sermonaudio.com/sermoninfo. asp?SID=10300514137.

7. Day, "Mental Illness Awareness Sunday."

8. Stephen Arterburn, *Healing Is a Choice: Ten Decisions That Will Transform Your Life and Ten Lies That Can Prevent You from Making Them* (Nashville: Thomas Nelson, 2005), 206. Reprinted by permission. All rights reserved.

9. Kathryn Greene-McCreight, *Darkness Is My Only Companion* (Grand Rapids: Brazos Press, 2006), 60.

10. Clay Nelson, "Messiahs Are from Mars; Syrophoenician Women Are from Venus," sermon preached 10 September 2006, at St Matthew-in-the-City Anglican Church, Aukland, New Zealand. Accessed October 2006 at http://www.stmatthews.org.nz/?sid=265&id=641.

11. Susan Palwick, "All Hail, Uppity Women!" *Rickety Contrivances of Doing Good: Science Fiction, Progressive Christianity, and Other Improbable Contrivances,* 10 September 2006. Accessed at http://improbableoptimisms.blogspot.com/2006_09_01_improbableoptimisms_archive.html.

12. Larry Keefauver, *When God Doesn't Heal Now* (Nashville: Thomas Nelson, 2000), 7.

Chapter 8: "No Matter What I Do, I'm Never Enough" The Weariness of Constant Striving

1. Pam Vredevelt, in Steve Stephens and Pam Vredevelt, *The Wounded Woman: Hope and Healing for Those Who Hurt* (Sisters, OR: Multnomah, 2006), 225.

2. Paula Rinehart, *Strong Women, Soft Hearts: A Woman's Guide to Cultivating a Wise Heart and a Passionate Life* (Nashville: W Publishing Group, 2001), 60–61.

3. The only physical description we have of Leah is found in Genesis 29:17, which uses a Hebrew verb that literally means "weak, soft, delicate, or tender." But translators and commentaries disagree about how to interpret this word. Some present Leah as a plain woman with pretty or soft and gentle eyes. Others say her eyes were dull, that they didn't sparkle. Still others think the eyes have something wrong with them—poor eyesight, chronic infections,

or even a disfiguring "wandering" eye. It's clear, though, that Rachel was considered the beautiful sister and Leah ran a poor second. (Note: I found this information in a variety of sources, but I recommend Dawn Adamy's wonderful sermon, "Looking for Love," given 25 July 2005 at the Presbyterian Church of Lawrenceville, New Jersey, accessed 1 October 2006 at http://www.ourmeetinghouse.org/sermons/sermon340.html.)

4. Karen Burton Mains, *Lonely No More: A Woman's Journey to Personal, Marital, and Spiritual Healing* (Dallas: Word, 1993), 154.

5. I don't know for sure that this happened. It's just my educated guess, based on my research and what seems logical. The Bible never actually says that Rachel returned Jacob's love or that his love was based on anything other than her physical beauty and outward charm. It does depict Rachel as the kind of person who would steal and lie in a pinch (see Gen. 31:19, 35). So I'm thinking she might be a bit conniving at home, the kind of person who depends on her beauty and charm to get her through life and who gets snippy when thwarted.

6. Ilene Lelchuk, "Girls Reporting High Stress Over Looks, Weight," *San Francisco Chronicle,* 29 October 2006.

7. Steve Stephens, in Stephens and Vredevelt, *The Wounded Woman,* 127.

8. Don Osgood, *Listening for God's Silent Language: Hearing God Speak in the Unexpected Places of Life* (Minneapolis: Bethany House, 1995), 26.

9. Joanna Weaver, *Having a Mary Spirit: Allowing God to Change Us from the Inside Out* (Colorado Springs: Waterbrook, 2006), 182.

10. Wendy M. Wright, *The Vigil: Keeping Watch in the Season of Christ's Coming* (Nashville: Upper Room, 1992), 42.

Chapter 9: "How Much Longer, Lord?" Practical Grace for the Chronically Discouraged

1. Brennan Manning, *The Signature of Jesus* (Sisters, OR: Multnomah, 2004), 20.

2. Jean M. Blomquist, *Wrestling Till Dawn: Awakening to Life in Times of Struggle* (Nashville: Upper Room, 1984), 129.

3. The actual text of Exodus contains three different kinds of references to the hardening of the heart. In 4:21, 7:3, and 14:17, God warned that He (God) was going to harden Pharaoh's heart. Yet 8:15; 8:32; 9:34; and 13:5 (plus 1 Sam. 6:6) say specifically that Pharaoh hardened his own heart. Though 7:13–14, 22; 8:9; 9:7; and 9:35 simply state that Pharaoh's heart "grew hard," the implication is that it grew hard on its own—Pharaoh is still hardening his own heart. But 9:12; 10:1, 20, 27; 11:10, 14:4, 8; and 14:17 show how God stepped in after the sixth plague (boils) and actually made things harder for the Israelites in Egypt by hardening Pharaoh's heart and influencing him to be more stubborn and arrogant than before.

Notes

4. Henri Nouwen, "A Spirituality of Waiting: Being Alert to God's Presence in Our Lives," *Weavings,* January 1978, in Robert Durback, ed., *Seeds of Hope: A Henri Nouwen Reader* (New York: Doubleday, 1989, 1997), 158–60.

5. Angela Thomas, *When Wallflowers Dance: Becoming a Woman of Righteous Confidence* (Nashville: Thomas Nelson, 2005), 111.

6. For more passages of lament, see the appendices of Michael Card, *A Sacred Sorrow: Reaching Out to God in the Lost Language of Lament* (Colorado Springs: NavPress, 2005), 146–200.

7. Emilie Barnes with Anne Christian Buchanan, *Fill My Cup, Lord* (Eugene, OR: Harvest House, 1996), 129–30.

8. Karen Burton Mains, *Lonely No More: A Woman's Journey to Personal, Marital, and Spiritual Healing* (Dallas: Word, 1993), 49.

Chapter 10: "Lord, That Was So Cool!" The Deeper-Still Adventure of Being God's Christian Girl

1. Nan E. Cook, "Thanks Eugene," 11 October 2006 entry on Web log. Accessed at http://nangirl.blogspot.com/2006_10_01_nangirl_archive.html.

2. Pam Vredevelt, in Steve Stephens and Pam Vredevelt, *The Wounded Woman: Hope and Healing for Those Who Hurt* (Sisters, OR: Multnomah, 2006), 41–42.

3. Jimmy Dorrell, *Trolls and Truth: 14 Realities About Today's Church That We Don't Want to See* (Birmingham: New Hope, 2006), 138–39.

4. Henri Nouwen, *Out of Solitude: Three Meditations on the Christian Life* (Notre Dame, IN: Ave Maria Press, 2004).

5. According to Sharon Betters in *Treasures of Encouragement: Women Helping Women in the Church* (Phillipsburg, NJ: P&R, 1996), the word translated "spur" means to sharpen, to come alongside, and to abide—the same ministry as the Holy Spirit.

6. Ibid., 9–10.

7. Paula Rinehart, *Strong Women, Soft Hearts: A Woman's Guide to Cultivating a Wise Heart and a Passionate Life* (Nashville: W Publishing Group, 2001), 122.

8. Emilie Barnes with Anne Christian Buchanan, *My Cup Overflows* (Eugene, OR: Harvest House, 1998), 124.

Tammy Maltby is a compelling speaker, author, Bible teacher, and media personality with a heart for helping real Christian women live richly and fully in the real world.

A cohost of the four-time Emmy-nominated television talk show *Aspiring Women*, Tammy has also been featured on *Focus on the Family*, *Family Life Today* with Dennis Rainey, *Life Today* with James and Betty Robison, *The 700 Club*, *Midday Connection*, and hundreds of other radio and television programs. She was the ongoing MC for the John Maxwell's international THRIVE! Event and has spoken at numerous fundraising events for crisis pregnancy. She serves on the board of the National Women's Ministry Association, Christian Women in Media and Arts, and Women of Courage International.

In her keynote addresses for women's events around the country, Tammy expands on themes developed in this book and her previous titles, *Lifegiving: Discovering the Secrets to a Beautiful Life* and *A Discovery Journal to a Beautiful Life*. Her passions (and topics) range

273

from the serious (healing and hope for those in pain) to the seriously lighthearted (fun and gracious homekeeping and hospitality), and she has a special heart for mothering issues, including adoption and crisis pregnancy. (She is the mother of four teenagers, two of whom were adopted internationally.)

For more on Tammy's upcoming books, media appearances, and speaking schedule, visit her blog at http://tammymaltby.typepad. com or the Aspiring Women Web site (http://www.aspiringwomen. tv). To book a speaking engagement, you can e-mail her directly at TMaltbyspeaks@aol.com.